Publisher's note

Ancient Chinese classic poems are exquisite works of art. As far as 2,000 years ago, Chinese poets composed the beautiful work *Book of Poetry* and *Elegies of the South*. Later, they created more splendid Tang poetry and Song lyrics. Such classic works as *Thus Spoke the Master* and *Laws Divine and Human* were extremely significant in building and shaping the culture of the Chinese nation. These works are both a cultural bond linking the thoughts and affections of Chinese people and an important bridge for Chinese culture and the world.

Mr. Xu Yuanchong has been engaged in translation for 70 years. He won the Lifetime Achievement Award in Translation conferred by the Translators Association of China (TAC) in 2010, and won the "Aurora Borealis" Prize for Outstanding Translation of Fiction Literature, conferred by the Federation of International Translators (FIT) in 2014. He is honored as the only expert who translates Chinese poems into both English and French. After his excellent interpretation, many Chinese classic poems have been further refined into perfect English and French rhymes. This collection of Classical Chinese Poetry and Prose gathers his most representative English translations. It includes the classic works *Thus Spoke the Master, Laws Divine and Human* and dramas such as *Romance of the Western Bower, Dream in Peony Pavilion, Love in Long-life Hall* and *Peach Blooms Painted with Blood*. The largest part of the collection includes the translation of selected poems from different dynasties. The selection includes various types of poetry. The selected works start from the pre-Qin era to the Qing Dynasty, covering almost the entire history of classic poems in China. Reading these works is like tasting "living water from the source" of Chinese culture.

We hope this collection will help English readers "understand, enjoy and delight in" Chinese classic poems, share the intelligence of Confucius and Lao Tzu (the Older Master), share the gracefulness of Tang poems, Song lyrics and classic operas and songs and promote exchanges between Eastern and Western culture. We also sincerely invite precious suggestions from our readers.

出版前言

中国古代经典诗文是中国传统文化的奇葩。早在两千多年以前，中国诗人就写出了美丽的《诗经》和《楚辞》；以后，他们又创造了更加灿烂的唐诗和宋词。《论语》《老子》这样的经典著作，则在塑造、构成中华民族文化精神方面具有极其重要的意义。这些作品既是联接所有中国人思想、情感的文化纽带，也是中国文化走向世界的重要桥梁。

许渊冲先生从事翻译工作70年，2010年荣获"中国翻译文化终身成就奖"，2014年荣获国际译联颁发的"北极光"杰出文学翻译奖。他被称为将中国诗词译成英法韵文的唯一专家，经他的妙手，许多中国经典诗文被译成出色的英文和法文韵语。这套"许译中国经典诗文集"荟萃许先生最具代表性的英文译作，既包括《论语》《老子》这样的经典著作，又包括《西厢记》《牡丹亭》《长生殿》《桃花扇》等戏曲剧本，数量最多的则是历代诗歌选集。这些诗歌选集包括诗、词、散曲等多种体裁，所选作品上起先秦，下至清代，几乎涵盖了中国古典诗歌的整个历史。阅读和了解这些作品，即可尽览中国文化的"源头活水"。

我们希望这套许氏译本能使英语读者对中国经典诗文也"知之，好之，乐之"，能够分享孔子、老子的智慧，分享唐诗、宋词、中国古典戏曲的优美，并以此促进东西文化的交流。也敬请读者朋友提出宝贵意见。

PROJECT FOR TRANSLATION AND PUBLICATION
OF CHINESE CULTURAL WORKS
中国文化著作翻译出版工程项目

CLASSICAL CHINESE POETRY AND PROSE

ROMANCE OF WESTERN BOWER

WANG SHIFU

TRANSLATED BY XU YUANCHONG & FRANK M. XU

许译中国经典诗文集

西厢记 | 【元】王实甫 著
许渊冲 许明 译

五洲传播出版社　　　中华书局
China Intercontinental Press　　Zhonghua Book Company

Contents
目　　录

	Preface	/ 1
	序	/ 225

ACT I
第一本

Scene 1 Enchantment	/ 12
第一折 惊艳	/ 236
Scene 2 Renting of Quarters	/ 21
第二折 借厢	/ 241
Scene 3 Verse Exchange	/ 34
第三折 酬韵	/ 248
Scene 4 Religious Service	/ 43
第四折 闹斋	/ 253

ACT II
第二本

Scene 1 Alarm	/ 50
第一折 寺警	/ 257
Scene 2 Invitation	/ 70
第二折 请宴	/ 267
Scene 3 Promise Broken	/ 77
第三折 赖婚	/ 271
Scene 4 Lute	/ 88
第四折 琴心	/ 277

ACT III
第三本

Scene 1 First Expectation	/ 97
第一折 前侯	/ 282
Scene 2 Billet-doux	/ 106
第二折 闹简	/ 287
Scene 3 Repudiation	/ 121
第三折 赖简	/ 294
Scene 4 Further Expectation	/ 129
第四折 后侯	/ 298

ACT IV
第四本

Scene 1 Tryst	/ 139
第一折 酬简	/ 303
Scene 2 Rose in the Dock	/ 149
第二折 拷艳	/ 307
Scene 3 Farewell Feast	/ 159
第三折 哭宴	/ 312
Scene 4 Dreams	/ 169
第四折 惊梦	/ 317

ACT V
第五本

Scene 1 Report of Success	/ 179
第一折 捷报	/ 322
Scene 2 Guess	/ 189
第二折 猜寄	/ 327
Scene 3 Contest for the Beauty	/ 197
第三折 争艳	/ 331
Scene 4 Union	/ 207
第四折 团圆	/ 336

CLASSICAL CHINESE POETRY AND PROSE

ROMANCE OF WESTERN BOWER

WANG SHIFU

TRANSLATED BY XU YUANCHONG & FRANK M. XU

China Intercontinental Press   Zhonghua Book Company

Preface

The *Romance of the Western Bower* written by Wang Shifu is the most important lyrical drama in the history of Chinese literature. It is as well-known in China as Shakespeare's *Romeo and Juliet* in the West, yet it was written about three hundred years earlier than Shakespeare's tragedy. Like the English play, it consists of a narrative part written in prose and a lyrical part written in verse. It is divided into five acts and twenty scenes. Act One describes the first meeting in the temple between the lovers, Zhang Gong, a young scholar, and Cui Yingying, nineteen-year-old daughter of former Prime Minister Cui. Act Two relates how Zhang saves the temple from attack by bandits and Madame Cui promises her daughter can marry Zhang, but she soon goes back on her word. Act Three describes the lovers' longing for each other. Act Four depicts their meeting in Scene I. In Scene II, Madame Cui will not approve their marriage unless Zhang wins honor in the civil service examinations. Scene III depicts their parting when Zhang leaves to attend the examinations in the capital. Scene IV ends with a dream in which the lovers meet again. The last Act describes their reunion.

As Jin Shengtan (1608–1661) said in the preface to *Romance*, "Before reading *Romance*, one should read the *Book of Poetry* (China's earliest anthology of poetry compiled in the 6th century BC), because there are correlations between *Romance* and *Book of Poetry*". For instance, the first lyric in the *Book of Poetry* reads as follows:

By riverside are cooing
A pair of turtledoves;
A good young man is wooing
A fair maiden he loves.

Water flows left and right
Of cresses here and there.
The youth yearns day and night
For the good maiden fair.

His yearning grows so strong,
He cannot fall asleep;
He tosses all night long,
So deep in love, so deep!

Now gather left and right
The cresses sweet and tender.
O lute, play music bright
For the fiancee so slender!

Feast friends at left and right
On cresses cooked tender;
O bells and drums, delight
The bride so sweet and slender!

If we compare this lyric with the parting scene in Act Four, we shall find similarities as well as differences between them, which shows the development of love poetry from the 6th century BC to the 14th century AD. In the lyric the young man seeing a pair of turtledoves cooing by the riverside longs for his beloved. In Act

Four, Scene III, the heroine sings:
   ... Two lovebirds torn apart bewail. ...
   Eastward the oriole and westward the swallow flies. The lovebirds, the oriole and the swallow are symbols of the lovers. She sings:
   My tears would make the Yellow River overflow.

We see the heroine's grief symbolized by the river, depicted from a more subjective viewpoint, while in the lyric the water flowing left and right of the cresses has nothing to do with the yearning of the young man, and we have only a simple description of the lover who cannot fall asleep and tosses all night long. But in the parting scene of *Romance*, the heroine has more intense feelings and is not only unable to fall asleep but also afraid "to see the curtained bed" for "Last night in warm embroidered coverlet spring dwelt." Here we see that the tradition of romantic love during the 14th century has developed from twenty centuries before. As well, in *Romance* there is a more pictorial description of the lover who sits at table,

   Slanting his head,
   Knitting his brows, as if half-dead.
   He dare not let his tears fall from his brimming eyes
   For fear his grief be known.
   Seeing himself observed, he utters sighs,
   Pretending to arrange his white silk gown.

In the passage cited from the *Book of Poetry*, the food is only sweet cresses cooked tender; but in Act Four, Scene III of *Romance* the food and wine "taste like muddy water," but

>   As mud the food is not so fine;
>   As water the wine is not so sweet.

In the former we find only an objective description; in the latter, the subjective sentiment of the heroine at parting. Here we see the poet of the Yuan dynasty (1271–1368) more skilled in his description of scenery and situation, persons and things, thoughts and feelings.

Even in the description of the relationship, we may compare a poem in the *Book of Poetry* with Act Four, Scene I of *Romance*, see the differences between them and find out how much progress has been made from vague suggestion to more detailed description. First, let us read the love story between a deer-killer and a beautiful maiden in the *Book of Poetry*.

>   An antelope is killed
>   And wrapped in white afield.
>   A maid for love does long,
>   Tempted by a hunter strong.
>
>   He cuts down trees amain
>   And kills a deer again.
>   He sees the white-drest maid
>   As beautiful as jade.
>
>   "Oh, soft and slow, sweetheart!
>   Don't tear my sash apart!"
>   The jade-like maid says, "Hark!
>   Do not let the dog bark!"

Preface

Here we see the hunter loves the maiden because she is "beautiful as jade" and she loves him because he is strong and skilled. The description of their love-making is rather implicit and suggestive only by saying "Don't tear my sash apart!" and "Do not let the dog bark!" On the other hand, in *Romance* Zhang loves Cui because

> She speaks like an oriole warbling 'mid flowers; each pace
> She takes awakens love.
> When she does move,
> Her supple waist is full of grace
> Like that of a dancer or drooping willow trees
> Waving in the evening breeze.

And she loves him

> Not that he's wise to give advice,
> But that he's not afraid of sacrifice.
> ... the point of his pen
> Would sweep away five thousand men.

In short, he loves her for her beauty and she loves him for his talent. The description of their love-making is explicit and symbolic.

> No fragrance is so warm, no jade so soft and nice,
> Ah! I am happier than in paradise.
> Spring comes on earth with flowers dyed.
> Her willowy waist close by my side,
> Her pistil plucked, my dewdrop drips
> And her peony sips
> With open lips.

The progress made by the Yuan dramatist was based not only on the *Book of poetry* but also on poetry of the Tang dynasty (618–907) and on lyrics of the Song dynasty (960–1279). For example, Zhang says during the parting in Act Four, Scene III:

> I retain my tears,
> and try to conceal them by hanging my head
> Though overwhelmed by my feelings,
> I assumed a look of delight. (Tr. by S. I. Hsiung)

And Yingying says:
> My soul has already gone from me,
> How can I follow you even in my dreams? (ibid)

These verses are an imitation of the following stanza by Wei Zhuang of the Tang dynasty:

> Holding back my tears,
> Bashfully I pretend to bow
> And draw together half my brow.
> Not knowing that my heart is broken,
> I follow you in dreams unwoken.

For another example, the parting scene ends by

> All the world's grief seems to fill my breast.
> How can such a small car bear such a heavy load!

Preface

This is an adaptation of the following verse of the Song dynasty poetess Li Qingzhao:

> But I'm afraid the grief-overladen boat
> On the Twin Creek can't keep afloat.

Therefore, the parting scene in *Romance* may be said to have reached the apex of farewell poetry in China for it has profited from poetry of the Tang and Song dynasties. If we compare *Romance* with Shakespeare's *Romeo and Juliet*, we shall find the Chinese lovers more reticent and the Western pair more outspoken. Both the Chinese and the Western hero fell in love at first sight, but Romeo kissed Juliet at their first meeting while Zhang and Cui dare not declare their love but reveal it in their verse:

> (Zhang) All dissolve in moonlight,
> Spring's lonely in flowers' shade.
> I see the moon so bright.
> Where's her beautiful maid?
> (Cui) In a lonely room at night,
> In vain spring and youth fade.
> You who croon with delight,
> Pity the sighing maid!

Their reticence shows the influence of Confucianism in China: Everything should be done in accordance with the rites. On the other hand, the following dialogue between *Romeo and Juliet* reveals the influence of Christianity in the West.

> Romeo: Have not saints lips, and holy palmers too?
> Juliet: Ay, pilgrim, lips that they must use in pray'r.
> Romeo: O, then, dear saint, let lips do what hands do!
> They pray; grant thou, lest faith turn to despair.

Master Zhang compares his lover to an oriole warbling amid the blooms and her waist to a drooping willow tree waving in the breeze, which shows his love of nature. At the sight of Juliet, Romeo says:

> O, she doth teach the torches to burn bright!
> It seems she hangs upon the cheek of night
> Like a rich jewel in an Ethiop's ear...
> Beauty too rich for use, for earth too dear!
> ...
> It is the East, and Juliet is the sun!
> Arise, fair sun, and kill the envious moon,
> Who is already sick and pale with grief
> That thou her maid art far more fair than she.

Both Master Zhang and Romeo call their lover the moon's maid, but the former is more suggestive and realistic while the latter is more imaginative and romantic.

If the Chinese and Western lovers seem different when they meet, they are alike when they part.

(Zhang): If you but look at me without turning away,
   I would thyme with your verse till the break of the day.
Clever loves clever
For ever and ever.
(Romeo): Love goes toward love as schoolboys from their books;
   But love from love, toward school with heavy looks.
(Juliet): Good night, good night! Parting is such sweet sorrow,
   That I shall say good night till it be morrow.

Both the Chinese and the Western heroine love the hero, but Yingying is ingenious while Juliet is straightforward. This can be illustrated by what their maids say of them.

(Nurse): Then hie you hence to Friar Laurence' cell;
   There stays a husband to make you a wife.
(Rose): Who has ever see
   A messenger befooled by the sender?
She is so clever,
Though she appears so young and tender.
She tells her love to climb
Over the eastern wall for a tryst.
Five words hint at the time;
Four lines appeal to the lover missed.
About this critical affair. O mark!
I was kept in the dark.
You want the cloud
To bring fresh showers
For thirsting flowers,

Romance of Western Bower

> But order me to use my leisure
> To gratify your pleasure.

The theme of *Romance* and of *Romeo and Juliet* is the conflict between love and family honor. The former ends by a reconciliation between them: The lover should win honor in the civil service examinations so that both love and honor can be preserved. The latter ends in the death of the lovers so that the two households are reconciled. Both the plays are full of vicissitudes. In *Romance*, the alarm in Act Two, Scene I, the promise broken in Act Two, Scene III, and the repudiation in Act Three, Scene III, prevent Master Zhang from winning his love. In *Romeo and Juliet*, the hostility between the two households, the death of Tybalt and the fixed marriage between Juliet and Paris lead to the tragic death of the two lovers. The conflict is internal in the former and external in the latter. On the other hand, characterization in *Romance* is indirect and suggestive: The inner world of the persona is revealed by the description of the external world. The characterization in *Romeo and Juliet* is direct and concrete: we know the inner world of the persona by what he says and what he does. The conclusion of the Chinese drama is the reunion of the two lovers; that of the English tragedy, death which reunites the hero and heroine. In the one we see love's triumph in life and in the other, over death.

Xu Yuanchong
June 24,1996
Peking University

ACT I

Scene 1 Enchantment

Madame Cui enters with Yingying (Oriole), her daughter; Rose, the maid; and Merry Boy, the adopted son, and says:

My surname is Zheng and that of my late husband is Cui, former Prime Minister who died unfortunately in the capital. We have only this nineteen-year-old daughter, Yingying, able to sew and embroider, to compose verse, to write a good hand and to make calculations. She was betrothed, when my husband was alive, to my nephew Zheng Heng, eldest son of Minister Zheng; but as the period of mourning has not expired, their marriage has not yet taken place. This little maid, Rose, has been in the service of my daughter since her childhood. This lad, Merry Boy, was adopted by my husband so that he might have a descendant. After my husband's death, I and my daughter wanted to convey his coffin to the burial ground at Boling, but, obstructed on the way, we were unable to proceed, so we deposited his coffin temporarily at the Salvation Monastery in the Mid-river Prefecture. This monastery was erected by the imperial favor of Her Majesty the Empress Wu Zetian (A. D. 690–712). The Abbot, Fa Ben, was originally presented for ordination by my husband, so the western bower is reserved for our use. I have written to Zheng Heng at the capital, requesting him to come to help us in the conveyance of the coffin. How sad I feel in company only of three or four close relatives when I think of the

ACT I

hundreds of attendants and the sumptuous food spread before us while my husband was alive!

She sings to the tune of *ENJOYING FLOWERS IN COMPANY OF FAIRIES*:

My husband ended at the capital his life,
Leaving helpless his orphaned child and widowed wife.
Now in the temple stays his coffin on its way.
When can we reach the burial ground so far away?
Alas! azaleas turn red
With tears of blood we shed.

She says:

Now in the time of late spring, one feels rather weary.
Look, Rose, if there is no one in the front courtyard, you may go with your young Mistress to divert yourselves there for a while.

Rose says:

Yes, Madame.

Yingying sings to the tune of *PETTY SONG*:

Here we are, east of District Pu, when spring is late,
Shut up in lonely temple with barred door and gate.
The flowing stream is red with fallen blooms.
Laden with glooms,
Mutely I bear a grudge against the eastern breeze,
Blowing down flowers from the trees.   (Exeunt.)

Master Zhang enters with his lute-bearer page and says:

I am Zhang Gong, styled Junrui, born in the family of the late President of the Board of Rites west of Luoyang. Having not yet obtained my official rank, I am traveling here and there early in the second moon of the year 801, and I want to go to the capital to attend the highest civil service examinations. On the way I pass the Mid-river Prefecture, where I have an old friend, Du Que, styled Junshi, my fellow countryman, fellow student and sworn brother, who gave up the pen for the sword, came out first on the list in the military examinations and was appointed general of the Western Front, commanding a hundred thousand men and stationed at the Pass of Pu. I want to pay him a visit before I proceed to the capital. Having studied hard in summer as in winter, I have acquired a deep knowledge of literature, but I am still a wanderer here and there and do not yet know when I can realize my noble aspiration. Mine is really the following case:

"My precious sword lies hidden in the autumn stream;
My sorrow-laden saddle's bursting at the seam."

He sings to the tune of *ROUGED LIPS OF A FAIRY*:

In Central Plain I travel up and down,
Rootless like floating thistledown.
I look toward the sky:
The sun seems nearer than the capital to the eye.

Tune: *DRAGON IN TROUBLED WATER*

Into the ancient classics I have bored my way
Just as a bookworm delves in volumes all the day.
My seat is warm: so long I've read alone;
Writing so much, I've worn out my ink-stone.
Before I rise like roc to the celestial spheres,
I must first study day and night for twenty years.
The higher talent can't in vulgar places fill;
A noble man in troubled times can't do his will.

ACT I

    What can I be but a poetaster mere,
    To whom are ancient literary fragments dear!
He says:
    Walking along, I have arrived at the bank of the Yellow River.
    Look, what a magnificent sight!
He sings to the tune of *FIELD CRICKET*:
    Of the tortuous, turbulent Yellow River, where
    Is the perilous part?
    Surely it's there.
    The River girds two Eastern States
    And keeps two Western States apart
    And bars the Northern Gates.
    White-crested waves upsurge as high
    As autumn clouds that roll in the boundless sky.
    The floating bridge, boats joined by ropes of bamboo,
    Looks like a crouching dragon blue.
    From east to west its waves through nine States go;
    From south to north a hundred streams into it flow.
    How swift are home-bound ships? Behold and lo!
    Just like an arrow shot from a bow.
          Tune: *UNIVERSAL JOY*
    The River like the Milky Way falls from the sky;
    Beyond the cloud its source hangs high.
    It runs its course unchanged till the Eastern Sea.
    It makes a thousand Luoyang flowers dance in glee,
    And fertilizes ten thousand acres in Eastern land.
    Skyward I'd sail till sun and moon are near at hand.

He says:
> Here I am in the city, and this is an inn. Lute-bearer, Hold my horse. Where is the inn-keeper?

Inn-keeper enters, and says:
> I am an inn-keeper in the High Street. Do you want to put up here, sir? We have clean rooms.

Master Zhang says:
> I will put up in your best room. Inn-keeper, come here. Tell me if there is any place for sight-seeing.

Inn-keeper says:
> We have the Salvation Monastery erected by the Imperial Order of Her Majesty the Empress Wu Zetian. It is an extraordinary building passengers from north or south never fail to visit. This is the only sight worth-while seeing in the city.

Master Zhang says:
> Lute-bearer, see to my luggage and unsaddle my horse. I am going to visit the monastery.

Lute-bearer says:
> Yes, sir.

(Exeunt.)

Fa Cong enters and says:
> I am Fa Cong, monk of the Salvation Monastery and disciple of Abbot Fa Ben. My master has gone to conduct a religious ceremony and told me to stay and take note of visitors so that I may inform him on his return. Now I am standing at the gate to see if anyone is coming.

Master Zhang enters and says:
> "The winding path leads to secluded rooms
> Shaded by thick foliage and heavy blooms."

ACT I

Now I have arrived.

(They meet.)

Fa Cong says:

Where do you come from, sir?

Master Zhang says:

I have come from the west of Luoyang. Having heard of your renowned monastery, I am coming to worship Buddha and pay my respects to the abbot.

Fa Cong says:

The abbot is out. I am his disciple Fa Cong. May I invite you to have tea in the hall?

Master Zhang says:

Since the abbot is out, don't bother to give me tea. Will you please show me around the monastery?

Fa Cong says:

With pleasure, sir.

Master Zhang says:

It is really a fine building!

He sings to the tune of *VILLAGE DRUMS*:

I've visited the Buddha hall

And quarters of the monks withal.

I've passed the kitchen to the west.

And to the north the hall of Scriptures blest,

In front of the tower of bells.

I've visited the monks' cells,

Climbed the pagoda,

Gone through all the passages.

I've counted the arhats, worshiped the Buddha,

And made my bow to saints and sages.

He says:
> There is another fine building. What place is that?
> May I have the pleasure to visit it?

Fa Cong, stopping him, says:
> Please do not go there, sir. It is the residence of the family of His Excellency the late Prime Minister Cui.

> (Master Zhang sees Yingying, who enters with Rose.)

Master Zhang says:
> Who is there if not the beauty who has sown love seed in my heart for five hundred long years!

He sings to the tune of *SONG OF PEACE*:
> Thousands of beauties I have seen before,
> But not such charming face as this one I adore.
> I'm dumb-found, dazzled are my eyes,
> My soul has soared up to the skies.
> Regardless of my admiration, still she stands,
> Rubs shoulders with and fondles flowers with her hands.

Tune: *CHARMING ON HORSE*
> Is this a paradise or a sorrowless sphere?
> Who would have thought I'd meet an angel here!
> Pleased or displeased, she's always a vernal vision fair.
> Her profile most becomes the ornaments on her hair.

Tune: *BETTER THAN GOURD*
> Her eyebrows arch like crescent moon
> And slant upward into her cloudy forehead.
> Before she says a word, she blushes soon.
> Her lips are cherry-red,
> Her teeth as white as jade.
> She's speaking hesitantly to her maid.

ACT I

Yingying says:
> Rose, I am going to see Mother.

Master Zhang sings to the tune of *PETTY SONG*:
> Like an oriole warbling amid the flowers. Every pace
> She takes awakens love,
> When she is seen to move,
> Her supple waist is full of grace
> Like that of a dancer or drooping willow trees
> Waving in evening breeze.
> What a captivating sight!
> What an intoxicating delight!

(Exeunt Yingying and Rose)

Master Zhang sings to the tune of *BACKYARD FLOWERS*:
> On a petal-softened pathway, see the trace
> In fragrant dust of her light and easy pace.
> The Love her glance inspires apart,
> Her gait transmits the sentiments of her heart.
> Slowly advancing, she arrives at her threshold;
> Within one pace
> She turns her face,
> And on myself I've lost my hold.
> The angel has returned to her paradise,
> In vain the willows weep and the bird cries.

Tune: *WILLOW LEAVES*
> Shut is the gate within which bloom pear trees;
> The white-washed wall seems as high
> As azure sky.
> Why will not Heaven help men to do what they please!
> How can I while the time away?

How can I linger here and stay?
I am at a loss what to do this life long day.

Tune: *PARASITIC GRASS*

The musk's and lily's fragrance she spread is still here;
Her tinkling ornaments I can no longer hear.
The willow branches wave in eastern breeze;
Gossamer threads retain the petals of peach trees.
Behind the beaded screen her lotus face disappears.
Is this the residence of former premier Cui
Or Temple of Goddess of the Southern Sea?

Tune: *EPILOGUE*

My eyes gaze with pain;
My mouth waters in vain.
Lovesickness penetrates the marrow of my bone.
How can I bear her bewitching glance when she's to part!
Even if I were made of iron or stone,
I could not forget her in my heart,
Flowers and willows still vie
In beauty on the lovely ground;
At noon the sun is high
And the pagoda throws a shadow round.
With beauties of the spring in view,
It grieves me not to see her face of rosy hue.
When I saw her in the monastery stand,
The temple was converted into a fairyland.

ACT I

Scene 2 Renting of Quarters

Madame Cui enters with Rose and says:

Rose, go and ask the Abbot when it will suit him to perform religious service for my late husband. When you are told the time, come back and let me know it.

Rose says:

Yes, Madame. (Exeunt.)

Fa Ben enters and says:

I am Abbot Fa Ben of the Salvation Monastery. Last night I went to perform a religious ceremony in a village. I do not know if anyone has come here to pay a visit.

(He calls Fa Cong and asks him.)

Fa Cong enters and says:

Last night a scholar from Luoyang came to visit you and went back in your absence.

Fa Ben says:

Go and keep watch at the gate, and let me know if he comes again.

Fa Cong says:

Yes, master.

Master Zhang enters and says:

Since I saw that young lady yesterday, I could not sleep all night. Today I am coming again to call on the Abbot and have something to say to him.

(He makes his bow to Fa Cong.)

21

Master Zhang sings to the tune of *PINK BUTTERFLY*:
> If thou hast no help to give me,
> Fa Cong, I will not forgive thee.

Fa Cong says:
> So you have come, sir. But I don't understand what you say.

Master Zhang continues to sing:
> I want thee to let me a cell
> So that I may live opposite the door
> Of one who can make a paradise of a hell.
> Though I can't steal her heart that I adore,
> On her cloud-like dress I can feast
> My eyes at least.

Fa Cong says:
> I do not understand what you say, sir.

Master Zhang sings to the tune of *INTOXICATED EAST WIND*:
> Formerly when I saw a powdered face,
> I truly thought it to be a disgrace;
> At the sight of a penciled brow,
> I seemed to hear a broken vow.
> But now I see my heart's desire,
> I seem to feel vibrate the strings of a lover's lyre,
> My mind bewildered, dazzled my eye,
> And a whirling sensation rising high.

Fa Cong says:
> I still do not understand what you say, sir. My master has been waiting for you. I will go to inform him.

(Master Zhang meets Fa Ben.)

ACT I

Master Zhang sings to the tune of *MEETING THE IMMORTAL*:
>I see before me one with snowy head
>And hair like frost,
>And face like one whose youth inbred
>Is never lost.
>He looks divine and profound;
>His voice is strong and clear.
>If he had but a halo around,
>I would think Buddha did appear.

Fa Ben says:
>Please come in and take a seat, sir. Last night I was not at home and failed to welcome you. I hope you will forgive me.

Master Zhang says:
>I have long heard of your renown and wished to come and hear you preach. But I am sorry to have missed you yesterday. Now that I have met you, I feel I am really happy.

Fa Ben says:
>May I ask you, sir, about your family, your name and surname, and why you have come here?

Master Zhang says:
>I am a native of Luoyang; my surname is Zhang and my name is Gong, styled Junrui. I am passing here on my way to the capital in order to attend the highest examinations.

He sings to the tune of *POMEGRANATE FLOWER*:
>You've asked me why I've paid this call;
>I'll tell you these things one and all.
>Coming from Luoyang,
>I am travelling up and down,

Leaving my family settled at Xianyang.
My late father had a great renown:
President of the Board of Rite,
He died at over fifty years of age.
During his life he was just and upright;
After his death he left no heritage.

Tune: *FIGHT OF QUAILS*

Brilliant as you're, you condescend to humble sphere;
Pure as the wind and bright as the moon you appear.
As for me, no office will I beseech;
What I want is to hear you preach.

He says:

As a traveller has no means to show his respect to you, I can only offer an ounce of silver for the expenses of the monastery. Would you kindly accept it?

He continues to sing:

Like a piece of paper a scholar's gift is light;
He does not know the price in gold or silver white.
He cares not for reproach or renown;
He fears not being weighed up or down.

Tune: *ASCENDING THE ATTIC*

I have come to pay a visit to you;
You need not refuse my gifts, be they so few.
They're not enough to purchase firewood
For the monastery nor to buy food.
At best, they can be used to provide some tea.
If you will undertake to speak a word for me
To those richly-dressed and nobly-bred,
I will never forget you, alive or dead.

ACT I

Fa Ben says:
>Why should you offer us gifts while travelling? You must have something to say to me, sir.

Master Zhang says:
>May I request a favor of you? As I cannot study the classics in a crowded inn, I wish to rent a room here so that I may hear your teaching morning and evening. As for the rent, I will pay what you wish by the month.

Fa Ben says:
>There are a lot of spare rooms in our monastery; You may choose which you want, or, if you like, you may share my couch with me.

Master Zhang sings to the tune of *PETTY SONG*:
>I do not want the incense store,
>
>Nor the old wooden hall;
>
>I want no room at southern door
>
>And none by eastern wall,
>
>But one near Western Bower where the lane goes by
>
>And where the anteroom arrests the eye.
>
>This is a place I like well.
>
>Do not mention the room you dwell.

Rose enters and says:
>My Mistress has ordered me to inquire of the Abbot when it will suit him to perform the religious service for my late Master, and when I am told the time, to return and report to her.
>
>   (She meets Fa Ben.)
>
>Ten thousand blessings, Abbot! My Mistress has sent me to inquire when it will suit you to perform the religious service for my late Master.

Master Zhang says:
> What a pretty girl!

He sings to the tune of *DOFFING THE CLOTHES*:
> Her manners show her not a maiden cheap;
> There is no slightest sign of coquetry.
> Having made to the Abbot a curtsy deep,
> She opens her lips and speaks with propriety.

> **Tune: *SMALL LIANGZHOU***
> Her lightly powdered face affords delight,
> Though she's in mourning dress of pure white.
> With unusual clever eyes like those of a bird,
> She steals a look, but her eyes speak to me not a word.

> **Tune: *PETTY SONG***
> Could I on your Young Mistress' pillow put my head,
> I would not trouble you to make for us the bed.
> I will ask her and her mother to set you free;
> If not allowed, I would myself write a guarantee.

Fa Ben says:
> Will you please sit here for a moment while I go with the young maid to the Hall of Buddha? I will soon be back.

Master Zhang says:
> What if I go there with you?

Fa Ben says:
> You are welcome.

Master Zhang says:
> Let the young maid go in front, and I will keep a little distance behind.

He sings to the tune of *THE HAPPY THREE*:
> The maid's attractively arrayed

ACT I

So that her charms may be displayed.
If she does not flirt with your halo of light,
Why should she be dressed so fair and bright?

Tune: *HOMAGE TO EMPEROR*

The winding passage leads to your cell;
Out of the blue comes the charming belle.

Fa Ben says angrily:

How can you who look so fine talk so indecently?

Master Zhang says:

You must not blame me for what I cannot help saying.

He continues to sing:

My looks so fine and talk so rude
Have offended and angered the Abbot so good.
But how can such a family have no servant male
That it must send as messenger a maiden frail?
If you insist on having your say,
Can you explain the reason why, I pray?

Fa Ben says:

It is the filial feeling of the Young Mistress for her late father that prompts her to hold a religious service for him, so she sends no other than her personal maid Rose to inquire about the date.

He turns and says to Rose:

The offerings are ready and other preparations are made for the service. The fifteenth is the day for the Buddha to receive offerings, so I request Madame Cui and your Young Mistress to come on that day to offer in cease.

Master Zhang says in tears:

"Alas! Alas I My parents late,
Who gave me birth with toil and pain!

> How to repay their kindness great
> As Heaven and deep as the main!"

Even the young lady will show her gratitude to her father. How can I not fulfil my filial duty toward mine! Will you be kind enough to allow me to subscribe five thousand cash so that I may be included in the religious service for the salvation of the souls of my deceased parents? I think Madame Cui will not object to my wish when she knows it.

Fa Ben says:

Of course not. Fa Cong, arrange to include Master Zhang into the service.

Master Zhang asks Fa Cong apart:

Will the young lady be present at the service?

Fa Cong says:

How could she be absent at a service for her own father?

Master Zhang says:

Then I have made good use of the five thousand cash.

He sings to the tune of *FOUR-SIDE TRANQUILLITY*:

> The sight of Yingying on earth or in paradise
> Would give more blessings than a sacrifice.
> So warm and sweet, she is softer than jade;
> Not to speak of the joy of an embrace,
> At the touch of her face,
> All pain and grief would fade.

Fa Ben says:

Let us have tea in the hall.

Master Zhang says:

Please excuse me for a moment.

ACT I

He goes to a corner and says aside:
> The maid is sure to come out and I will wait for her here.

Rose, bidding goodbye to Fa Ben, says:
> I cannot take tea lest my Mistress should wonder why I am delayed. I must go and report to her. (She departs.)

Master Zhang, meeting her with a salute, says:
> I make my bow to you, fair maid.

Rose says:
> Ten thousand blessings to you, sir.

Master Zhang says:
> Are you not Rose, personal maid of Mademoiselle Yingying.

Rose says:
> Yes, sir. Why should you ask?

Master Zhang says:
> May I be allowed to say something to you?

Rose sings and says:
> "Like arrows, word
>
> Must not be freely spread,
>
> Once they are heard,
>
> They cannot be unsaid."
>
> Now, if you have anything to say, speak fitly.

Master Zhang says:
> I am Zhang Gong, styled Junrui, a native of Luoyang. Born on the seven-teenth of the first moon, I am twenty-three years old, not yet married.

Rose says:
> Who asked you all these? I am not a fortune-teller who needs to know such particulars. What is the use of telling me the year, the moon and the day of your birth?

Master Zhang says:
> I have another question to ask you. Does your Young Mistress sometimes go outdoors?

Rose says angrily:
> What has that to do with you? You are an educated gentleman. Don't you know what Confucius taught you: "Speak not a word and make not a movement which are contrary to propriety!" Cold as ice and frost, my Mistress rules her family strictly. Even a boy dare not enter her chamber if not summoned. How dare you, who are in no way connected with the family, ask such questions!
>
> (Exit.)

Master Zhang says:
> I am afraid I'll die of lovesickness.

He sings to the tune of WHISTLING AROUND:
> Having heard what she said, I feel sad as if lost;
> My knitted eyebrows show my bitter grief and gloom.
> She said her Mistress is as cold as ice and frost,
> And no one, unless summoned, dare enter her room.
> Yingying, if you stand in awe of your mother stern,
> Why should you turn your eyes on me before you part?
> If I must give up, how can I for you not yearn?
> Your image is so deeply engraved in my heart.
> If we can't in this life be joined like lilies twin,
> Is it because the incense I burned was not lit?
> O could I hold you in
> My warm embrace and sit
> You in my heart! O at least I
> May on your image feast my eye!

Tune: *PLAYING THE CHILD*

The Amorous Hill's far in the celestial sphere,
But our meeting place seems even farther away.
My lovesick body stands though in the passage here,
My yearning soul for a long time has gone astray.
Would she tell the feeling in her heart to lonely me?
Or does she, fear her love be known to her mother stern?
Seeing the butterflies flying in pairs, would she
Not be aflame with love in her turn?

Tune: *LAST STANZA BUTF OUR*

Rose, you are young and will not listen to my plea.
Could I but hold her in my embrace,
I would steal her fragrance like a bee
When she begins to like a poet's painted face.
Such a meeting as would enravish my soul
Might result in making a husband of me
And setting her free from her mother's control.

Tune: *LAST STANZA BUT THREE*

Rose, are you overthoughtful or am I dreaming now?
Cannot my talent match with your Young Mistress fair?
Should she wait long for one to paint her brow
Until her youth and spring vanish into the air?
I dare say if she is a peerless beauty,
I know how to fulfill my glorious duty.

Tune: *LAST STANZA BUT TWO*

Rose, her lightly penciled brows and thinly powdered face,
Her jade-white neck and green skirt and lily-like feet,
Her crimson sleeves and taper fingers full of grace!

How can I banish from my thoughts her image so sweet!
Oh, if she were deprived of her charming elegance,
I would not be lovesick for her lingering fragrance.

Master Zhang says:

I forgot to say goodbye to the Abbot.

(Turning round and meeting Fa Ben.)

May I ask you for the room?

Fa Ben says:

There is a room near the Western Bower; it is delightful and quite suitable for you. You may take it at your earliest convenience, sir.

Master Zhang says:

I will return to the inn and bring my luggage here.

Fa Ben says:

Be sure to come back, sir. (Exeunt)

Master Zhang re-enters and says:

Now I have moved to the monastery. But how can I while away my lonely hours!

He sings to the tune of *LAST STANZA BUT ONE*:

Alone in lonely room with mat and pillow cold,
A single lamp throws fitful shadows on books old.
E'en if my aspiration can be fulfilled,
How can the time of this endless night be killed?
Sleepless all night,
I toss from left to right.
How many times I've uttered sigh and groan
And beaten bed and pillow all alone!

Tune: *EPILOGUE*

Her bashful beauty would make flowers fade;
Her tenderness might sweeten lifeless jade.
Seen only once, I can't remember her charming face;
Sleepless, I'll ruminate hand on cheek o'er her grace.

(Exit.)

Scene 3 Verse Exchange

Yingying enters and says:
>   My mother has sent Rose to inquire of the Abbot on what day he will perform the religious service. She has been absent for a long time without coming back.

Rose enters and says:
>   I have already reported to my Mistress. Now I must go and tell my young Mistress.

Yingying says:
>   What about the religious service?

Rose says:
>   I have just made a report to my Mistress, and now I want to report to you. The fifteenth of the second moon is the date on which is offered I know not what sacrifice to Buddha, and the Abbot requests your mother and you to burn incense to that day. (She laughs.) I have something amusing to tell you. The young scholar we met the other day was today sitting in the hall. He went out to wait for me and, seeing me out, he made a deep bow and said, "Are you not Rose, personal maid of Mademoiselle Yingying?" And he went on to say, "I am Zhang Gong, styled Junrui, a native of Luoyang. Born on the seven-teenth of the first moon, I am twenty-three years old. not yet married."

Yingying says:
>   Who told you to question him?

ACT I

Rose says:
>Yes, indeed, who? He also mentioned your name and asked if you sometimes went outdoors. But I scolded him to the face and came back.

Yingying says:
>It would be as well if you had not scolded him.

Rose says:
>I don't know what on earth he was thinking about. When I saw such a fool, why shouldn't I scold him?

Yingying says:
>Have you told my mother about it?

Rose says:
>No, not a word.

Yingying says:
>You need not breathe a word to her. It is getting late; arrange the table for incense-burner and we shall go to the garden to offer incense to Heaven.
>
>How unexpected love affects my heart!
>
>Leaning on brazier, I wait for moonrise apart.
>
>(Exeunt.)

Master Zhang enters and says:
>Having moved to the monastery, I occupy now my desired rooms near the Western Bower. As I was told by the monk, the young lady burns incense in the garden every night. Fortunately the garden is separated from my quarters only by a wall, so I can wait for her by the rocks at the corner and feast my eyes on her when she comes out. What could be better than that! It is now midnight and there is no one about; the moon is bright and the air is clear, a truly delightful hour!

(Singing): At leisure I beseech
To hear the Abbot preach;
Sad in the room, I croon
In the light of the moon.

He sings to the tune of *FIGHT OF QUAILS*:
No speck of cloud in jade-like sky,
The Milky Way casts gentle light;
The silver moon sails up on high,
The courtyard shaded with flowers bright.
Through her silk sleeves she'd feel the cold;
In her tender heart she'd know it's late.
I incline my ear
So as to hear;
I walk on tiptoe
So as to be slow.
Furtively I go so that none may behold.
And silently for her I wait,

Tune: *VIOLET FLOWER*

For Yingying so full of charm and grace I wait.
After first watch the world is mute,
To Yingying's courtyard I'll go straight.
Should I confront at the winding passage the cute,
Dear Yingying, I'd hold you tight in my embrace,
And ask you why our meeting seems
So hard that I could only see in dreams
Your shadow fair more than your shining face.

Yingying enters with Rose and says:
Open the side door and take out the table for the incense-burner.

ACT I

Master Zhang sings to the tune of *GOLDEN BANANA LEAF*:
    Suddenly I hear the creaking of the side door
    And smell the fragrance of her dress the wind conveys.
    On tiptoe I intently fix on her my gaze,
    And find her even more beautiful than before.

                Tune: *SONG OF FLIRTATION*
Now that I see her charm and grace tonight,
The Goddess of the Moon is not so fair and bright.

He says:
    I think she is the Goddess so weary of restrictions and so inconsiderate as to flee from the Palace on high. See her fair face and charming person. She stands there, neither speaking nor moving, with her long sleeves flowing and her silk skirt hanging down. She looks like the Fairy Queen leaning against the crimson door of the imperial temple or the riverside Nymph worthy of the praise of a great poet. Truly she is a beauty!

He continues to sing:
    Dimly I see her pass along the fragrant pathway;
    I am afraid her feet
    Are too small to be fleet.
    When she approaches near,
    A hundred charms appear.
    Oh, how can my soul not be enticed away!

Yingying says:
    Bring the incense here.

Master Zhang says:
    I would like to hear her pray.

Yingying says:
    In burning the first stick of incense, I pray that my deceased

father may soon ascend to Heaven. In burning the second, I pray that my dear mother may live long. As to the third, ...
(She hesitates.)

Rose says:
Why are you always silent when it comes to the third? Let me pray for you. I pray that my Young Mistress may marry a husband whose literary talents are second to none, and who may come out first in the highest examinations, and who, gallant and gentle, may live together with my Young Mistress all his life long.

Yingying puts the third stick into the burner, kneels and says:
Would the act of worship impart
The secret yearning of my heart!
(She heaves a deep sigh.)

Master Zhang says:
What is there in your heart that makes you sigh so deeply while leaning on the balustrade?

He sings to the tune of *RED PEACH BLOSSOM*:
Late in the night the clouds of incense pervade
The courtyard; in east wind the curtain seems asleep,
Her worship done, she leans on the balustrade,
And utters sigh on sigh so deep.
The bright full moon looks like a mirror round,
Which neither clouds nor mist surround.
I see but smoke of incense and the breath we exhale,
Which mingle and cloud her face like a veil.

He says:
On reflection, I think her sighs must arise from some innermost feeling. Although I am not the good lutist, she may be a lute-

lover. Let me try to compose a poem, read it to her and see what she will say:

All dissolve in moonlight,

Spring's lonely in flowers' shade.

I see the moon so bright.

Where's her beautiful maid?

Yingying says:

Someone is chanting a poem at the corner of the wall.

Rose says:

It must be that foolish scholar who is twenty-three years old and still unmarried.

Yingying says:

It reads as pure as moonlight. Rose, I will compose one to rhyme with his.

Rose says:

Please compose one for me to hear.

Yingying reads:

In lonely room at night,

In vain spring and youth fade.

You who croon with delight,

Sympathize with the maid!

Master Zhang, surprised and overjoyed, says:

How promptly she has responded to my verse!

He sings to the tune of *THE BALD HEAD*:

Her face so full of charms has enticed me away,

And what is more, I find

Deep wisdom in her mind.

She has responded to my verse without delay.

Each word reveals

What her heart feels;
It is pleasant to hear
For the listening ear.

Tune: *SOVEREIGN OF MEDICINE*

Your words and rhymes are soft and clear,
Yingying, you are worthy of your name so dear.
If you but look at me without turning away,
I would thyme with your verse till the break of the day.
Clever loves clever
For ever and ever.

He says:

What if I go to the other side of the wall?

He sings to the tune of *THE POCKMARKED FACE*:

I tuck up my silk robe, ready to go.
Would she welcome me with a smile? I do not know.
O Rose, be not unkind to me,
And say nothing against my plea!

Tune: *PETTY SONG*

But suddenly I hear a sound which startles me.

Rose says:

We ought to go in, or else our Mistress will be displeased,

(Exeunt Yingying and Rose, shutting the side door)

Master Zhang continues to sing:

The birds which were asleep fly up with fluttering wing,
And moonlight plays with shadows of the shivering tree.
Shower by shower fall red blossoms of late spring.

Tune: *SPINNER*

I see on green, green moss glisten cold dew;
Through flowers' shadows the bright, bright moon sifts its light.

Lonely by day, in vain I am longing for you;

How can I cure my lovesickness tonight?

Tune: *JOY OF THE EASTERN PLAIN*

Your curtains drawn and closed your door,

The verse I dared to croon

And your reply in soft voice can be heard no more.

It's second watch when winds are soft and bright the moon.

Oh, how unfortunate!

It seems decreed above

You should not fall in love

And I fall victim of the Fate.

Tune: *BROCADE AND WILLOWDOWN*

On my backward way,

In empty court I stop and stay.

In the breeze the bamboo branches sway;

The Dipper slants across the sky.

Oh, lonely tonight, I see good signs above.

What matters though at me she did not cast an eye?

Does she need speaking eyes to show her love?

I understand what she did not say.

He says:

But how can sleep come to me tonight?

He sings to the tune of *RASH SPEED*:

A single lamp sheds green, green. flame and shadows grim;

An old screen looks so cold and drear.

The flickering lamp is dim;

I cannot even dream of my dear.

The wind through lattice window strikes a chill

And makes torn slips of window paper flutter.

My pillow feels the midnight still;
My coverlet my loneliness utter,
Which chills me to the bone
And would e'en move a heart of stone.

Tune: *PETIY SONG*

I can nor hate nor complain,
But restless and sleepless remain.
Some day, 'mid flowers and 'neath willow-tree,
In mist-like curtain or surrounded by cloud-like screen,
We'd make an oath e'erlasting as mountain and sea
At the dead of a night serene.
We would enjoy our love at will,
Facing a future bright;
We might even love our fill
Till in our painted hall spring has attained its height.

Tune: *EPILOGUE*

So what good fortune to me beams!
The verse exchanged is evidence clear.
I need not seek her locked chamber in my dreams
But wait beneath the flowering peach tree for my dear.

(Exit.)

ACT I

Scene 4 Religious Service

Master Zhang enters and says:
>Today is the fifteenth of the second moon. The priest has requested me to join in the service by burning incense, so I must go along.
>The preachers utter words as rain falls from the cloud;
>Like waves raised by the wind they turn palm leaves over loud.

He sings to the double tune of *SONG OF NEW WATER*:
>Over Buddha's Temple high the full moon shines in the skies;
>Around its green-tiled roof the smokes of incense rise.

Fa Ben enters with all the other priests and says:
>Today is the fifteenth day of the second moon when Sak-yamuni entered Nirvana and Bodhisattva Manjusri and Auysman Cunda made offerings to Buddha. Those who perform religious service today, men and women, will secure great happiness and advantage. Master Zhang, you are early to come here. Priests, play your sacred instruments now. When it dawns, I will request Madame Cui and her daughter to come to burn incense.

Master Zhang continues to sing:
>The smoke of incense forms of clouds a canopy;
>The prayers sound like rolling waves of the sea.
>The banners undulate with shadows to and fro,
>All benefactors have come from high and low.
>
>**Tune: *HALTING THE HORSE***
>
>The sacred drums and brazen cymbals sound

> In every corner of the temple and all around
> Like thunder in the second moon of spring;
> The prayers to Buddha and the bells ring
> Like a half skyful of rain mingled with strong breeze,
> Sprinkling among the tips of green pine-trees.
> The lordly house forbidden to the priest,
> Rose has not left her windowsill.
> O how I thirst to feast
> My hungry eyes on her and have my fill!

Fa Ben sees Master Zhang and says:
> You make your offering first. If Madame Cui asks you, please tell her you are a relation of mine.

Master Zhang burns the incense and sings to the tune of *INTOXICATED EAST WIND*:
> May those who are alive enjoy long life with glee!
> Be happy in Paradise, those who have passed away!
> For my ancestors' souls I worship the "Holy Three"
> And then I burn the incense and in secret pray:
> May Rose not slap my wrist!
> May Madame be kept in the dark!
> May dogs not bark!
> O Buddha, show your favor on our tryst!

Madame Cui enters with Yingying and Rose and says:
> We are now going to burn the incense as requested by the Abbot.

Master Zhang sings to the tune of *WILD GEESE'S FALL*:
> She seems a fair angel from the blue skies,
> But she's a lovely maiden coming to say grace.
> Lovesick for her, can I refrain from heaving sighs

ACT I

For such a beauty with such a captivating face?

Tune: *TRIUMPHANT SONG*

Her lips are cherry-red, you see,
Her nose jade-white,
 Her face like the flower of a pear-tree,
Like willow branch her figure slight.
Lovely and sweet,
In her charms she's complete;
Slim and slender,
She's delicate and tender.

Fa Ben says:

I have something to tell you, Madame. A relation of mine, who is a scholar on his way to the capital, has asked me to include him in the religious service to show his gratitude to his deceased parents. I have promised him I would, but I am afraid I might have incurred your displeasure.

Madame Cui says:

How can I be displeased to see anyone show his gratitude to his deceased parents? Please ask him to come and see me.

(Master Zhang meets Madame Cui.)

Master Zhang sings to the tune of *PSEUDO-MELODY*:

The Abbot, though advanced in years,
From his high seat, bends his eyes on the belle.
What a fool the head monk appears!
He's striking Fa Cong's head and not the bell.

Tune: *SONG OF SWEET WATER*

The old and young, the foul and fair,
All stand in great confusion there

As on the Lantern Day.
Their looks beseeching
And hers bewitching
As if all had something to say.
She casts a furtive glance from her eyes full of tears
As if she had some lurking fears.

Tune: *PICKING LAUREL*

She fills my heart
With a longing that cannot be put apart.
All hear her weep
Like an oriole warbling in a forest deep,
And see her tears
As pearly dew on a flower appears.
The inimitable Abbot grieves
And hides his kindly face with both his sleeves.
The acolyte
Forgets the candles he should light,
And the monk who should burn
The incense forgets his concern.
So flicker candles red
And cloud-like smokes of incense spread.
To Yingying they are so devout
That incense ceases to burn and candles all go out.

Tune: *GREEN JADE FLUTE*

My love's revealed at the point of my brows;
She knows my lovesickness.
Her heart which sorrow plows
Is stirred by love, I guess.

ACT I

But I dislike
The loud sound of the gong the monks strike
And the prayers the novices recite,
For I would not be robbed of my delight.

Tune: *LOVEBIRDS'EPILOGUE*

A longing heart is sadder than a longing eye;
For the enchantress I, enchanted, can only sigh.

Fa Ben reciting the prayers for the service and burning paper money, says:

It is dawn now. Please return to your quarters, Madame and Mademoiselle.

(Exeunt Madame with Cui Yingying and Rose)

Master Zhang says:

Another day like this would be a joy indeed! What am I to do now?

He continues to sing:

A busy night,
The moon is out of sight;
The bell has rung;
The cock has sung.
The fair is gone,
The service done,
Deserted is the place,
At an easy pace
All worshippers go on their homeward way.
Soon breaks the day. (Exeunt)

To sum up the four scenes of Act I:

Madame Cui welcomes spring.
Yingying burns incense at night.
What good news will Rose bring?
Master Zhang drinks in delight.

ACT II

Scene 1 Alarm

Sun Feihu (The Flying Tiger) enters with a company of soldiers and says:

> I am Sun the Flying Tiger. Now the Empire is in a state of disorder. My Commander-in-chief has failed to discharge his duties. I have been given a separate command of five thousand men to guard the Bridge on the River. It is said the late Prime Minister Cui has a daughter called Yingying whose black eyebrows with winning expressions and whose face as beautiful as the lotus in spring are of such an overwhelming charm that she matches the most famous beauties of old. She is now in the Salvation Monastery where the coffin of her late father is resting. She was seen by many people on the fifteenth of the second moon when a religious service was held in memory of her father. When I come to think that even my chief has not discharged his duties, why should I not follow his example? Officers and men, listen to my command! All you men, with your mouth gagged and your horse bitted, march all night long to the Mid-river Prefecture. If I could have Yingying as my wife, then the desire of my life will be fulfilled.
>
> (Exit with his troops)

Fa Ben, entering in agitation, says:

> A calamity has come upon us. Who would have thought that Sun Feihu would have led five thousand men to surround

ACT II

the monastery as tightly as iron hoops round a barrel? They are sounding gongs, beating drums, waving flags and loudly shouting that Sun would make the Young Lady his wife. I dare not hush up the matter but must inform Madame and her daughter at once.

Madame Cui, entering in agitation, says:
What is to be done? What is to be done? Abbot, let us go to discuss the matter outside my daughter's room.

(Exeunt)

Yingying enters with Rose and says:
When I saw Master Zhang the other day at the religious service, I was so beside myself that I could scarcely eat or drink. My feelings are intensified by the fact that it is late spring when

The moon which shines so bright

Pities my lonely night;

Blooms fallen from the trees

Resent the eastern breeze.

She sings to the tune of *EIGHT BEATS OF GANZHOU SONG*:
Sorrow and grief are wearing me away.

How can I bear late spring's departing day!

My robe of silk becomes too large for me to wear.

How many lonely nights can I still bear?

The curtain not uprolled, the incense wafts in breeze;

I shut the door and let the rain beat on pear trees.

I dare not lean on balcony:

The clouds are blown as far as the eye can see.

Tune: *DRAGON IN TROUBLED WATER*

What's more, red flowers

Are falling in showers.

It saddens me to see.
Ten thousand petals twirl in wind and flee.
Last night I dreamed of seeing poolside green grass grow,
This morning spring has left my chamber in the west.
White butterflies and willow down mingle like snow;
The soil from fallen blooms is made the swallows' nest.
The willow branch so long can't make spring stay;
The man beyond the blooms seems farther off than the sky.
How many beauties like me have pined away
  By heaving sigh on sigh!

Rose says:

My Young Mistress is pensive and melancholy. I will make her coverlet fragrant so that she may sleep well.

Yingying sings to the tune of *FIELD CRICKET*:

My coverlet and broidered mattress grow so cold
That you can't warm them with musk perfumes spread.
Even if you used all the perfumes manifold,
You could not warm and sweeten a lonely bed.
It is clear his fine verse tried to lure me away.
Why can't I get in touch with him today?
I do not like to sit on the one hand
Nor on the other to stand.
No vista brings me pleasure;
I'm wearied when I walk at leisure.
Lost in a love so strong,
I'm drowsy all day long.

        Tune: *UNIVERSAL JOY*

I can but on my pillow rest my head
In my embroidered bed.

ACT II

When I go out of door,
My maid won't leave me, shadow-like, no more.
Of late she's been so cautious as not to let me free,
Ever in close attendance on me.
My mother rules me with a strict control
Lest I should play an indecent role.

Tune: *SONG OF CHERUBIN*

You know whenever I see a stranger, I'm annoyed;
Even relations I would fain avoid.
But on that day when I saw him appear,
At once I felt he was my dear.
So I composed a verse the other night
To thyme with his so bright.

Tune: *MAGPIE ON THE BRANCH*

Not only were the words so fine,
But also natural was each line.
Two poems read as one.
Oh, who would thread the needle and run
Over the eastern wall to reveal
To him what in my heart I feel?

Tune: *PARASITIC GRASS*

He's gallant and benign,
With handsome face and figure fine.
He must be kind and constant in love.
Can I not repeat his name and think of him alone?
Although he writes as brilliantly as stars above,
Who will regret his labor for ten years unknown?

(Madame Cui enters with Fa Ben and knocks at the door.)

Rose says:

Why has my Mistress invited the Abbot to come straight to our door?

(Yingying salutes her mother.)

Madame Cui says:

Have you not heard, my dear child, that Sun Feihu has besieged the monastery with his five thousand men? He says that you have black eye-brows with winning expressions, a face as beautiful as the lotus in spring and such overwhelming charms as to match the most famous beauties of old. He wants to take you by force and make you his mistress of the camp! My dear child, what is to be done?

Yingying sings to the tune of *PRELUDE TO GREEN WAIST*:

My soul is gone, my body full of woe,
My sleeves can't stop my tears which overflow.
I cannot stay
Nor go away.
Where can we find a friend
On whom we can depend?
My widowed mother finds not one before;
At such a crisis my blessed father is no more.
I hear the drums resounding loud;
The bandits raise a dust as high as the cloud.

Tune: *PETIY SONG*

It is reported the bandits say
I have black eyebrows with winning way
And a face full of such overwhelming charm
As to disarm
Those who behold.

ACT II

Such a peer of famous beauties of old
Might do away with priests and bandits in mass
Just as uprooted grass.
How could I bear the bandits to loot and rob their fill
And burn the palace-like monastery at will?

Madame Cui says:

I am fifty now. For me death would not be premature. But you, my dear child, you are still young and not yet married. How can I bear to see you fall victim to this disaster?

Yingying says:

I think all that can be done is to hand me over to the bandit so that the lives of our family can be saved.

Madame Cui, weeping, says:

In our family not a man has ever violated law and not a woman has ever remarried. How can I bear to hand you over to the bandit so as to disgrace our family!

Yingying says:

My dear mother, do not think much of your daughter. I think there will be five advantages in handing me over.

She sings to the tune of BACKYARD FLOWER:

Firstly, dear mother, your safety may be ensured;
Secondly, the temple from fire may be secured;
Thirdly, the priests may pray without alarm;
Fourthly, my father's coffin protected from harm;
Fifthly, Merry Boy, although young, will be
A scion of our family.
Should I not make this sacrifice
And disobey the bandit steeped in vice,
The temple with the coffin would be burned to ashes

And the monks stained with bloody splashes.
Can I be so unkind to my adopted brother
And so ungrateful to my widowed mother?

Tune: *WILLOW LEAVES*

Not a child would be left to continue our race.
Should I follow the rebel host,
To our family it would be a disgrace.
The best for me to do is to give up the ghost
So that you may present to the head
Of the brigands my body dead.
Thus you all may escape injury
And save our family.

Fa Ben says:

Let us go to the preaching hall and inquire of the monks and laymen in the two corridors if they have any suggestions to offer so that we can make a workable plan.

(They all go and arrive there.)

Madame Cui says:

My dear child, what is to be done? I have something to say to you. Not that I can bear to be separated from you, but that I know no way out. If any one in the corridors, priest or layman, is able to induce the bandits to withdraw, I will present you to him as his wife and give him a handsome dowry. Though a lop-sided alliance, such a match would be better than falling into the hands of the brigand.

(Weeping) Abbot, please proclaim my proposal in the preaching hall. My dear child, it is you who will suffer.

Fa Ben says:

This is a better proposal.

ACT II

Yingying sings to the tune of *BLUE SONG*:
>You think of none but me, my mother dear;
>What you have said is not for other ears to hear.
>But be not anxious for poor me!
>It matters little who it be.
>So long as he can display
>His bravery to drive the bandits away,
>With handsome dowry I would be his wife
>To the end of my life.
>
>>(Fa Ben proclaims the above conditions.)

Master Zhang enters applauding the declaration and says:
>I have a plan for driving away the bandits. Why not ask me?
>
>>(He greets Madame Cui.)

Fa Ben says:
>I beg to tell you, Madame, this scholar is my relative who joined in the religious ceremony on the fifteenth of the moon.

Madam Cui says:
>What is your plan?

Master Zhang says:
>I beg to say, Madame, large reward will secure brave men. Since a handsome reward is offered, I think my plan will work.

Madame Cui says:
>I have just told the Abbot: I will give my daughter as wife to any one who can drive the bandits away.

Master Zhang says:
>If that is the case, I have a plan which, first of all, requires the assistance of the Abbot.

Fa Ben says:
>An old priest is no fighter. I must ask you, sir, to find someone

else in my place.

Master Zhang says:

Be not afraid. I do not want you to fight. You just go out and tell the rebel chief the decision of Madame that her daughter in mourning cannot marry a general in arms. If he wishes the marriage, he must take off his armour, lay down his arms and withdraw as far as an arrow can shoot. He must wait three days until the religious service is finished. After she bids farewell to her father's coffin and changes into her bridal robes, she will be escorted to him. If she should be escorted at once, it would be unlucky for his army because she is still in mourning. Go and tell him as above.

Fa Ben says:

What is to be done after the three days?

Master Zhang says:

I have a friend whose name is Du Que and whose title is General on the White Horse. He is now in command of an army of a hundred thousand men, guarding the Pu Pass. He and I are sworn brothers. If I write a letter to him, he is sure to come to my rescue.

Fa Ben says:

If the General on the White Horse comes. Madame, we need not be afraid even if there were a hundred Flying Tigers. Please be not worried, Madame.

Madame Cui says:

Our warmest thanks are due to you, sir. Rose, see your Young Mistress back to her chamber.

Yingying says:

Rose, what a lucky strike!

ACT II

She sings to the tune of *PSEUDO-EPILOGUE*:

> The priests for their own lives would flee.
> Who would take care of our family?
> Although an unacquainted outsider mere,
> To help us he would volunteer.
> Not that he's wise to give advice,
> But that he's not afraid of sacrifice.
> We've no relation near;
> Upon a thread hangs our lives dear.
> Sink or swim, live or die,
> Upon this scholar we can but rely.
> O that his letter would restore order
> And conquer brigands as generals did on the border!
> I wish the point of his pen
> Would sweep away five thousand men.

(Exeunt Yingying and Rose.)

Fa Ben says loud:

> I request the General to come out.

Sun Feihu enters with soldiers and says:

> Send Yingying to me at once!

Fa Ben says:

> Calm down your anger, General. I am ordered by Madame Cui to inform you that...

(He repeats the order.)

Sun Feihu says:

> If such is the case, I limit you to three days. If Yingying is not sent to me by the end of that time, I will have you put to death one and all. Go and tell Madame what an excellent son-in-law I

will make. Say she ought to accept me.

(Exit Sun Feihu with his soldiers.)

Fa Ben says:

The bandits have withdrawn. You must write your letter without delay, sir.

Master Zhang says:

The letter is already written. What we need is a man to send it.

Fa Ben says:

I have a disciple in the kitchen called Hui Ming, who is good at fighting and drinking. If you ask him to send the letter, he is sure to refuse but if you can arouse his perverse spirit, nothing will deter him from going. He is the only man on whom we can rely.

Master Zhang says loud:

I have a letter to send to the General on the White Horse. Who dare to take it? But I would not allow Hui Ming of the kitchen to go.

Hui Ming enters and says:

I will go. I will go.

He sings to the tune of *CALM DIGNITY*:

I won't recite the Scripture nor pray;
In Imperial Confession I do not believe.
I have thrown my monk's cowl away
And doffed my robe which has only one sleeve.
If anyone arouses my desire to kill,
There's nothing but my iron poker could fulfill.

Tune: *ROLLING BALL*

Not that I am perverse,
Nor that I care a curse
What they call Buddha worship,
But that I only know

ACT II

> To take big strides and go
> To kill the tiger, heedless of hardship.
> Not that I'm full of greed,
> Nor that I hate the creed,
> But that the meatless diet is tasteless indeed.
> Five thousand bandits need not be fried or stewed first.
> Their blood would quench my thirst,
> Their flesh would satisfy my appetite.
> Can you say I'm not right?

Tune: *MURMURING SONG*

> Your soup so thin
> And noodles thick
> With flour mixed in
> Would make my stomach sick.
> Your yellow leek and strong-smelling bean-curd
> Are tasteless and absurd.
> Ten-thousand-catty dumplings are good to eat,
> With these five thousand bandits as minced meat.
> Deter me not! Deter me not!
> If any of their flesh were left unserved,
> I'd sprinkle it with salt and have it well preserved.

Fa Ben says:

> Oh Hui Ming, don't you know that Master Zhang will employ anyone but you? Why should you venture to go? Are you not afraid of the bandits?

Hui Ming sings to the tune of *PSEUDO-SCHOLAR*:

> Don't ask me if I dare to go,
> But tell me if I'll be employed. Yes or no?
> You say Sun is a flying tiger indeed;

I say he is a beast of lust and greed.
How can I bear a brute of such breed!

Master Zhang says:
How is it that you, a monk, will not recite your sacred books and follow other priests for spiritual instruction, but want to bear message for me?

Hui Ming sings to the tune of *ROLLING BALL*:
I will not read my sacred books
Nor meditate in my religious nooks.
My newly polished sword remains
Without rust or stains,
When other priests look like laymen
Shut up by daylight in their den.
They care not if the entire
Monastery is on fire.
If you do know a general miles away,
To whom you have a message to convey,
I will send it for you
And brave the foe in view.

Master Zhang says:
Will you go by yourself or do you need someone to accompany you?

Hui Ming sings to the tune of *WHITE CRANE*:
Send with me some young monks with banners and parasols
And weakling acolytes with rolling pins and poles.
If you are firm to calm down the whole community,
I'll boldly go to meet the enemy.

Master Zhang says:
What if they don't let you pass?

ACT II

Hui Ming says:
> Don't worry if they don't let me pass!

He sings to the tune of *A SECOND STANZA*:
> My angry glance would make the billows leap and bound;
> With my thundering voice the mountains would resound.
> I stamp my feet and there would come an earthquake;
> I raise my arms and Heaven's gates would shake.
> Those who stand afar,
> I'd sweep away with my iron bar;
> Those who are nigh,
> I'd cut in two while passing by.
> Those who are small,
> I'd pick up and kick like a ball,
> And smash the head of those who are tall.

Master Zhang says:
> Now I give you the letter, when will you start?

Hui Ming sings to the tune of *PLAYING THE CHILD*:
> Explosive I have always been;
> I do not know what fear could mean.
> Tempered through fighting, I'm not outworn;
> Intrepid I was born.
> I've ever been decisive and determined,
> Unlike the thoughtless straw in the wind.
> Even to death I'm not afraid to go.
> With sword in hand, would I stay my horse before the foe?

Tune: *A SECOND STANZA*

> I'd help the weak; the strong I'd beat,
> Preferring the bitter to the sweet.

Don't worry about me more than your would-be wife.
If no armed troops of White-horsed General came,
It is not I but your letter that is to blame.
Fair words alone could not persuade,
And a mistake once made
Would cause you shame for the rest of your life.

He says:

I am off!

He sings to the tune of *THE EPILOGUE*:

You beat the drum three times to stir my spirit high,
And blessed by Buddha, I'll utter a loud war-cry.
Behold from far a hero amid their flags appear
And five thousand bandits tremble with fear!

Master Zhang says:

Madame, you may tell the Young Lady not to worry. As soon as my letter is received, the army will come at once.

If through the night my letter flies,
The White Horse would come from the skies.

(Exeunt.)

General Du enters with his soldiers and says:

I am Du Que, styled Junshi, born west of Luoyang. While young, I studied Confucian classics together with Zhang Junrui. Then I gave up the pen for the sword and came out first in the military examinations. I was appointed General of the Western Front, commanding a hundred thousand men stationed at the Pass of Pu. A man coming from the Mid-river Prefecture told me my sworn brother Junrui is staying in Salvation Temple. Why does he not come to see me? I do not understand. Recently Ding Wenya,

ACT II

instead of fulfilling his duty, has allowed his men to plunder the people and I must despatch my troops to wipe them away. But as I do not yet know the whole truth, I cannot make a well-considered decision. Yesterday scouts were sent for information. Now I am going to the tent to see if they have come back.

(He opens the entrance of his tent and sits down.)

Hui Ming enters and says:

Having left the Salvation Monastery, here I am at the Pass of Pu. This is the encampment of General Du. I must get in at once.

(He is arrested by soldiers who report to the general.)

General Du says:

Bring him in!

(Hui Ming enters and kneels down.)

General Du says:

Hello, monk! Are you not a spy?

Hui Ming says:

I am not a spy. I am a monk of the Salvation Monastery. It is now surrounded by Sun the Flying Tiger with his five thousand men, declaring he would force the daughter of the late Prime Minister Cui to be his wife.

I have brought a letter from Zhang Junrui, who requests Your Excellency to come to their rescue as soon as possible.

General Du says:

Attendants, release the monk! Zhang Junrui is my sworn brother. Hand his letter to me.

(Hui Ming prostrates himself and presents the letter.)

General Du opens the letter and reads:

Zhang Gong, your former fellow-student and sworn brother,

65

makes his bow once and again and presents this letter to Your Excellency General Du Junshi. Two years have passed since we met last, and I can never forget the windy and rainy night when we shared the bed together. On my way from home to the capital I passed the Mid-river Prefecture and intended to pay you a visit. But the journey had so exhausted me that I fell ill. Now I am far better and there is no cause for worry. I have taken up quarters in a quiet monastery which unexpectedly became a scene of arms. The widow of the late Premier Cui has brought her husband's coffin to the monastery But, at the sight of her beautiful daughter, a bandit named Sun Feihu has besieged the temple with his five thousand men. Anyone who should see their helpless state would feel indignant and try all means to drive the bandits away. But, to my regret, as I am a mere scholar unable to truss a chicken, I could do nothing to help them even at the sacrifice of my life. Then I think of you who have received full powers to control the area and are able to lull the storm. You who follow the tradition of the heroes of old are in no way unworthy of them. I am now in danger; the matter is pressing. Words fail me to express my longing for your help. I beseech you to come to the Mid-river Prefecture as soon as possible and wish you would start in the morning and arrive in the evening. We should be grateful to you as a fish stranded on dry land to the water brought from the far-off West River. The late Minister Cui, though in the eternal Shades below, would also be grateful to you for your timely arrival. Hoping you will give this matter enough attention, Zhang Gong salutes you again on the sixteenth day of the second moon.

ACT II

General Du says:
> Since the matter is urgent, I will give orders at once. Monk, you go back ahead and I will follow this very night. By the time you reach the monastery, probably I may have already captured the brigand.

Hui Ming says:
> The monastery is in a dangerous situation. I pray Your Excellency to speed up.
>
> (Exit)

General Du, giving orders, says:
> Officers and men, listen to my orders! Select five thousand soldiers and start this very night for the Salvation Monastery in the Mid-river Prefecture to the rescue of my sworn brother.

All answer:
> Your orders will be obeyed. (Exeunt)

Sun Feihu rushes in with his men and says:
> The General on the White Horse has come. What is to be done? What is to be done? Let us dismount, doff our armour, lay down our arms, kneel down and await the General's decision on us.

General Du enters and says:
> Why have you all dismounted, doffed your armour, laid down your arms and knelt down? Do you expect me to forgive you? All right. Sun Feihu is to be beheaded. As for the rest, those who will not be enlisted may go home, those who will may give their names and be enlisted.
>
> (Exeunt all the bandits)

Madame Cui enters with Fa Ben and says:
> The letter was sent two days ago, but no reply has come.

Master Zhang enters and says:
> Thunderlike noises are heard from outside the gate:

probably it is my sworn brother who has arrived.

(Du and Zhang meet and bow to each other.)

Master Zhang says:

So long I have not heard from you since we parted that our meeting seems like a dream.

General Du says:

I have just heard you were travelling in my neighborhood, but I have not been able to pay you a visit, and I beg you to forgive me.

(General Du and Madame Cui meet and bow to each other.)

Madame Cui says:

We were in such a hopeless situation that we deemed death inevitable. It is due to you that we can still enjoy life today.

General Du says:

I have not taken proper precautions against these bandits so that you have been alarmed, for which I should bear the blame.

(To Master Zhang) May I ask you why you did not come to my place?

Master Zhang says:

I happened to be indisposed, so I failed to pay you a visit. I ought to accompany you back today, but Madame promised to give me her beloved daughter in marriage. I should be grateful to you if you could defer your departure and act as go-between. My plan is that a month after the wedding ceremony I will pay you a visit and express my gratitude to you.

General Du says:

My hearty congratulations and best wishes to you, Madame. I shall be delighted to act as go-between.

Madame Cui says:

I have still other arrangements in mind. Let dinner be served.

ACT II

General Du says:
> As five thousand men have just surrendered, I must go and deal with the matter. I will certainly come some other day to renew my congratulations.

Master Zhang says:
> I dare not detain you lest it should interfere with your duties.
>
> (General Du mounts his White Horse.)
>
> The horsemen leave the temple amid the cymbals' sound;
> The soldiers sing victorious songs, for Pu Pass bound.
>
> (Exit General Du)

Madame Cui says:
> We are deeply grateful for your invaluable help. From now on you should no longer dwell in your present quarters but move to the library of ours. A dinner will be prepared tomorrow and Rose will come to invite your presence. You must not refuse to come.
>
> (Exit)

Master Zhang bids goodbye to Fa Ben and says:
> I am going to pack up my things and remove to the library of Madame's quarters.
> The fire ignited by the bandits brings a shower
> Unexpectedly to satisfy the thirsting flower.
> Sun Feihu, you can never know how much I am indebted to you.

Fa Ben says:
> When you have leisure, Master Zhang, I hope you will come to my cell and we may have a chat as usual.
>
> (Exeunt)

Scene 2 Invitation

Master Zhang enters and says:
>Yesterday Madame said that Rose would come to invite me to a feast. I rose before dawn to await her arrival, but up to now I have not seen her. Oh! where is my dear, dear Rose?

Rose enters and says:
>My Mistress has ordered me to invite Master Zhang. I must go there as early as possible.

She sings to the tune of *PINK BUTTERFLY*:
>Five thousand bandits shouting loud
>Were wiped away like floating cloud.
>Our family in midst of death
>Can breathe again our breath.
>We'll make a feast voluntarily
>Of delicacies from land and sea
>To show to Zhang Junrui our thanks and our respect.
>Who would expect
>The hope that seemed vain in those days
>Has been fulfilled by what a letter says!
>
>   **Tune: *INTOXICATED EAST WIND***
>
>The mist-veiled East Pavilion's opened today;
>No longer need you outside Western Bower stay
>With the moon overhead.
>The coverlet and pillow will be warmed on your bed.

Henceforth you won't feel cold.

The incense from the burner's a joy to behold;

The gentle breeze won't roll up your embroidered screen.

None will disturb you two within your windows green.

She says:

Here I am in front of the library.

She sings to the tune of *DOFFING THE CLOTHES*:

A quiet spot

With none in sight,

There's but green moss with dot

On dot of dewdrops white.

Outside the window I must cough.

Master Zhang says:

Who is it?

Rose says:

It is I.

(Master Zhang opens the door and sees her.)

She continues to sing:

I see him open the door and come right off.

Tune: *SMALL LIANGZHOU*

He greets me with clasped hands and many, many bows;

I can return no more salute than time allows.

Wearing a black-gauze hat, he looks so bright,

Attired in a scholar's robe of Pure white

With a gilt-buckled belt.

Tune: *PETTY SONG*

His splendid garments put apart,

His fine appearance's sure to win my Young Mistress' heart.

His talent shown and gentleness felt

Would make a maid like me with envy green,

Hard-hearted though I've always been.

She says:

By Madame's order ...

Master Zhang says:

I am off at once.

Rose sings to the tune of *ASCENDING THE ATTIC*:

Before I say a word,

He answers though nothing is heard.

His soul has flown to my Young Mistress dear;

His heart's no longer here.

Eager to make her an address,

He keeps on saying: "Yes."

When scholars are invited, they

Regard it as an order to obey.

Master Zhang says:

May I ask you, Miss Rose, why this banquet is held?

Will there be other guests present?

Rose sings to the tune of *PETTY SONG*:

It's held to ease the alarm, in the first place;

And secondly to thank you for your act of grace.

Nor neighbours nor relations will appear;

No gifts will be received, however dear.

All priests are kept away;

Alone you are invited to be betrothed today.

I see he's but too eager to obey.

ACT II

Tune: *COURTYARD FULL OF FRAGRANCE*
While walking to and fro.
Admiring his own shadow,
The brilliant scholar has a gallant air,
Taking such pains to polish his hair,
On which may slither flies
And which may dazzle one's eyes.
His wretched looks might set on edge one's teeth
When he arranges to lock up his rice
And put some wreath
Upon his jars of little price.

Tune: *THE HAPPY THREE*
This man who's clever in one thing is wise in all,
Unlike those who fail in everything, great or small.
Even unfeeling plants and trees
Will grow together in the vernal breeze,

Tune: *HOMACE TO EMPEROR*
Could such a youth as he be free from lovesickness?
Wise and well-dressed, could she bear nightly loneliness?
I've heard a genius' love despised by a beauty
May make him lose his life and forget his duty.
But you will have good proof tonight
Of my Young Mistress' faith and true delight
And her sincerity.

Tune: *FOUR-SIDE TRANQUILITY*
But such an ecstasy
May thrill our delicate Yingying with fright,
So you should be gentle and light.

When you cross her legs by lampside,
You may contemplate your bewitching bride,
And love your fill
At your sweet will.

Master Zhang says:

May I ask you, Miss Rose, what arrangement has been made and how the chamber is decorated for today? Is it appropriate for me to go there without due preparation?

Rose sings to the tune of *PLAYING THE CHILD*:

The grounds there covered with rouge-red flowers,
Don't miss the pretty scene and happy hours!
My Mistress ordered me not to delay.
Dear sir, don't fail to go at once, I pray.
We have prepared a curtain embroidered above
With a round moon and below with birds of love;
Two screens of jade adorned with peacocks standing at ease
Enjoying the vernal breeze;
A music band consisting of phoenix flute,
Ivory castanets and wild swan lute.

Master Zhang says:

May I ask you, Miss Rose, as a traveller has brought nothing with him as a ceremonial gift, how can I go to see Madame with bare hands?

Rose sings to the tune of *LAST STANZA BUT THREE*:

When no betrothal money is needed,
The marriage will be all the more speeded.
Your happy union is determined by fate:
You are to ride on phoenix' back to Heaven's gate,

ACT II

And I will watch you like the Cowherd meet
His Weaving Maiden sweet.
How lucky to be joined in nuptial bed
Without the tying of a red silk thread!

Tune: *LAST STANZA BUT TWO*

The rebels being driven away,
The General coming in array,
I think your merits worth more than a red silk thread.
You have entirely won Miss Oriole's heart,
And you're as strong as a million soldiers in your head.
Since olden days true talents take a leading part.
Who has ever seen a pearl-adorned maiden bright
Not wed to one who studied by a dim lamplight?

Tune: *LAST STANZA BUT ONE*

My Mistress here has only her own family,
And you, sir, have no other company.
It will be quiet ceremony indeed.
You are awaited with hearty welcome, so speed!
We won't invite a priest who cares
Not for worldly affairs.
So do not disobey
My Mistress. Come without delay!

Master Zhang says:

If so, will you please go ahead, Miss Rose? I will follow at once.

Rose sings to the tune of *THE EPILOGUE*:

Be not too modest, sir, I pray.
My Mistress only waits for you.
To be polite is not so good as to obey.
Don't let me come to invite you anew! (Exit)

Master Zhang says:
>Rose has gone. Let me close the door of the library. When I arrive in the presence of Madame, she will say, "Here you are, Master Zhang. You and my Yingying will make a happy couple, so drink two cups of wine before you go to the bridal chamber." (Laughing) Sun Feihu, you are indeed my benefactor. I owe you so much. When I have leisure, I will not grudge spending ten thousand coins and asking Fa Ben to perform a religious ceremony to save your soul. I wish the Dragon's rain would wash away his vice to help the Flying Tiger rise to paradise.
>
>(Exit)

ACT II

Scene 3 Promise Broken

Madame Cui enters and says:
> Rose has gone to invite Master Zhang. Why has she not yet returned?

Rose enters, sees Madame Cui and says:
> Master Zhang told me to go ahead and he will follow at once.
>
> (Master Zhang enters and salutes Madame Cui.)

Madame Cui says:
> If it had not been for you the other day, Master Zhang we could not have survived till today. Our survival is due to you. I have prepared for you a feast. Although it is not in any way a return for what you have done for us, I hope you will not regard it as unworthy.

Master Zhang says:
> It is said that on the good fortune of one person may depend that of the millions. The defeat of the bandits was due to your good fortune, Madame. As it is a thing of the past, it is not worthy of mention.

Madame Cui says:
> Bring wine here. Drink off this cup please, sir.

Master Zhang says:
> I will comply with the order of my elder.
>
> (He drinks at once and pours out wine for Madame Cui.)

Madame Cui says:
> Sit down please, sir.

Master Zhang says:
> I should remain standing before you as prescribed by the rite. How could I presume to sit down in your presence?

Madame Cui says:
> Do you not know the old saying that politeness is not so good as compliance?
>
> (Master Zhang, asking to be excused, sits down.)
>
> (Madame Cui tells Rose to ask Yingying to come.)

Yingying enters and says:
> The foe like smoke by wind are swept away.
> The sun and moon will shine on festive day.

She sings to the tune of *PROVISION*:
> If Master Zhang had not such a good friend,
> To the armed riot none else could have put an end.
> The banquet spread,
> The music played,
> Incense like thread,
> Flowers never fade.
> The eastern wind uprolls curtain and screen
> For one who saved our family from woe.
> On him it's proper to be keen;
> To him it's right respect to show.

Rose says:
> My Young Mistress, how early you have got up this morning!

Yingying sings to the tune of *NEW WATER*:
> I have just painted my eyebrows near the window screen,
> And swept away the powder soiling my robe green.
> I've with my fingertips adjusted my hair-pin.

ACT II

Had I not been awakened in my bed,
On my embroidered pillow I'd still rest my head.

Rose says:

You have finished your toilet, my Young Mistress? Will you please wash your hands? I see your face seems so delicate that it would be hurt by a breath of air. What a lucky man is Master Zhang! My Young Mistress, you were indeed born to be the wife of a lord.

Yingying sings to the tune of *PETTY SONG*:

What are you talking without thyme or reason there?
Could my fair face be hurt by a breath of air?
Don't talk nonsense and freely wag your tongue!
How could you know his fate and mine while we're still young?

Tune: *BRUSHWOOD*

You say I am lovesick for him and he for me,
But cured today our lovesickness will be.
Our gratitude should be shown by a special feast.
Why should my mother worry in the least?

Tune: *ZITHER AND GUITAR*

My marriage would cause loss to our family, true,
So mother'd show her gratitude and celebrate
It by one feast instead of two.
The General's coming to exterminate
The foe is worth the money we can give
For one to live
The rest of his life.
Why should my mother fear
It would cost her dear
To make me his wife?

Tune: *CELEBRATION OF HARMONY*

>Outside the curtained door,
>Before I move my lotus feet,
>I take a furtive glance to explore …

Master Zhang says:
>Please excuse me for a moment.

>>(He pretends to meet Yingying by chance.)

Yingying continues to sing:
>Who would have thought -what can I do? —
>He has such insight as to see me through
>So that I cannot but retreat.

Madame Cui says:
>Come near, my dear daughter, and pay your respect to your elder brother.

Master Zhang says:
>Ah! This is not a good augury.

Yingying says:
>Oh! My mother has changed her mind.

Rose says:
>Oh! They will be lovesick again.

Yingying sings to the tune of *FALLING SWAN*.
>Surprised, he can nor move
>Nor react, faint with love.
>Confused, he can't reply
>Nor sit down with a sigh.

Tune: *TRIUMPHANT SONG*

>You are indeed an olde worlde mother.
>How can I call him elder brother?

Before me water rises higher and still higher;

The monastery seems consumed by roaring fire.

The two inseparable fish

Are separated by green waves against their wish.

How can I not be worried for it!

How can I not keep my eyebrows knit!

Tune: *SONG OF SWEET WATER*

My head bent down,

My neck is shown;

My locks undone,

My heart by woe is overrun.

What can I say to him when we do meet?

Dim are my starry eyes,

My breath consumed in sighs;

I cannot stamp my feet.

Can this be called a feast

Where there is no joy in the least!

Madame Cui says:

Rose, bring heated wine for your Young Mistress to fill the cup of her elder brother.

(Yingying fills a cup for him.)

Master Zhang says:

I am not a drinker.

Yingying says:

Rose, remove the wine-cup.

She sings to the tune of *PICKING LAUREL*:

He cannot drink another cup of wine,

Even if it be nectar divine.

How could he know the delight enjoyed beneath moonbeams
Would turn into empty dreams!
His eyes are drowned in tears,
He wipes them with the sleeve which also wet appears,
He tries to open his eyes,
So listless like a lump that he can't rise.
He cannot shrug his shoulders and
Not even lift his hand.
He is so incurably ill
That I don't know how long he can live still.
Oh, mother, you have made him half-dead.
What more is there to be said!

Madame Cui says:

My dear daughter, you must fill a cup of wine for your elder brother.

(Yingying fills a cup of wine.)

Master Zhang says:

I have said I am not a drinker.

Yingying says:

Master Zhang, please take this cup of wine.

She sings to the tune of *THE MOON OVER CRABAPPLE*:

When I present this cup of bitter wine to you,
Why should you grieve in silence, bending your head?
You cannot be intoxicated with such brew.
Why should you hold this large glass cup in dread?
Oh! Listen to me, please!
When the wine mounts, your heart will be more at ease.

Tune: *PETTY SONG*

Your sorrow now is still not hard to bear.
What's to be done with our secret love affair?

I should like in you to confide,

But how can I do so with mother at my side?

Although you're but a foot away,

You seem as far off as the Milky Way.

>> (Master Zhang drinks the cup of wine.)
>> (Yingying sits down at the feast.)

Madame Cui says:

Rose, pour out some more wine. Please drink this cup dry, sir.

>> (Master Zhang does not respond.)

Yingying sings to the tune of *PSEUDO-MELODY*:

You have changed your mind,

But do not think we cannot find

Out your riddle. You try to coax with honeyed word,

We feel all the unhappier when it's heard.

Tune: *A CLEAR RIVER*

The beauty always has a hapless fate,

And never bold is a scholar great.

Sad is the daughter when her father's lost

And when her marriage may dearly cost.

I know not what my mother will do with me.

>> (Master Zhang laughs ironically.)

Yingying sings to the tune of *BEFORE THE PALACE*:

How can he laugh apart?

He must be filled with tears in his heart.

Without his letter, who'd have beaten the enemy

And saved the lives of all our family?

What could be his desire if not to marry me?

It's hard to guess:

You have abused your power over me;

The failure or success
In this matter rests with no other
Than you, Oh! mother.

Tune: *FAREWELL FEAST & EPILOGUE*

Henceforth my lonely face will no longer be fair
As blossoms of the pear;
Nor cherry-red my lips will be
For lovesickness I cannot stand.
My grief is as deep as the dark, dark sea,
As boundless as the vast, vast land,
And as endless as the blue, blue sky.
You looked up first to him as mountain high
And thirsted for him as for ocean deep.
How can you be so cruel now as to make him weep!
You're crumpling tender, tender twin buds of the flower,
Severing lovers fragrant, fragrant knot,
And breaking long, long branches joined before the bower.
It's hard for white-haired one to bear her lot.
Who would have thought the hope of youth is hard to gain?
You've shattered a future kindling our hearts' flame:
On the one hand you've flattered him with promise vain,
And on the other tricked me by a sister's name.

Madame Cui says:

Rose, conduct your Young Mistress to her bed chamber.

(Yingying bids goodbye to Master Zhang.)

(Exeunt Yingying and Rose.)

Master Zhang says:

I am overcome with wine and beg to hid you farewell. If I may be permitted, I still have a word to say to you, Madame. When the bandits threatened violence and danger menaced, Madame promised to give Yingying as wife to anyone who could make the bandits withdraw. Is this not what you said?

Madame Cui says:

Yes, it was.

Master Zhang says:

Then, who was it who came forward to brave the bandits?

Madame Cui says:

It was you to whom we owed our lives. But when the late Prime Minister was alive...

Master Zhang says:

Will you please stop a moment, Madame? When I wrote that letter in haste, requesting General Du to come, was it only because I wanted something to eat and drink today? When Rose came this morning to summon me, I thought you were going to fulfill your promise and I was to marry your daughter. Who knows what has made you suddenly change your mind and call me her elder brother? May I beg to ask what use the Young Lady can have for me to be her elder brother and what use I can have for her to be my younger sister? As the old saying goes, it is never too late to mend. I request you, Madame, to reconsider the matter.

Madame Cui says:

My daughter was betrothed, when my late husband was still alive, to my nephew Zheng Heng, and I have written to summon him to come here. What if he comes? Now I think the best we can do is to reward you with a large sum of money so that you may select another lady of a noble family and that both of us may carry out our matrimonial arrangements to our satisfaction.

Master Zhang says:
>Do you really think so? What if General Du had not come and Sun Feihu had done what he would? What use have I for your money? I will now bid you farewell.

Madame Cui says:
>Stay a moment, sir! You have been drinking today. Rose, support the elder brother to the library. Tomorrow we will discuss other arrangements.

>> (Exit.)

Rose, supporting Master Zhang, says:
>Master Zhang, would it not have been better if you had drunk a cup less?

Master Zhang says:
>Alas! Miss Rose, how can you be so simple? How much wine have I drunk? Since I saw your Young Mistress, I have neither eaten nor slept well. Up to now I have suffered so much. I cannot tell my suffering to others. But how can I not tell you? The letter I wrote to General Du the other day may not be worthy of mention. But Madame is a lady of the first rank, whose word should be as good as gold. How could she break her promise of marrying her daughter to me? Oh, Miss Rose, her promise was not only heard by us two, but by all the priests and laymen in the monastery, and even by the Buddha above and the Abbot below. How could she suddenly have changed her mind and reduced me to my wits' end without any way out? How can this matter be ended? It seems all I can do is to unloose my girdle and commit suicide before your eyes so that
>Within the doors a stranger hanging on the beam

ACT II

Would only wander to his far-off home in dream.

(He unlooses his girdle.)

Rose says:

Don't be so rash, sir! I understand your sentiments for my Young Mistress. My offense against you the other day was owing to my unacquaintance with you. It was so sudden that you should not blame me for that. As to the present matter, Madame did make her promise. As Confucius said, one good deed deserves another, I will do my best to help you.

Master Zhang says:

I will be grateful to you to the end of my life. But may I ask you what you can do to help me?

Rose says:

I have seen your lute, so I think you must be a good lute player. My Young Mistress also loves the music of the lute. She will go with me to the garden to burn incense tonight. I will cough as a signal, and when you hear it, you may begin to play your lute. I will observe what she will say, and at the right moment I will tell her your sentiments. If she says anything, I will let you know early tomorrow morning. Now I am afraid my Mistress may call me at any moment, so I had better go back at once.

(Exit.)

Master Zhang says:

I pass my lonely night in lonely temple still.
When in her bridal chamber can I love my fill?

(Exit.)

Scene 4 Lute

Master Zhang enters and says:

Rose told me to wait for her Young Mistress to burn incense in the garden and to play my lute so as to see what she will say. I have thought it over and found it reasonable. The night is already dark. Oh, Moon, can't you come out a little earlier for my sake? Oh, I have heard the drum beat. Oh, I have heard the bell ring.

(He tunes his lute.)

Oh, Lute, my travel companion, on you I depend for the success of tonight's matter. Oh, Heaven, will you lend me a fair breeze to waft the song of my lute to my Young Lady's ears carved from jade and moulded of powder?

(Yingying enters with Rose.)

Rose says:

My Young Mistress, let us go to burn incense. How bright the moon is tonight!

Yingying says:

How can I have the heart to burn incense, Rose? Oh, Moon, why have you come out?

She sings to the tune of *FIGHT OF QUAILS*:

Clouds break and clears the sky;
The moon dazzles the eye.
The wind sweeps off red flowers;
They fall in fragrant showers.

The grief to be kept apart

Now and then wrings my heart.

Oh, mother, why should something well begun

Be in the end undone?

He will be now to me but a dream lover dear,

And I shall be to him a beloved picture mere.

Tune: *VIOLET FLOWER*

I can but long for him in vain;

From talking of him I'll refrain.

We cannot meet

But in dreams sweet.

A feast was given yesterday;

I fondly thought of my bridal array.

My visions fade:

I raised green sleeves to fill with wine his cup of jade.

How could I know

My mother showed her love

By parting fish from water below

And severing love-birds above!

Rose says:

Look, my Young Mistress, there is a halo around the moon.

It will probably be windy tomorrow.

Yingying says:

Yes, there is a halo around the moon.

She sings to the tune of *RED PEACH BLOSSOMS*:

A lovely jade-like face

Is locked up within the broidered curtains of lace;

It's feared to be profaned

By the touch of a mortal hand

　　　　Just like the Goddess of the Moon
　　　　Traversing the sky from east to west, all alone.
　　　　And we complain
　　　　Her lover cannot visit her Palace again,
　　　　Which is surrounded by screen on screen
　　　　Lest she be seen
　　　　And her heart above
　　　　Be moved to love.

　　　　　　　　　　　　　　　　(Rose coughs slightly.)

Master Zhang says:
　　　　It must be Miss Rose coughing. Her Young Mistress has come out.

　　　　　　　　　　　　　　　　(He plays on the lute.)

Yingying says:
　　　　What is that sound, Rose?

Rose says:
　　　　Will you guess, my Young Mistress?

Yingying sings to the tune of *CLEAR SKY OVER THE SAND*:
　　　　Is it the tinkling headdress on a lady's hair
　　　　Or ringing ornaments on the skirts women wear?
　　　　Is it the creaking iron hinges in shape of steed
　　　　When the wind blows with speed,
　　　　Or ding-dong sound of golden hooks
　　　　Knocking against the curtain frame in cozy nooks?

　　　　　　　　Tune: *SONG OF FLIRTATION*

　　　　Is it the evening bell
　　　　In the temple where Buddhists dwell,
　　　　Or the rustling made
　　　　By sparse bamboos in the winding balustrade?
　　　　Is it the sound

ACT II

Of ivory foot-measure and scissors around,
Or of water that drips
Incessantly into the clepsydra's lips?
Concealing myself, I listen again
At eastern corner of the wall,
And find it is the strain
Of the lute coming from the western hall.

Tune: *A BALD HEAD*

The strain seems strong
Like the clash of horsemen's sabres short and long;
Then soft it seems
Like flowers falling into smoothly flowing streams.
The strain is high
Like the cry of the crane in breezy moon-lit sky;
Then it is low
Like lovers' whispers about what we do not know.

Tune: *SOVEREIGN OF MEDICINE*

He is at his wits' end,
And sorrow will be his eternal friend.
I'm sad to hear the phoenix wail
For his lost mate to no avail.
The strains have not expressed what he might mean,
But I can understand what's in between:
He regrets the separation of two love-birds
In music without words.

Rose says:

Will you stay here to listen, my Young Mistress? I am going to see if the old Mistress may need me.

(She pretends to leave.)

Yingying sings to the tune of *A POCKMARXED FACE*:
>Not that an outsider, I have a good ear
>To know the feelings of my dear,
>But that two lovers have the same heart
>Which feels the grief to be kept apart.

Master Zhang says:
>There is a slight sound outside the window. It must be the Young Lady. I will try a tune now.

Yingying says:
>I will go nearer the window.

Master Zhang sighs and says:
>Oh, my lute! I remember an ancient scholar wooing a beautiful lady played a tune called Phoenix Seeking His Mate. Though I cannot presume to compare myself to the ancient sage, Miss Oriole, you are in every way a worthy rival of the beautiful lady. So I will play this tune in accordance with the original score:
>There is a lady fair
>I can't forget, I swear.
>Not seen a single day,
>She makes my mind go stray.
>See up and down the phoenix fly,
>Seeking his mate low and high.
>Alas! the lady fair
>Can't be found anywhere.
>I can but play my lute
>To show my grief acute.
>When will you give your word
>To the wandering bird:

ACT II

> United we will stand
> Together hand in hand?
> If wing to wing we could no fly,
> I would prefer to die.

Yingying says:

> It is beautifully played. Sad tune and bitter words move me to tears without my knowledge.

She sings to the tune of *PETTY SONG*:

> The notes from first to last are varied well,
> Unlike the nightly ringing bell,
> The cry of the drunken old man's golden crane
> Or the unfortunate phoenix's strain.

> **Tune: *SPINNER***
>
> Word by word drips like waterdrop
> From clepsydra of long, long night;
> Sound by sound shows without a stop
> He pines away with belt no longer tight.
> His grief of separation melts into a song.
> How can I not admire him for long?

Master Zhang, putting down the lute, says:

> Your mother may be ungrateful and unjust, but you, my dear Young Lady, how can you deceive one who believes in you!

(Rose reenters secretly.)

Yingying says:

> Your plaint is unjustified.

She sings to the tune of *JOY OF EASTERN PLAIN*:

> This is a strategem of my old mother.
> How can you lay the blame on another?

Were I allowed to rule my fate,
I would do like a phoenix seeking for a mate.
I'm ordered to do needlework night and day,
And have no leisure whate'er.
How could my mother care
About the blame on me another might lay?

Tune: *WADS OF COTTON*

Outside the window screen the breeze is light;
Inside his lonely room the lamp's not bright.
Between us there is only a sheet of paper red
On lattice window spread.
No cloudy mountains keep us far apart.
Who would send him the message of my heart?
High as the Twelve Mountain Peaks seem,
The lovers could still cross them to meet in dream.

Rose suddenly appears and says:

What dream, my Young Mistress? What if my Old Mistress gets to know it?

Yingying sings to the tune of *AWKWARD AND HEADLONG*:

Hurriedly she appears;
About my grief she does not care.
She has struck in me sudden fears,
Though I have not moved anywhere.
Why should a girl speak in such a loud voice?
But I must pat her and keep her here
Lest she should make much noise
Before my mother dear.

Rose says:

I have just heard that Master Zhang will be leaving. What is to

ACT II

be done, my Young Mistress?

Yingying says:

You may go, Rose, and tell him to stay two or three days longer.

She sings to the tune of *EPILOGUE*:

Tell him my mother still has something to say,
And good or bad, he'd not go empty away.
Why don't you keep your word, oh, mother most unkind,
And sever me from one who loves with heart and mind?

Rose says:

You need not give me orders, my Young Mistress. I know what should be done. I will go to see him tomorrow.

(Exeunt Yingying and Rose.)

Master Zhang says:

The Young Lady has gone. Why did you not stay a little longer, Miss Rose, so that you might tell me her response tonight? But as things are, what I can do is only to go to bed.

(Exit.)

To sum up the four scenes of Act II:

Master Zhang plans to drive the bandits away.
Hui Ming, the monk, is heedless of the rite.
Rose invites the guest by day;
Yingying listens to the lute at night.

ROMANCE OF WESTERN BOWER

ACT III

ACT III

Scene 1 First Expectation

Yingying enters with Rose and says:
> I have been feeling uneasy since I heard the lute last night. Rose, as you have nothing to do at the moment, you had better go to see Master Zhang in the library, hear what he has to say and come back to tell me.

Rose says:
> I dare not go there. What if my Mistress were to know it?

Yingying says:
> How can she know anything if I tell her nothing? You had better go now.

Rose says:
> All right, I will go just to tell him that you are no less ill than he is.
> You've not yet drunk your cup of nuptial day
> But heard on chilly night his lute's sweet lay.

She sings to the tune of *ENJOYING FLOWERS IN COMPANY OF FAIRIES*:
> She won't attend to needle and thread
> Nor renew the rouge and powder on her face.
> Spring sorrow knits the brows on her forehead,
> Which only mutual love can erase.

(Exit.)

Yingying says:
> Now Rose is gone. I'll wait and see what she has to tell me on

her return.
I can express in words only one-tenth of what I'll say;
Thinking of him all night long, I'm drowsy all day.

(Exit.)

Master Zhang enters and says:
How terribly I suffer! I requested the Abbot to tell them I am ill. Why is there no one sent to pay me a visit? Now I am tired. I'll go and sleep for a while.

(He sleeps.)

Rose enters and says:
On my Young Mistress' order, I am going to see Master Zhang. If it were not for him, how could our family be still alive?

She sings to the tune of *ROUGED LIPS OF A FAIRY*:
The Premier's coffin had to rest
In lonely Temple for the Blessed,
When suddenly
Came a calamity:
My fair Young Mistress in an alien land
Was in danger of falling in the bandit's hand.

Tune: *DRAGON IN TROUBLED WATER*
To Master Zhang we owe our thanks:
A letter sent, there came the files and ranks.
It's true that letters had their worth;
It's not the merit of heaven and earth.
If the five thousand bandits had not been wiped out,
Our family could not survive, no doubt.
The lovers should be man and wife
Throughout their life,

ACT III

But Madame broke her words
Under one pretext or another,
And they were severed like two single birds,
And called each other sister and brother.
Now the marriage is never talked about.
The Scholar's literary thought then disappears;
The Beauty's rouge and powder are bedewed with tears.

Tune: *FIELD CRICKET*

I see him waste
And pine away
With grizzled hair;
I see her not so fair
As in her better day,
Her girdle wider than her slender waist.
He will not read his classics and history;
She pays no heed to her embroidery.
He plays on lute the tune revealing grief to part;
She writes a poem with broken heart.
What does her poem express?
What does his lute confess?
Nothing but lovesickness.

Tune: *UNIVERSAL JOY*

This is indeed a case
Of Scholar and Beauty who interlace,
O how peculiar they seem to my eyes!
But all frustrated lovers act likewise.
He's lovesick for the fair.
For whom should I then care?

> I should bury my head
> And pine away until I'm dead.

She says:

> Here I am. I'll lick the window's paper screen and break it so as to see what he is doing in the library.

She sings to the tune of *VILLAGE DRUMS*:

> I peep in after breaking the window's paper wet,
> And seem to see him get
> Up after having gone
> To bed with clothes on.
> Creased is the front of his silk gown.
> How sad is he to sleep alone
> with none to attend on!
> Behold! His brightness gone.
> Listen! His breath is weak With hollow cheek.
> Oh, Master Zhang, without relief,
> You'd die, if not of sickness, at least of grief.

Tune: *SONG OF PEACE*

> I will knock at the door with the pin in my tress.

Master Zhang says:

> Who is there?

Rose continues to says:

> I am the spirit spreading lovesickness.

> *(Master Zhang opens the door and Rose enters.)*

Master Zhang says:

> I am very grateful for what you told me last night, and I will never forget your kindness. But I wonder whether your Young Mistress said anything to you last night.

ACT III

Rose covering her mouth with sleeve, laughs and says:
>As for my Young Mistress, I'll tell you what she said.

>She continues to sing:

>When the moon was bright

>And the wind was fresh in the deep of night:

>She ordered me

>To come to see

>Her lover from her heart she could not erase.

>Even now she neglects to rouge her powdered face.

>She only thinks of you

>Who are a talent true.

Master Zhang says:
>Since your Young Mistress has shown so much love for me, Miss Rose, I have a letter to send to her, but I don't know whether I may trouble you to take it for me.

Rose sings to the tune of *CHARMING ON HORSE*:
>When of your verse she comes in sight,
>She'll be beside herself with sweet delight.

She says:
>But she will pull a long face and say: "Rose, from whom is this message you dare to bring to me?"

She continues to sing:
>"You little minx! How dare you be so impudent!"
>And see the letter she will tear up in fragment.

Master Zhang says:
>I am sure your Young Mistress will not do this. It is only an excuse for you not to take this letter for me. Will it do for me to give you a handsome reward for your trouble?

Rose sings to the tune of *BETTER THAN GOURD*:

You are a wretched, vulgar registrar;
You want to make a show of how rich you are.
Do you think I have come to see
What I can get out of you?
If you give me the salary
You have in view,
Do you believe I could be sold
For your reward in gold?

Tune: *PETTY SONG*

You think we are like branches of peach or plum trees
Waving in vernal breeze
And smiling to all passers by,
But such is not the case of decent girls as I.
You ought to say:
"Have pity on poor, lonely me, I pray."
In that case, we may try
To find for you a way.

Master Zhang says:

As you say, Miss Rose, have pity on poor, lonely me, I pray. Will that do?

Rose says:

Yes, that is it. Now write your letter and I will take it.

(Master Zhang writes.)

Rose says:

How nice your handwriting looks! Read it to me, please.

Master Zhang reads:

Zhang Gong salutes a hundred times and presents this letter

ACT III

to Miss Oriole. The other day your kind mother rewarded my service with unkindness so that I felt more dead than alive. When the feast was over, I could not fall asleep. So I played on my lute to express my helpless feelings so that you might see from then on both the lute and its player would be gone for ever. Now that Rose comes, I will send you a few lines in the hope that you, who are so near and yet so far away, may have pity on me and come to the rescue of my life. While awaiting your decision, I add a poem which I hope you will condescend to read:

Gnawed by lovesickness,

I play on my lute.

Spring is happiness.

Can your heart be mute?

Love can't be disobeyed.

Of vain fame make light.

Pity the flower's shade;

Don't miss the moon bright!

Zhang Gong once more salutes a hundred times.

Rose sings to the tune of *BACKYARD FLOWER*:

I thought you'd smooth the paper for a draft,

But you have written like the frost and snow that waft.

Your letter begins with greetings you send;

A poem of eight lines comes at the end.

In a moment you've got

It folded up in lover's knot.

You are so clever,

Thoughtful forever

You are so free

And full of gallantry.
Even if you pretend to do something, none
Could have succeeded as you've done.

Tune: *BLUE BOY*

Writing "birds love" instead of "love-birds," you reverse
The word order to show your deep feeling in verse.
I must watch if the letter will annoy
The one whom you adore
Or cause her joy.
Make your mind easy, sir, on that score!
I'm only pleased to do
All this for you.
I won't refuse you, nay,
I know what I should say:
The dear lute-player of last night
Told me to give you the letter he did write.

She says:

I will take this letter for you, sir. But you must not forget your ambition and your career.

She sings to the tune of *PARASITIC GRASS*:

Your hands that wish to carry off the lady fair
Must be ready to pluck the laurel crown;
Your brilliant handwriting beyond compare
Should not be used to profane your renown.
Don't let love's rope bind a roc's wing
Nor let his ears listen to an oriole sing!
The silk bed-curtain for a beauty made
Should not detain the-golden horse from the Hall of Jade.

ACT III

Tune: *EPILOGUE*

Don't waste through lovesickness nor pine away
Like sick and sad scholars night and day!

Master Zhang says:

Your kind words I will bear in mind for the rest of my life.
But as to the letter, dear Miss Rose, you must be careful.

Rose says:

Make yourself easy, sir.

She continues to sing:

Before your love's revealed in your exchange of glances,
Day and night I reflect on your chances.
Now you entrust this jade-white letter to my care.
Could I neglect to send it to my Mistress fair?
I'll use my word
To convey your feelings true
So as to make it heard
And my Young Mistress pay a visit to you.

(Exit.)

Master Zhang says:

I dare say without boasting that this talisman will make lovers meet.
When she comes back tomorrow, she is sure to bring me good news.
If no fair breeze should send to her my poem fine,
How could the fairy come into sweet dreams of mine?

(Exit.)

Scene 2 Billet-doux

Yingying enters and says:
>Rose may come back at any moment. As I got up earlier than usual, I will go again to sleep for a little.
>
>(She sleeps.)

Rose enters and says:
>My Young Mistress ordered me to see Master Zhang and I have brought her a letter. Why don't I hear any sound of her? Has she gone to sleep again? I must go in and see.
>
>The rising sun peeps slowly in her window screen;
>A pair of swallows enlivens the lonely scene.

She sings to the tune of *PINK BUTTERFLY*:
>The curtains hang around
>The windows whence a fragrance of lily is spread;
>My copper rings resound
>When I open the doors painted red.
>On crimson stand with golden leaf-like plate the light
>Of silver candle is still bright.
>I gently draw aside the curtain on her bed
>And lift up the silk valance red
>So as to have a peep
>At her who's still asleep.

Tune: *INTOXICATED EAST WIND*
>I see her slanting hairpin of jade
>And her cloud of hair unmade.

Although the sun is high in the sky,
She has not opened her bright eye.
How lazy she appears!

(Yingying rises, stretches herself and sighs deeply.)

Sitting up and scratching her ears,
She heaves a deep, deep sigh.

Rose says:

In such a case, how can I give her the letter? It would be better to put it in her toilet case and let her find it herself.

(She puts it there.)

(Yingying makes her toilet. Rose casts a furtive glance.)

Rose sings to the tune of *UNIVERSAL JOY*:

Faded her rouge of previous night,
Down falls the black cloud of her hair.
She puts upon her face a powder light
And arranges her locks without much care.
She takes the letter then
And reads it over and over again
Without indeed a sign of weariness and pain.
Suddenly now
Displeased, she knits her brow
And bends her head,
With anger her fair face turns red.

Rose, revealing her sentiment by dumb show, says:

Alas! The game is up.

Yingying says in anger:

Come here, Rose!

Rose says:

Yes.

Yingying says:
> Where has this come from, Rose? I am the daughter of the late Prime Minister. Who dare to make fun of me with such a letter as this? When have I been used to read such a thing? I shall tell my mother so that she may give you, little imp, a good thrashing on the bottom.

Rose says:
> It was you who sent me to him and he who sent me back with the letter. If you had not sent me to him, how could I have dared to ask him for it? Besides, I can not read. How could I know what he has written?

She sings to the tune of *HAPPY THREE*:
> The fault is yours, it is quite clear.
> Why should you shift on me the blame, my dear?
> You want to make me suffer for what you have done.
> If you were not, then who is used to such a fun?

She says:
> Do not make so much fuss, my dear Young Mistress! It would be better for me than for you to take this letter to your mother and tell her all about it.

Yingying says in anger:
> About what?

Rose says:
> About Master Zhang.

Yingying, revealing her sentiment by dumb show, says:
> Let me think it over, Rose. Perhaps it would be better to pardon him this time.

Rose says:
> My dear Young Mistress, are you afraid he will be given a good

ACT III

thrushing on the bottom?

Yingying says:

I have not yet asked about Master Zhang's health.

Rose says:

I will not tell you.

Yingying says:

Oh, Rose, do tell me!

Rose sings to the tune of *HOMAGE TO EMPEROR*:

His face becomes so thin

As to make me feel chagrin.

He has no desire to drink or to eat

And fears to move his feet.

Yingying says:

Why not call in a doctor to examine his illness?

Rose says:

He has no special illness. He said himself:

She continue to sing.

"I was sighing away

For our union night and day.

I forgot to eat and to sleep

Till evening faded into night deep.

I gazed at eastern wall

And copious tears began to fall.

My sickness would get worse

Unless my sweat be sweetened by hers."

Yingying says:

You are always discreet of speech, Rose. What if others know of this? What will become of the honor of our family? Don't tell me from now on whatever he says in such language as this! The relations between us are merely those of brother and sister, and nothing more.

Rose says:

Fine words!

She sings to the tune of *FOUR-SIDE TRANQUILLITY*:

His flirting with you, you fear,

Might lead to harm

When it's discovered by your mother dear.

It would create alarm

For you and me.

Why should you care for him under any pretense

Since you've encouraged him to climb up the tree,

Removed the ladder and gazed with indifference?

Yingying says:

Although my family is under obligation to him, how can he be allowed to do this? Hand me pen and paper so that I may write him an answer, telling him not to do in this way again.

Rose says:

What are you going to write to him? Why should you trouble yourself again?

Yingying says:

You do not understand, Rose.

(She writes.)

She says:

Take this letter and say to him: "When my Young Mistress sent me to see you, sir, it was simply a matter of courtesy between sister and brother and it meant nothing else. If you repeat what you have just done, my Young Mistress will be obliged to tell her mother." And Rose, you will have to answer for this!

ACT III

Rose says:
> Why, my dear Young Mistress, are you fussing again? I will not take your letter and you need not trouble yourself for that.

Yingying, throwing the letter on the ground, says:
> How dare you, little chit!

(Exit.)

Rose, picking up the letter, sighs and says:
> Ah! my Young Mistress, why do you show such temper?

She sings to the tune of *DOFFING THE CLOTHES*:
> You maiden young
> Don't know how to restrain your tongue,
> Abusing others and making them feel sad
> By giving vent to your own temper bad.
> You think but of the scholar you cannot forget
> Instead of the example to others you've set.

Tune: SMALL LIANGZHOU

> In his dreams you and he were twain;
> When he awoke, he was single again.
> For your sake he forgot to eat and sleep;
> His silken robe felt cold when night was deep.
> Boundless his grief appears:
> In solitude his face is crisscrossed with tears.

Tune: A SECOND STANZA

> He longed for the happy union in vain
> As for the rising wain.
> I've never shut the side door
> So that you two may meet no obstacle any more.
> I wish you would in full bridal array be seen
> While I play the role of tacit go-between.

Tune: *POMEGRANATE FLOWER*

Making your toilet in your boudoir, you're afraid
Your thin robe cannot keep out the cold when flowers fade.
Then when you heard the lute beneath the moon so bright,
Why didn't you fear the cold on dewy vernal night?
Was it because you were devoured by your flame
For the scholar so that you felt no shame?
For that sour, crazy gallant alone,
You weren't afraid of being frozen into stone.

Tune: *FIGHT OF QUAILS*

You are a flower
Thirsting for shower,
So I will be
A bearer of letters for you.
But you find fault with me
And won't reproach yourself for the folly you do.
I can't but bear
What is unfair
Like burning scar.
O how crafty you are!
Your speech in public plausible appears;
In private your brows knit, your eyes are filled with tears.

She says:

If I do not go with her letter, she will say I disobey her.
And Master Zhang is waiting for me to bring an answer.
What can I do but go again to the library?

(She knocks at the door.)

Master Zhang enters and says:

So you have come, Miss Rose. What about the letter?

ACT III

Rose says:
> It has failed. Don't be silly, sir.

Master Zhang says:
> My letter is a talisman to make lovers meet. How can it have failed? It must be you, Miss Rose, who were not zealous enough.

Rose says:
> Was I not zealous enough, sir? Heaven above knows the truth. It was your letter that was anything but good.

She sings to the tune of *ASCENDING THE ATTIC*:
> It's you who were unlucky, sir,
> Your message I dare not defer;
> It turned out to be your confession clear,
> A summons for you to appear,
> A proof I'm also concerned in this case.
> If my Young Mistress should not save my face,
> And pardon your impertinent flame,
> E'en I should bear the undeserved blame.

Tune: *PETTY SONG*

> From now on meetings will be hard and visits rare;
> The moon will no more shine on Western Bower,
> The phoenix will leave the Pavilion fore'er,
> And clouds won't bring on Mountain-crest fresh shower.
> You may take the road high
> And I the low.
> I pray, sir, do not sigh.
> The feast is over and guests are bound to go.

She says:
> This is the end of the matter. You, sir, need not tell me again your innermost feelings. My Mistress may be looking for me. I

must return at once.
Master Zhang says:
Miss Rose!

(He remains motionless for a long time.)

(Weeping)

Miss Rose, once you have gone, who can I expect to plead my cause with?

(Kneeling down)

Miss Rose, Miss Rose, you must help me to have this matter put right and save my life.

Rose says:
A learned scholar as you are, sir, can you not understand how the matter stands?

She sings to the tune of COURTYARD FULL OF FRAGRANCE:
Don't play the cunning with a foolish air!
While you want to enjoy your love-affair,
Why not think of the torture I shall stand?
My Young Mistress may beat me, rod in hand.
Like a thick rope, could I
Go through a needle's eye?
If beaten, on a crutch I'd lean,
Could I still act as go-between?
If I should have my lips kept sealed,
How could I help you to be healed?

Master Zhang, still kneeling and weeping, says:
There is no other way for me. The only hope of saving my life depends on you, Miss Rose!

Rose says:
Why should I explain to you? Here is her answer to your letter.

ACT III

You can read it for yourself.

(She hands him the letter.)

Master Zhang, having opened and read the letter, gets up and says smilingly:

Ah, Miss Rose!

(Reading once more)

Today is indeed a happy day, Miss Rose!

(Reading still once more)

If I had known your Young Mistress' letter was to arrive, I should have prepared for its reception. Now it is too late so I hope I may be excused. I am sure, Miss Rose, you will rejoice too.

Rose says:

What about?

Master Zhang says smilingly:

Her abuse of me is all put on. In the letter she says the contrary.

Rose says:

Really?

Master Zhang says:

In her letter she tells me to go to the garden tonight.

Rose says:

What for?

Master Zhang says:

For an assignation.

Rose says:

What is an assignation?

Master Zhang says:

To have a secret meeting with her, Miss Rose.

Rose says:

I do not believe it.

Master Zhang says:
>You may believe it or not as you like.

Rose says:
>Try to read me the letter.

Master Zhang says:
>There are four verses of five characters, very implicit.
>
>Wait for moonrise in Western Bower,
>Where the breeze opens half the door.
>The wall is shaded by dancing flowers
>Then comes the one whom you adore.
>
>Now, Miss Rose, do you still not believe it?

Rose says:
>What does it mean?

Master Zhang says:
>Don't you understand it?

Rose says:
>I don't.

Master Zhang says:
>Well, then I will explain it to you "Wait for moonrise in Western Bower" tells me the time to go to the garden. "Where the breeze opens half the door" means the door will be open for me. "The wall is shaded by dancing flowers" tells me to climb over the wall screened by the shadows of the flowers lest I should be seen. "Then comes the one whom you adore" needs no explanation. It simply means: "I am coming."

Rose says:
>Are you sure it is what she means?

Master Zhang says:
>What else can she mean if not this, Miss Rose? To tell the truth,

ACT III

I am a master in solving riddles, full of romance and gallantry.
If it is not explained in this way, how else can it be explained?

Rose says:
Can this be what she writes?

Master Zhang says:
Here it is.

(Rose remains motionless for a long time.)
(Master Zhang reads the letter again.)

Rose says:
Is it really what she writes?

Master Zhang says smilingly:
You are absurd, Miss Rose. Here it is.

Rose says angrily:
Then my Young Mistress has made a fool of me.

She sings to the tune of *PLAYING THE CHILD*:

O Who has ever
 Seen a messenger befooled by the sender?
She is so clever,
Though she appears so young and tender.
She tells her lover to climb
Over the eastern wall for a tryst.
Five words hint at the time;
Four lines appeal to the lover missed.
About this critical affair, O mark!
I am kept in the dark.
You want the cloud
To bring fresh showers
For thirsting flowers
Rising above the crowd,

But order me to use my leisure
To gratify your pleasure.

Tune: *LAST STANZA BUT THREE*

As brilliant jade her letter paper is as neat;
As lily's fragrance her words are as sweet.
The lines are wet
Not with her fragrant sweat
But with the rosy tear
Wept for her lover dear.
The ink is not yet dried,
Like grief of rainy spring at rising tide.
You need not doubt, sir from now on
But do your best to win high literary renown!
Then you may do what you will of your lady fair
With golden bird on cloudy hair.

Tune: *LAST STANZA BUT TWO*

To him you've shown affection, my Young Mistress dear,
But of me you make light.
When has he become the husband you revere?
Your honeyed words would make him warm in winter's height;
Even mid-summer your disfavor would make me cold.
Today I'll keep a watch on you and behold
How can a metamorphosed lady fair
Attract her handsome lover with a lovely pear.

Master Zhang says:

How can a student like me climb over a garden wall?

Rose sings to the tune of *LAST STANZA BUT ONE*:

The wall's not high, caressed by full-blown trees;
The door is only half-closed in the breeze.

ACT III

If you attempt to steal a lady sweet,
You should have nimble hands and feet.
If you're afraid of the height of the wall,
How can you climb o'er glorious Dragon's Gate at all?
If amid thickset rose-bushes you're not free,
How can you pluck the flower on the laurel tree?
Make haste and have no fear!
Don't weary the longing eyes of your lady dear
Nor let her eyebrows still,
Knit like distant vernal hill!

Master Zhang says:

I have already visited the garden twice.

Rose sings to the tune of *EPILOGUE*:

Though you have been there twice,
This visit will be far more nice.
Your verse exchange was mere by-play,
The real thing is her letter of today.

(Exit)

Master Zhang says:

Alas! all things are fated. When Rose came here, I was depressed beyond words. But who could have anticipated the happiness my young lady would send me in her letter? I am indeed a master in the art of solving riddles, full of romance and gallantry. If her verse were not interpreted in this way, how else then should it be interpreted? "Wait for moonrise in Western Bower" tells me the time to go to the garden. "Where the breeze opens half the door" shows me the place. "The wall is shaded by dancing flowers, then comes the one whom you adore." These lines tell me how to climb over the wall unperceived. But the damned daylight seems unwilling to depart. O

Heaven! You give everything to everyone. Why won't you give me a single day! O Sun! Will you go down quickly!

When I talk with a happy friend,

The sun will soon westward descend.

Today I am to meet my love;

The sun seems glued and rooted above.

It is now only midday. I must still wait for a long time. When I look again, I find everything seems against the sun's setting today.

No cloud in azure sky

With fragrance drifting by.

Who could shorten the day,

Driving the sun away?

Ah! The sun begins to sink in the west. I have to wait still for a long while.

The sun's a golden crow

In Heaven's palace high.

I'd shoot it with a bow

Down from the western sky.

Thanks to Heaven and Earth! The sun is down at last. Ah! lamps are lit. Ah! drums are beaten. Ah! evening bells are ringing. I'll close the door of the library and go out. When I arrive there, I'll clasp the branch of the drooping willow-tree and climb over the wall in a trice. I'll hold my young lady in my arms. O my dear young lady! I feel sorry only for you.

Your letter's twenty words hide twenty pearls below;

I'll pluck the fruit whose seed was sown three lives ago.

(Exit)

ACT III

Scene 3 Repudiation

Rose enters and says:
> When my Young Mistress ordered me to take her letter to Master Zhang, she pretended to assume a cool air, but actually she made a secret assignation with him in her poem. Since she did not tell me the truth, I will not give her away, but simply ask her to burn incense and see how she can humbug me when he comes.
> (Respectfully) Will you go to burn incense, my Young Mistress?

Yingying enters and sings:
> The evening breeze is heavy with fragrance of flowers;
> The rising moon has brightened the deep, silent bowers.

Rose sings to the double tune of *NEW WATER*:
> The evening breeze so cold has come through window screen;
> The golden hooks have not kept up the curtains green.
> The door is open to the evening haze,
> The bower steeped in the sun's departing rays.
> Before her mirror in her boudoir my Young Mistress
> Has just put on her evening dress.
>
> **Tune: *HALTING THE HORSE***
>
> From bustle far away,
> In the light-green pool the ducks sleep.
> Beautiful is the day,
> On the pale yellow willow-tree crows are perched deep.
> She crushes peonies' young shoots with her small feet,

Her jade hairpin entangled in red flowers sweet.

Slippery is the mossy way;

Her stockings wet with pearls of dewdrops indiscreet.

She says:

My Young Mistress and Master Zhang seem impatient for the nightfall.

She sings to the tune of *PSEUDO-MELODY*:

Ever since sunrise

They have wearied their eyes

For the rising moon;

A moment seems as long as the month of June.

Beyond the willow-trees now slowly sinks the sun,

They wish it buried by the Holy One.

Tune: *ZITHER AND GUITAR*

In bewitching attire,

She brings her cloud and rain to quench his flame and fire.

Seeing the orioles and swallows in pairs,

Could she not think of love affairs?

She will nor drink nor eat,

And looks more bashful and sweet.

Is she not true?

It is hard to construe,

And I'm not sure what to do.

She says:

My Young Mistress, will you please stand below the poolside rock? I will shut the side door lest we should be overheard.

(She looks outside the door.)

Master Zhang enters and says:

It is time to go there.

(He looks inside the door.)

ACT III

Rose sings to the tune of *INTOXICATED EAST WIND*:
>The evening crow
>Amid the trees
>Seems to shiver and throw
>Its shadow in the breeze.
>No, it's the scholar, I guess,
>In his black silk headdress.
>Behind the winding balustrade he seems to hide;
>With her back to the rock she stands by the poolside.
>How can they interchange a word?
>How can their speech be heard?

Master Zhang, embracing Rose, says:
>My dear young lady!

Rose says:
>You beast! It is I. Luckily the mistake is made with me. What if it were my Mistress!

She continues to sing:
>Are you so eager
>For an embrace
>That hungry and meager,
>You see stars in my face!

She says:
>Let me ask you once more if you were told to come here.

Master Zhang says:
>I am a master in solving riddles, full of romance and gallantry
>So I am sure to captivate her.

Rose says:
>Don't go through the door, or she will say I have let you in. You must climb over the wall, you see? Such a beautiful night is

really good for a tryst.

She sings to the tune of *PSEUDO-MELODY*:

> Behold! the fleecy cloud veiling the moon so bright
> Serves as the shade of silver candlelight;
> The weeping willows and flowers as window-screen
> And verdant grass as spacious couch embroidered green.

Tune: *SONG OF SWEET WATER*

> Beautiful is your nuptial night.
> The court is tranquillized with leisure;
> The blooming branches weighed down for your pleasure.
> Knowing she is a maiden pure,
> You must be gentle to allure
> Her with caressing words and in your temper sweet:
> Don't take her for a flaunting flower you meet!

Tune: *PICKING LAUREL*

> Like flawless jade she's charming and full of grace.
> Do you not see her lovely face
> Exhaling spring,
> And her cloudy hair waved like a raven's wing?
> But your worry and fear won't worry me,
> For I don't hope from you a cup of wine or tea.
> When you're excited under the coverlet,
> Your fingers may be tired and sweetened with her sweat.
> When your sweat and hers blend,
> Your worry comes to an end.
> Your sorrow is no more,
> And you'll be ready to go on before.

(Master Zhang climbs over the wall.)

Yingying says:
>Who is it?

Master Zhang says:
>It is I.

Yingying calls:
>Rose!

>*(Rose does not answer.)*

Yingying says in anger:
>Oh, Master Zhang! What kind of a man are you! Why have you come while I am burning incense?

Master Zhang says:
>Ah!

Rose sings to the tune of *FLOWERS ON BROCADE*:
>Why is a go-between free from worry and fear?
>Skin to skin, man and wife of difference will be clear.
>I'd better go
>To listen on tiptoe.
>One of them full of shame;
>The other's ire in flame.

>**Tune: *A SECOND STANZA***

>One has nothing to say
>The other's changed her mind.
>The one does silent stay;
>The other chatters things unkind.

Rose, standing at a distance, says in a low voice:
>Master Zhang, what has become of all your bold talk behind her back? Go on! If this is brought before the court, do you think you will be the only one to be disgraced?

She continues to sing:
> You were full of romance and gallantry.
> Where did they flee?
> You clasp your hands and bow your head
> As if you're deaf and dumb, half dead.
>
> **Tune: *A CLEAR RIVER***
>
> You wag your tongue with none beside,
> But you are cunning and crafty in vain.
> Who would have thought by the poolside,
> So different you would remain?

Yingying says:
> Rose, there is a thief here.

Rose says:
> Who is it, my Young Mistress?

Master Zhang says:
> It is I, Miss Rose.

Rose says:
> Who told you to come, Master Zhang? What is your business here?
>
> (Master Zhang remains silent.)

Yingying says:
> Drag him off to my mother's place!
>
> (Master Zhang remains silent.)

Rose says:
> If we drag him off to my Mistress' place, it would unmake his reputation. Let me deal with him for you, my Young Mistress. Master Zhang, come here and kneel down. You have read the Books of Confucius, so you should understand the proper ways of behavior. What have you come here for at this late hour of night?

ACT III

She continues to sing:
>See what the lady fair and sweet
>Will do with pretty fruit not good to eat!
>>**Tune: *WILD GEESE'S FALL***
>
>Not that as judges we wish to pose,
>But something heartfelt I'd propose.
>I thought your scholarship profound as the sea;
>Who knows your lust amounts to bare audacity?
>>**Tune: *TRIUMPHANT SONG***
>
>You've come so late
>At dead of night.
>Do you want to steal sweet flowers by force?
>You are a scholar bright.
>Why don't you go to jump over the Dragon's Gate
>But over the garden wall as mounting a horse?

Rose says:
>Please forgive him once for my sake, my Young Mistress.

Yingying says:
>We are bound to repay your kindness for saving our lives. But since we have become brother and sister, how can you have such a desire? What if my mother should know of this? Now for Rose's sake I forgive you this time. But should it occur again, you will be dragged to my mother's place without leniency.

Rose continues to sing:
>Thanks to my Young Mistress, your mistake
>Has been pardoned for my sake.
>If we should bring before the court this case,
>None could have saved your skin and face.

Yingying says:
>Rose, remove the incense table and come in with me.
>
>(Exit)

Rose, mocking Master Zhang, says:
>For shame! For shame! Did you not say that you were a master in the art of solving riddles, full of romance and gallantry? From today on you may regard all your scheme as dead.

She sings to the tune of *FAREWELL FEAST AND EPILOGUE*:
>Say not one night of love is worth as dear as gold:
>Live ten years' single life more in your study cold!
>You are a master in solving riddles, you say,
>But mountains, not half-opened doors, stand in your way,
>And bar you from the sight of dancing flower,
>And clouds overshadow the moon over the Western Bower.
>You may powder your brazen face;
>She's painted her eyebrows with grace.
>You poor wretch want to force a shower
>Upon the thirsting flower.
>Your audacity you should regret;
>Your honeyed speech you should forget.
>No more seductive verse
>Nor any letter worse!
>You have no chance
>To boast of your romance.
>My Mistress Young,
>Do not be angry any more!
>O Master Zhang,
>Pursue your studies as before!
>
>(Exeunt)

ACT III

Scene 4 Further Expectation

Madame Cui enters and says:
>Early this morning the Abbot sent me word that Master Zhang was very ill. I sent for a doctor and ordered Rose to go with him, for I wish to know what medicine was prescribed, what the malady is, and how about his pulse. Now I am waiting for an answer.
>
>(Exit)

Rose enters and says:
>My Mistress has sent me to see Master Zhang. Oh, my Mistress, you know only his illness, but not the rebuff he suffered last night, which might lead to his death.
>
>(Exit)

Yingying enters and says:
>Master Zhang is very ill. I have written a letter for him, and I will tell Rose to take it to him in the guise of a prescription. Rose!

Rose reenters and says:
>Here I am, my Young Mistress.

Yingying says:
>Master Zhang is very ill. I have an excellent prescription for you to take to him.

Rose says:
>Oh, my Young Mistress, you are at it again. Very well, as my Mistress has just ordered me to go there, I will take it for you.

Yingying says:
> I will wait till your return.

> (Exeunt)

Master Zhang enters and says:
> I suffered such a rebuff in the garden last night that it has brought on my old malady and I am done for. Madame has told the Abbot to call in a doctor to see me, but mine is not a malady to be cured by a doctor but by some good prescription of the Young Lady.

Rose enters and says:
> My Young Mistress has caused him such a terrible illness, yet she bids me to take this prescription to him. I cannot but go as is bidden, but I am afraid it might make him worse.
>
> Homesickness in strange land
> Can't be cured by good hand;
> Nor can the finest art
> Heal a half-broken heart.

She sings to the tune of *FIGHT OF QUAILS*:
> You were the first to write
> A poem to the scholar bright
> So that he could not raise his head
> From the pillow of his bed,
> Forgetful of his food and sleep.
> And now his hair turns gray,
> His figure wastes away,
> For his regret and illness are both deep.
> But you rebuffed him to his face,
> Your icy words brought to him more disgrace.

ACT III

Tune: *VIOLET FLOWER*

You leaned upon the door alone,
Waiting for the rising moon;
You wrote a poem fine
To rhyme with his verse tine;
With ears intent, you listened mute
To his playing of lute.

She says:

But last night you suddenly talked nonsense, asking him what he should do as a brother to a sister.

She continues to sing:

You have entrapped the scholar bright.

She says:

Today you say you have a good prescription for me to take to him.

She continues to sing.

And of your handmaid you made light.
It's hard to bear.
I am kept going like the thread
Which never leaves the needle bare.
From now on I will let things go as they are led.
I won't believe your faith is ocean-deep
Nor your kindness mountain-high;
For they are beyond the sweep
Of my far-reaching eye.

She sees Master Zhang and says:

I feel very sorry for you, Master Zhang. How is your health today?

Master Zhang says:

It will be the death of me. Should I die, Miss Rose, you should be my witness at the tribunal of the King of Hades.

Rose says:

Of all the lovesick people in the world, none is so sick as you. O my Young Mistress, would that you realize his suffering!

She sings to the tune of *CLEAR SKY OVER THE SAND*:

For literature and learning you do not care;
You dream of willow's shade and lady fair.
Your heart is bent on secret meeting with dear one,
But so far you have nothing done.
I have seen lovesickness wring
Your heart since crabapple blooms in spring.

She says:

How is it that you are suffering so much?

Master Zhang says:

How could I dare to lie before you? It is all because of your Young Mistress. Back to the library last night, I burned with anger. How could a saviour be wronged by the one he saved? The old saw says that the maiden is doting but the swam is unfaithful. But today the case is reversed.

Rose says:

I am afraid it is not she who is to blame.

She sings to the tune of *SONG OF FLIRTATION*:

Examine your improper desire!
You are a skeleton whose blood is sucked by vampire.
You may say such has been a scholar's fate,
But your one-sided love had better abate.
I fear your literary ambition will fail
And your matrimonial attempts of no avail,

ACT III

She says:
> My Mistress has sent me to see you and ask what medicine you are taking. And there is another good prescription I have brought for you.

Master Zhang says:
> Where is it?

Rose hands it to him and says:
> Here it is.

> (Master Zhang opens and reads it.)

Master Zhang, standing up, says smilingly:
> How happy I am! It is a poem. (Bowing) Had I known this was a poem from your Young Mistress, I should have received it on my knees. O Miss Rose, my illness is suddenly and imperceptibly gone!

Rose says:
> You are at it again, But don't make another mistake!

Master Zhang says:
> How could I have made a mistake! Last night it was not I who made one, but she who would turn a gain into a loss.

Rose says:
> I don't believe it. Read the poem to me.

Master Zhang says:
> If you want to hear, you must first make a respectful bow.
> (Adjusting his hat and girdle, and holding the letter with both hands)

He reads:
> Do not trouble your heart with trifle mere,
> Nor extinguish your talent aglow!
> To keep my modesty without smear,
> I did not know it would bring you woe.
> To pay our debt I don't care for old rite

> But send new verse to the Western Bower.
> I'm sure to bring fresh showers tonight
> For the long, long thirsting flower.

He says:
> Miss Rose. this poem says more than that of the past.

Rose, bending her head and reflecting, says:
> Oh, I have got it. Now I understand you, my Young Mistress.
> Yours is indeed a good prescription.

She sings to the tune of *RED PEACH BLOSSOM*:
> The laurel flowers throw their shadows when night is deep.
> The medicine will give the poor scholar a good night's sleep.
> In the shade of the rocks by the poolside,
> In the innermost part he may find his bride.
> He may avail himself of such chance once or twice,
> But she's afraid her mother has not gone to bed,
> And her handmaid may leave her to her own device,
> So the poor scholar must have a cool head.

Tune: *THREE TERRACES*

You are a fool who tries
To look wise;
You are a scholar mad
Nowhere to seek news glad,
So try to find
Comfort in a letter of this kind.
If over bit of paper you're so wild,
Before the celestial beauty how can you be mild?
No wonder my Young Mistress should forget
Your kindness and our debt.

Tune: *A BALD HEAD*

You sleep under a simple coverlet.
And use as pillow your long lute.
Where could she sleep in your poor cabinet,
Shivering with cold from head to foot?
How could you start
To talk from heart to heart?

Tune: *KING OF MEDICINE*

If you love her and she loves you,
At dead of night in courtyard with a swing in view,
The moon was veiled and flowers veiled,
Of such a nuptial night why were you not availed?
Why should you croon
A verse beneath the moon?

Tune: *JOY OF EASTERN PLAIN*

I've pillows broidered with love-birds in pair
And coverlet of turquoise blue,
Which would captivate any lady fair,
But how could I lend them to you?
Why don't you doff your clothes with your fingers wet
With her imaginary sweat?
Could you fulfil your love,
Heaven would bless you above.

She says:

Master Zhang, to tell you the truth, do you know what my Young Mistress look like?

She sings to the tune of *WADS OF COTTON*:

Her eyebrows look like distant hills green,
Her eyes like autumn water serene,

>   Her skin milk-white,
>   Her waist like willow slender.
>   Her face beams bright,
>   Her heart is tender.
>   She's gentle, kind and sure;
>   She needs no holy needle for a cure,
>   For she's the Goddess in white dress
>   To relieve you from your distress.

She says:
>   Good as she is, I dare not believe she will come tonight.

She sings to the tune of *PEITY SONG*:
>   I still wonder
>   While you ponder.

Master Zhang says:
>   Miss Rose, the case of today is not the same as that of the past.

Rose says:
>   Ah, sir, I don't think so.

She continues to sing:
>   Your past is gone;
>   I'll talk about what's going on.

She says:
>   I don't believe my Young Mistress will come tonight.

She continues to sing:
>   Why should she come so late tonight?

Master Zhang says:
>   Miss Rose, let me tell you not to trouble yourself about whether she will come or not. All I hope for you is to do your best for me.

ACT III

Rose continues to sing:
> Have I not done for you with main and might?
> I don't want as reward your gold or jade,
> Nor flowers over my head nor carpet of brocade.
>> **Tune: *EPILOGUE***
> Even if my Mistress should shut the door tight,
> I will make you fulfil your heart's desire tonight.

She says:
> Now, sir, may I also tell you that all I hope for you is to do your best for yourself, and I will not trouble myself about whether she will come or not?

She continues to sing:
> Once coming here,
> How can she have her will?
> Meeting your dear,
> You may then love your fill!

(Exeunt.)

To sum up the four scenes of Act III:

Master Zhang writes a verse of love.
Rose arranges lovers' secret meeting.
Yingying pretends to stand above.
Madame Cui Sends a grateful greeting.

ACT IV

ACT IV

Scene 1 Tryst

Yingying enters and says:
> Rose has gone with my letter making an assignation with Master Zhang tonight. I must wait for her return and then decide what to do.

Rose enters and says:
> My Young Mistress bade me to take a letter to Master Zhang, making an assignation with him tonight. I am afraid she might change her mind again and cause his death, which would be no trifle. I must go and see her and hear what she has to say.

Yingying says:
> Get my bed ready, Rose. I am going to sleep.

Rose says:
> It is all right that you may go to sleep, but what is to be done with him?

Yingying says:
> With whom?

Rose says:
> My Young Mistress! There you are again. It would be no trifle to cause a man's death. If you should go back on your words, I would go and inform my Mistress that you told me to make an assignation with Master Zhang.

Yingying says:
> You little cat! How crafty you are!

139

Rose says:
> Not that I am crafty, but that you must not play the same trick again.

Yingying says:
> But I feel bashful.

Rose says:
> But who will see you? There is no one but me.
> (Urging her) Let us be off! Be off!
> (Yingying remains silent.)

Rose, urging her, again, says:
> My Young Mistress, what can we do but be off?
> (Yingying remains silent but reveals her feeling in dumb show.)

Rose, urging her, says:
> My Young Mistress, let us be off!
> (Yingying remains silent, goes and then stands still.)

Rose says:
> Why do you stand still, my Young Mistress? Let us be off! Be off!
> (Yingying remains silent and goes forward.)

Rose says:
> My Young Mistress is slow of speech but fleet of foot.

She sings to the tune of *CALM DIGNITY*:
> My Young Mistress is pure as jade
> And beautiful as flower,
> Which has made
> One long for her from dawn till dusk, from hour to hour.
> She is sincere tonight
> To heal the breach of promise, of which she made light.
> Leaving her bower
> For his cabinet,
> She brings fresh shower

ACT IV

    And dew to wet
    The thirsting flower
    With fragrant sweat.
    The Fairy Queen
    Will meet the King
    Behind the screen
    In dreams of spring.

(Exeunt.)

Master Zhang enters and says:
    The Young Lady bade Rose to bring me a letter making an assignation with me tonight. But the first watch of the night is passed. Why has she not yet come?
    The beautiful night on earth is silent far and nigh.
    When will the beautiful lady come from on high?

He sings to the tune of *ROUGED LIPS OF A FAIRY*:
    For long I stand and fret,
    When night is deep, the golden sphere gives out sweet breath.
    Lonely my cabinet,
    The scholar's bored to death.

    Tune: *DRAGON IN TROUBLED WATER*
    Where is my rainbow cloud?
    With flood-like moonlight my bower is overflowed.
    Priests in their cells repose;
    In courtyard trees cry crows.
    The wind plays with bamboo:
    I seem to hear her footsteps to our rendezvous:
    In moonlight dance the flowers:
    I seem to see my lady coming to my bower.
    I gaze with longing eyes:

I heave amorous sighs.
Where can I find
Repose for my body or my mind?
Petrified there, I wait
While leaning on the gate.
But the longer I do,
The later comes the Phoenix Blue.
Even the yellow dog will not bark
Far away in the dark.

Tune: *FIELD CRICKET*

I close my eyes,
Heavy with thoughts of love.
My head on lonely pillow lies,
My soul dreams of a flight
To the trysting place above.
Had I foreseen I'd be obsessed and day and night,
I would regret
Such an enthralling beauty I should have met.
When a mistake is made,
I'd blame myself and not be afraid
To mend my ways.
But when I try to raise
My love of beauty
To love of duty,
And tear myself from her apart,
Like a bolt from the blue she captivates my heart.

Tune: *UNIVERSAL JOY*

Leaning against the door I stand,
Resting my cheek upon my hand.

How can I know
Whether she'll come or no.
Perhaps it's difficult to leave her mother's side.
I gaze with longing eyes,
My mind at ebbing tide.
Perhaps she's also heaving heavy sighs. He says:
She has not yet come. Is she playing false again?

He sings to the tune of SONG OF CHERUBIN:

If she is willing to come,
She will have left her home.
If she is to arrive,
My cabinet with spring will revive.
If she won't come alone,
My hope will sink into the sea like a stone.
Counting my footsteps still,
To and fro I pace now and then.
Leaning against the windowsill,
I'll speak to her again.

Tune: *MAGPIE ON THE BRANCH*

Your rebuff was unkind,
But I've not borne it in my heart,
Wishing you'd change your mind
And promise me to come overnight and then depart,
We have exchanged love glances for half a year.
How much I've suffered, O my dear!

Tune: *PARASITIC GRASS*

I am ready to suffer and to die.
A stranger in a strange land, I try
To eat and drink enough to keep myself alive

> And wait until tonight you may arrive.
> I've steeled my heart
> To play a patient part.
> I'll make it clear
> That if I am not resolute and sincere,
> I cannot breathe my breath
> And preserve my body from death.
> If I were doomed to six months' grief,
> Ten years more could afford me no relief.

Rose enters and says:
> I'll go ahead while you wait here, my Young Mistress.
>
> (She knocks at the door.)

Master Zhang says:
> The Young Lady has come.

Rose says:
> My Young Mistress has come. Take her coverlet and pillow please.

Master Zhang says:
> Miss Rose, words fail to express my feeling at this moment, but Heaven knows it.

Rose says:
> Do not speak so loud or you will frighten her. Stay here and I will bring her in.
> (Pushing Yingying forward) Go in, my Young Mistress. I will wait outside the window.
>
> (Exit.)

Master Zhang, seeing Yingying, kneels and embraces her, saying:
> How fortunate I am to be favored with your visit, my dear Young Lady!

He sings to the tune of *VILLAGE DRUMS*:

>Of your sudden appearance assured,
>My sickness is already nine-tenth cured.
>Rebuffed into a wretched plight,
>How could I hope for your visit tonight?
>You're so considerate for me
>That I'd salute you on my knee.
>I have nor grace
>Nor handsome face;
>At writing I am not a good hand,
>But you pity me, stranger in a foreign land.

(Yingying remains silent.)

Master Zhang, rising and sitting close to her, sings to the tune of *SONG OF PEACE*:

>Your little shoes embroidered in silk thread,
>Your waist as slender as the willow,
>Bashful, you will not raise your head,
>But rest it on the love-bird's pillow.
>Your golden hairpin seems to fall from your cloud-hair,
>Your slanting locks make you look still more fair.

Tune: *CHARMING ON HORSE*

>I will unbutton your robe and untie
>Your silken girdle until you feel shy.
>A fragrance, lily-like, permeates my cabinet.
>You know how to enthral and entrance me, coquette!
>O why
>Do you not turn to me your face and eye?

(Embracing Yingying who remains silent.)

Tune: *BETTER THAN GOURD*

No fragrance is so warm, no jade so soft and nice,
Ah! I am better than in paradise.
Spring comes on earth with flowers dyed.
Her willowy waist close by my side,
Her pistil plucked, my dewdrop drips
And her peony sips
With open lips.

Tune: *A SECOND STANZA*

Overwhelmed with ecstasy,
I feel as happy and as free
As a fish swimming in the sea.
I gather your sweet fragrance like a butterfly;
You half refuse and half comply.
I'm filled with love as with surprise
And kiss your cheeks and eyes.

Tune: *WILLOW LEAVES*

With heart and soul I've loved you deep;
For you I have forgot to eat and sleep.
Had I not borne this with sincerity,
How could I win your virgin purity,
And end the bitterness
Of love with sweet caress!

Tune: *A BLUE SONG*

I have completed my happiness tonight;
Beyond the clouds my soul seems in flight.
I have met you so full of love, at last,
Though I've become so lean and pined away so fast.
The happy union of tonight still seems untrue,

ACT IV

But on the earth there's fragrant dew,
Over the lonely steps the wind dies away,
Into my cabinet the moon sheds its ray.
I see so clear our trysting bower
Still sweet with shower.
How can it seem
You came last night in dream?

Master Zhang, rising and kneeling again, says:
Having waited on you tonight, my dear Young Lady, I will remain your grateful servant for life.
(Yingying remains silent.)

Rose enters and, prompting Yingying, says:
Go back now, my Young Mistress, lest our absence be discovered.
(Yingying arises, starts to go and remains silent.)

Master Zhang, holding Yingying's hand and gazing at her, continues to sing:
What can I do
But part from you?

Tune: *PARASITIC GRASS*

A charming face
So full of grace,
To make you fall in love at first sight,
Regret when she's not seen,
And love your fill when she comes at night!
Tonight we've met behind the gauze bed-screen.
But when shall I again untie your girdle green?

Rose, urging Yingying says:
Let us go back at once, my Young Mistress, lest our absence

be discovered.

(Yingying, remaining silent, descends the steps.)

Master Zhang, holding both her hands and gazing at her, sings to the tune of *EPILOGUE*:

    Love is exhaled from her bosom snow-white,
    Her eyebrows dyed in vernal hue.
    Seeing her, you
    Of gold and jade would make light.
    Her rosy cheeks and flushed face
    Under the moon so bright,
    Look more charming and more strikingly red and white.
    She slackens her pace
    Down fragrant steps and on moss green,
    Not that her broidered shoes are lean,
    But that she lingers at the sight
    Of the unworthy scholar whom she does not slight.
    O would you come earlier another night!

(Exeunt.)

ACT IV

Scene 2 Rose in the Dock

Madame Cui enters with her adopted son, Happy Boy, and says:
>Yingying seems absent-minded and preoccupied these days, and her figure appears different. What is the matter with her?

Happy Boy says:
>The other night when you were asleep, I saw my sister and Rose go to burn incense in the garden and not come back before midnight.

Madame Cui says:
>Go and call Rose to come here.

>>(Happy Boy calls Rose.)

Rose enters and says:
>What are you calling me for, my Young Master?

Happy Boy says:
>My mother has learned that you and my sister have been to the garden and she wants to question you.

Rose says:
>Alas! My Young Mistress, you have compromised me. Go ahead, my Young Master, and I will come immediately.
>
>A pair of lovebirds sleep on water green;
>
>A parrot sees them through wind-opened screen.

She sings to the tune of *FIGHT OF QUAILS*:
>If you had gone by night
>
>And come back with daylight,
>
>Your joys might be secure

As long as sky and earth endure.
But you would bring fresh shower
Each night for thirsting flower,
And often make me feel in the wrong,
Gnawed by an anxiety strong.
You should have gone and come back by starlight.
Who'd have allowed you to sleep there all night?
Do you not know our Mistress' ingenious mind
Rather unkind?
She could see honeyed words through.
Even when there's nothing wrong, she would make much ado.

Tune: *VIOLET FLOWER*

She would suspect the scholar has become bridegroom
And you, my Young Mistress, his wife in golden room,
And I have pulled the string.
Seeing your eyebrows fresh as spring
And eyes as autumn water bright,
She'd guess all right.
If she just tries
To button up your robe and measure your girdle green
And compare it with the size
Of your former figure she has seen,
She's sure to find
You're lovely and coquette of a different kind.

She says:

I feel almost sure when I appear before my Mistress, she will say: O you little wretch!

She sings to the tune of *GOLDEN BANANA LEAVES*:

I ordered you to follow her wherever

ACT IV

>She went and keep an eye on her and never
>Lose sight of her. What made you lead her stray
>From the right way?
>If I am thus addressed.
>O what in my defence have I to say?

She says:
>Then I will simply tell her, "I have never dared to deceive you since my very childhood, my respectful Mistress."

She continues to sing:
>Then of the whole affair I will make a clean breast.

She says:
>What had I to gain from their liaison?

She sings to the tune of *SONG OF FLIRTATION*:
>Their heads were close together like two flowers;
>A pair of happy phoenix loved their fill.
>I stood alone outside the window of the bower,
>Ne'er daring cough e'en slightly, till
>In early morning hours
>My broidered shoes on mossy ground felt icy chill.
>Now my delicate skin will be beaten black and blue.
>What wrong has a go-between done in a rendezvous?

She says:
>Well, I am off, my Young Mistress. If I can explain matters to the satisfaction of my old Mistress, do not be overjoyed. If not, do not be overannoyed. Just stay there and wait for the news.

>>(Rose appears before Madame Cui.)

Madame Cui says:
>You little wretch! Why don't you kneel down? Won't you confess your guilt?

Rose says:
>Your maid knows of no guilt to confess.

Madame Cui says:
>How dare you deny it! If you tell the truth, I will pardon you; if not, I will beat you to death, you little wretch! Who allowed you to go with your Young Mistress to the garden at midnight?

Rose says:
>I did not go there. Who did see me?

Madame Cui says:
>Happy Boy saw you. How dare you still deny it!
>
>>(She beats Rose.)

Rose says:
>Please withdraw your noble hand, my Mistress. Do not be angry and listen to what I have to say.

She sings to the tune of *THREE TERRACES*:
>When we had finished our sewing at night,
>We talked about her elder brother's plight.
>We thought it was her due
>To inquire after his health without telling you.

Madame Cui says:
>To inquire? What did he say?

Rose continues to sing:
>"Your Mistress returned evil for good", he said,
>"And turned to grief my pleasure vain."
>He told me, Rose, to go ahead,
>And said my Young Mistress should alone remain.

Madame Cui says:
>Ah! you wretch! How could an unmarried maiden remain there alone!

ACT IV

Rose sings to the tune of *A BALD HEAD*:
>I thought she'd cure him with needle divine.
>Who knew like mating swallows they'd have done?
>They've slept together over a month, rain or shine.
>Why need you go into details one by one?
>### Tune: *KING OF MEDICINE*
>They know nor grief nor sorrow;
>They know today but not tomorrow.
>They love each other soul and heart;
>They cannot bear to be torn apart.
>My Mistress, overlook the matter if you can
>This is not an affair for you to probe or scan.

Madame Cui says:
>It is you, little wretch, who are to blame.

Rose says:
>It is neither Master Zhang nor Miss Yingying nor Rose who is to blame. The fault is yours, Madame.

Madame Cui says:
>You little wretch! How dare you shift the blame to me! How can it be my fault?

Rose says:
>It is fundamental for a man to keep faith. One who does not is not worthy of the name of a man. When the Salvation Monastery was surrounded by the bandits, you promised to give your daughter as wife to anyone who could make the bandits withdraw. If Master Zhang had not been an admirer of the beauty of my Young Mistress, would he, an outsider, have proposed a plan to such an effect? When the bandits retreated and you were left in peace, you repented and went back on your words. Was not this a breach of faith? Unwilling

to approve the match, you should have rewarded him with money and made him go far, far away. It was wrong of you to keep him in the library near the Young Lady's abode, so that the lonely maiden and bachelor had a chance to meet each other. If you did not cover up this scandal, in the first place, the family honor of the late Prime Minister would be compromised. In the second place, you would do wrong to Master Zhang who had done us good. In the third place, if you appealed to the court, you would be the first to be blamed for having not taken good care of the family. In my humble opinion, it would be far better to forgive the wrong he had done and not to return evil for good, but to fulfil the promise you have made to unite them as man and wife.

She continues to sing:

The proverb says: Don't keep in the household
A maiden who is growing old!

Tune: *A POCKMARKED FACE*

One of them is a leading light;
The other is a lady fair and bright.
One knows the secular and divine;
The other drawing and embroidery fine.

Tune: *A SECOND SONG*

When things appear
Good far and near,
Don't interfere!
Why make an enemy of a good friend
Who sent for General on White Horse to defend
The family and to the trouble put an end?

Tune: *SPINNER*

Why turn a benefactor into an enemy

ACT IV

And bring disgrace to your own family?
She's after all your flesh and blood,
Over which you should brood.

Madame Cui says:

What the little wretch has said is reasonable. It is my misfortune to have brought up this unworthy daughter. If the case were brought to the court, it would bring disgrace to our family. Well, well! Our family had no guilty man nor remarried woman. What can I do now but give my daughter to the beast! Rose, go and tell Yingying to come here!

Rose, calling Yingying, says:

My Young Mistress! The rod was brandished over me like a threatening shower. Fortunately I was spared by speaking straight. Now my Mistress asks you to go over.

Yingying says:

How dare I, so overwhelmed with shame, see my mother face to face?

Rose says:

Ah, my Young Mistress, you are at it again. You need not feel ashamed before your own mother. If you do, how could you have dared to do what you did?

She sings to the tune of *RED PEACH BLOSSOM*:

You had your tryst with Master Zhang as soon
As over the top of willows rose the moon.
As hamed, I hid my face amid willow leaves
And bit with my teeth into my sleeves.
When I turned my eyes on you,
I saw before the bed but your delicate shoe.
In bed he was loving his fill;

Silent, you let him have his will,
Why did you not feel shame
With your cheeks all in flame?

(Yingying meets her mother.)

Madame Cui says:

My dear child!

(Madame Cui weeps.) (Yingying weeps.) (Rose weeps.)

Madame Cui says:

My dear child, you have been wronged, but this was my fault. How could I blame anyone else? If I appealed to the court, it would bring disgrace to your late father. How could a prime minister's daughter have done such a thing!

(Yingying weeps bitterly.)

Madame Cui says:

Rose, help your Young Mistress. Well, well, what can I do with an unworthy daughter! Go to the library, Rose, and tell that beast to come.

(Rose calls Master Zhang.)

Master Zhang says:

Who is calling me?

Rose says:

Your affair has been discovered. My Mistress is calling for you.

Master Zhang says:

How can I get out of the difficulty? Miss Rose, will you please screen me a little? I wonder who would have told Madame this. I am so fearful that I dare not go to see her.

Rose says:

Don't appear fearful but put on a bold air and go to see her at once.

ACT IV

She sings to the tune of *A SECOND STANZA*:
>What leaked out could not be screened with success,
>So at once I had to confess.
>My Mistress now would entertain you with wine and tea.
>Why should you anxious be?
>Betrothal may not be arranged by a go-between.
>Am I a chaperon obscene?
>You look like a silver spear-head,
>But in fact it is made of lead.

(Master Zhang meets Madame Cui.)

Madame Cui says:
>Fine scholar as you are, have you not heard that deeds unworthy of the ancient sages should not be done? If I should hand you over to the court, that would bring disgrace to my family. There is left only for me to marry my daughter to you. But for three generations past our family has never had a son-in-law who had no official rank. So you must go to the capital to attend the civil service examinations. I will take care of your future wife. If you pass the examinations with honor, come back and marry my daughter. If not, do not come to see us!

(Master Zhang remains silent, kneels and makes his bows.)

Rose says:
>Thank Heaven and Earth, and thanks to my Mistress!

She sings to the tune of *JOY OF EASTERN PLAIN*:
>Your love affair
>Has been forgiven.
>Your eyebrows knit with care
>May now be riven.

Your lovesickness
Ends in your happiness.
O who would not embrace
Such a delightful maiden with a lovely face!

Madame Cui says:
Rose, give orders for the luggage to be packed and wine and viands to be prepared so that we may see Master Zhang off at the Pavilion tomorrow and give him a farewell feast.

Yingying sings:
Send word to riverside green willow trees
To see the rider off in vernal breeze!

(Exit Madame Cui with Yingying.)

Rose says:
Master Zhang, do you feel happy or sad?

She sings to the tune of *EPILOGUE*:
We must just wait till you come back again,
When flutes and drums will enliven the scene,
And like two lovebirds you are joined in twain,
Then I'll receive your reward for a go-between
And drink a cup of wine
For your union divine.

(Exeunt)

ACT IV

Scene 3 Farewell Feast

Madame Cui enters and says:
>We are going to see Master Zhang start for the Capital today, and Rose has gone to tell my daughter to come with us to the Pavilion of Farewell. I have ordered a feast prepared and an invitation sent to Master Zhang, and I think he must have finished his packing by now.

Yingying enters with Rose and says:
>We are going to see him off today. It is sad to say good-bye at any time, and how much sadder on a late autumn day!

Master Zhang enters and says:
>Madame told me last night to go to the Capital for the civil service examinations. She would marry her daughter to me if I come back with an official rank. What can I do but go as she directed? Now I am starting for the Pavilion of Farewell to wait for the Young Lady so that I may bid her farewell.
>
>(Exit)

Yingying says:
>We drink a cup of wine whether we part or meet;
>No matter where he goes, the rider must be fleet.

She sings to the tune of *CALM DIGNITY*:
>With clouds the sky turns grey
>O'er yellow-bloom-paved way.
>How bitter blows the western breeze!

From north to south fly the wild geese.
Why like wine-flushed face is frosted forest red?
It's dyed in tears the parting lovers shed.

Tune: *ROLLING BALL*

It's my regret
So late we met;
It grieves my heart
So soon to part.
Long as the willow branch may be,
It cannot tie his parting steed to the tree.
What would I not have done
If autumn forest could hang up the setting sun!
Go slowly, parting steed;
Cab, follow it with speed!
Of lovesickness just cured,
The grief of parting must now be endured.
"I'm going," when a voice is heard to say,
My body seems to waste away.
When the Pavilion of Farewell comes in sight,
My bracelet becomes no longer tight.

Rose says:

You have not made your toilet today, my Young Mistress.

Yingying says:

How can you know the feelings of my heart, Rose!

She continues to sing:

Who knows, who knows
My heart full of woes?

Tune: *MURMURING SONG*

Seeing the cab and steed ready to start,

ACT IV

How can I not feel grief and anguish gnaw my heart?
How can I rouge my cheeks and powder my face,
Adorn myself with winning charm and grace?
What can I do is but to bury deep
My head between my coverlet and pillow and sleep,
And let my hundred-folded dress with flowing sleeves
Drowned in a stream of tears no one perceives.
O what unconsolable grief!
O what unconsolable grief!
Could words and letters bring me any relief?

(Madame Cui, Yingying and Rose arrive at the Pavilion of Farewell.)
(Master Zhang salutes Madame Cui profoundly.)
(Yingying turns her face away.)

Madame Cui says:

Come nearer, Master Zhang. Now that you are my flesh and blood, there is no need for you to avoid my daughter. Come over here and meet him, my dear child!

(Master Zhang and Yingying meet each other.)

Madame Cui says:

Sit down, Master Zhang. I will sit here and my child there. Pour out wine, Rose. Drink up this cup, Master Zhang. Since I have promised to marry my daughter to you, you must go to the Capital and prove yourself worthy of our family and win the highest honor in the examinations.

Master Zhang says:

Though not born a literary talent or brilliant scholar, I will do my best, depending on the favor and fortune of your honorable family, to win the highest honor in the examinations so that the

Young Lady may be ennobled in due course.

(They all sit down.)

(Yingying sighs.)

Yingying sings to the tune of *DOFFING THE CLOTHES*:

The west wind drives the withered leaves here and there;
Decayed in mist, the grass has chilly, foggy air.
I see him sit at table, slanting his head,
Knitting his brows, as if half-dead.

Tune: *SAIALL LIANGZHOU*

He dare not let his tears fall from his brimful eyes
For fear his grief be known.
Seeing himself observed, he utters sighs,
Pretending to arrange his white silk gown.

Tune: *PETTY SONG*

Though we'll be man and wife in future years,
How can I now refrain from shedding tears?
My mind with him infatuated,
My heart with love intoxicated,
Just overnight
My slender waist has grown more slight.

Tune: *ASCENDING THE ATTIC*

Our joy of union not complete,
Our grief of parting comes so fleet.
You know how much for you I cared.
It was not till last night was our love declared.
But oh, today
You'll go away!
Having suffered from lovesickness on those days,
I know not parting grief still ten times heavier weighs.

ACT IV

Madame Cui says:
>Help your Young Mistress to pour out wine, Rose.
>
>(Yingying pours out wine.)
>
>(Master Zhang sighs.)

Yingying whispers:
>Drink up this cup of wine I hold in my hand.

She sings to the tune of *PETTY SONG*:
>While young,
>
>One makes light of a farewell long;
>
>Light-hearted,
>
>Lovers do not care to be parted.
>
>Canst thou forget thy leg across mine,
>
>My cheek against thine,
>
>Hand in hand we combine?
>
>The former Premier's son-in-law-to-be,
>
>Thy noble wife would ennoble thee
>
>Like on one stem twin lotus-flower,
>
>Far better than to win honor and power.
>
>>(Yingying sits down again at the table and sighs.)

She sings to the tune of *COURTYARD FULL OF FRAGRANCE*:
>So quickly passes the feast.
>
>We sit now face to face:
>
>We'll then be west and east.
>
>If Mother were not in her place,
>
>We might have enjoyed a bridal meal alone.
>
>Although the time will soon pass by,
>
>It might be called a dinner of our own.
>
>In vain I center on him my eye,
>
>Keep thinking on,

And nearly turn into a stone.

Madame Cui says:

Pour out wine, Rose.

Rose, pouring out a cup for Master Zhang and another for Yingying, says:

You have not had breakfast this morning, my Young Mistress. Will you please drink a little?

Yingying sings to the tune of *HAPPY THREE*:

They offer me both food and wine,
Which taste like muddy water 'neath the feet:
As mud the food is not so fine;
As water the wine is not so sweet.

Tune: *HOMAGE TO EMPEROR*

Even warmed wine as cold as ice appears:
It is diluted with my lovesick tears.
Not that I will not eat the food before my eyes;
But that my stomach's filled with grief and sighs.
For fame as empty as the horn of a snail,
For profit trifling as the head of a fly,
Two love-birds torn apart bewail.
One here, the other there, we're giving sigh for sigh.

Tune: *FOUR-SIDE TRANQUILLITY*

They remove in a moment dish and cup,
The cab goes down, the horse goes up.
Both linger till
The sun sinks behind the bar of a green hill.
Who knows tonight where thou shalt be?
Even in dreams I cannot find thee.

ACT IV

Madame Cui says:
> Rose, bid them to get ready the carriage and request Master Zhang to mount his horse. I am going back with your Young Mistress.
>> (They all get ready to start.)
>> (Master Zhang makes his bow to Madame Cui.)

Madame Cui says:
> I have no other wish but that you should win high rank and come back soon.

Master Zhang, thanking her, says.
> I will obey your instructions.
>> (Master Zhang and Yingying bow to each other.)

Yingying says:
> You are going now. Whether you win high rank or not, I just hope you will be back as soon as possible.

Master Zhang says:
> Make yourself easy on that score, my dear Young Lady. To which family will the highest literary honor belong if not to yours? I must bid you farewell now.

Yingying says:
> I have no other farewell gift for you but an impromptu quatrain:
> Now left alone, what can I say,
> I whom you loved deep night and day?
> Do not bestow your love of old
> Upon another whom you behold!

Master Zhang says:
> You mistake me, my dear Young Lady! How could I bestow my love on anyone else but you? As I am in a confused state of mind and you may not believe what I say, I will not respond to your poem until I come back with the highest literary honor.

Yingying sings to the tune of *PLAYING THE CHILD*:

    My sleeves in crimson tears of love are drowned;
    I know more soaked are yours, those of the blue-gowned.
    Eastward the oriole and westward the swallow flies;
    Before you start I ask when you'll return.
    Although afar, still you will be before my eyes;
    I'll drink a cup of wine to show my deep concern.
    Before I drink, my heart is drunk,
    My eyes shed blood, in ash my feeling's sunk.

        Tune: *LAST STANZA BUT FIVE*

Before your arrival, get used to harsh climate;
When you pursue your way, in food be moderate!
Take care of your own health,
Which is a mine of wealth!
Early to bed on journey long in rainy days
And late to rise at country inn in wind and haze
Riding in chilly autumn breeze, you yourself uncared-for, should take your ease.

        Tune: *LAST STANZA BUT FOUR*

To whom of my grief to complain?
Alone I know the pain.
Should I complain to Heaven? O, to what avail?
My tears would make the Yellow River overflow;
My grief would make three mountain peaks bend low.
At dusk I'll lean on Western Tower's rail
To watch the setting sun over ancient way
And withered willow trees along the bay.

ACT IV

Tune: *LAST STANZA BUT THREE*

Not long ago we came in laughter;
Alone I'll be back shortly after.
Once home, I'll dread
To see the curtained bed.
Last night in warm embroidered coverlet spring dwelt;
Tonight you'll dream of counterpane where cold is felt.
Can I detain you any longer here?
You have mounted your steed now,
Both of us are in tear
With a knitted eyebrow.

Tune: *LAST STANZA BUT TWO*

I care not if your talent won't build a career,
But fear you may give up the old wife for the new.
I wish wild geese and fish would bring your letters here.
While I shall send you tidings by the Phoenix Blue
O do not swear You won't come back unless you win the laurel crown!
Please note it down:
If you see elsewhere beauties fair,
Don't linger any longer there!

Master Zhang says:

My dear, your words as precious as gold and jade are imprinted on my heart.
We will meet again soon, so you need not be too sad. I am going now.
Holding back tears, I pretended to make bows;
Though feeling sad, I tried to unknit my brows.

Yingying says:

Not knowing that my heart is broken,
I'll follow you in dreams unwoken.

(Exit Master Zhang)

(Yingying sighs.)

Yingying sings to the tune of *LAST STANZA BUT ONE*:

> Green hills and forests standing between him and me
> Seem to extend a thousand li.
> Thin mist and evening vapours screen him from my view.
> No human voice is heard on sun-lit ancient way
> But rustling of the crops in autumn wind and horse's neigh.
> I am reluctant to enter the car,
> So eager to have come with you;
> So slow to go back afar!

Madame Cui says:

> Rose, help your Young Mistress to her carriage.
> The time is late. Let us go home.
> Although to give way to my daughter I appear,
> I've acted after all as proper mother dear.

(Exit)

Rose says:

> Your mother's carriage is a long way ahead. You must go back quickly.

Yingying says:

> Rose, can you see where he is now?

She sings to the tune of *THE LAST STANZA*:

> Surrounded by mountains east and west,
> He flips his whip on sun-lit road.
> All the world's grief seems to fill my breast.
> How can such a small car bear such a heavy load!

(Exeunt)

ACT IV

Scene 4 Dreams

Master Zhang enters with his Lute-bearer and says:
>We are already twenty li east of the Prefecture of Pu, and before us appears the thatched-roofed Inn at the Bridge. I will pass the night there and go on early tomorrow morning. My horse is unwilling to go further at any price.

He sings to the double tune of *NEW WATER*:
>The distant temple in a shroud
>Of evening cloud,
>My parting grief
>Arises from each faded leaf.
>The horse goes slow;
>The rider in a spirit low.
>Strong is the breeze,
>And broken the row of wild geese.
>I feel regret gnawing my heart:
>It's the first night we're torn apart.
>
>**Tune: *CHARMING PACES***
>
>Last night in our green coverlet sweet fragrance spread,
>Upon our pillow we reclined our head.
>We slept together face to face;
>I gazed at her in my embrace:
>What an enchanting grace!
>In her cloud-hair was inserted a comb of jade,
>Which looked as if of crescent moon it were made.

He says:
> Here I am before the inn. Where is the innkeeper?

The Inn-keeper enters and says:
> This is the well-known Bridge Inn, sir. The best room is at your disposal, sir. (Exit)

Master Zhang says:
> Look after my horse, Lute-bearer, and have a lamp lit. I do not want to eat but to sleep.

The Lute-bearer says:
> I am also tired and need a rest. I will spread my bedding in front of your bed.

> (The Lute-bearer falls asleep first.)

Master Zhang says:
> How could sleep close my eyes tonight?

He sings to the tune of *THE WIND BLOWING DOWN MUMES*:
> Reclining on my lonely pillow in the inn,
> I find my coverlet too cold and thin.
> I hear the sound
> Of autumn insects all around,
> To make my sorrow keen,
> The wind cracks paper windows green.
> I try to sleep alone in vain.
> Lonely and cold, when can I feel warmed up again?
> (He tries to sleep, tosses about and finds sleep impossible.
> He tries again and falls asleep.)

He says in dream:
> Is this the voice of my Young Lady? Where on earth am I now? I must get up and listen.

ACT IV

He hears sing to the tune of *BRUSHWOOD*:
>Walking in lonely wilds and barren plain,
>My heart beating with fear I can't refrain,
>I pant and gasp for breath to overtake my man
>As quickly as I can.

Master Zhang says:
>No doubt that is my Lady's voice, but whom is she trying to overtake?
>I must listen again. (He hears her continue to sing:)
>I beat the grass
>For fear of snakes, alas!
>
>### Tune: *ZITHER AND GUITAR*
>
>I feel my heart
>Is torn apart.
>So I am not afraid
>Of this long journey, hard though it may appear.
>I come, unknown to my maid
>And to my mother dear.

Master Zhang says:
>It is clear this is my Young Lady. Let me listen again.

He hears her continue to sing:
>When I saw him mounting his steed and sighing sad,
>I wept as if I had gone mad.
>Not that I had a wicked heart,
>But from the moment we did part
>To the setting of the sun,
>My grief could never be undone.
>And I began to waste away

So much within half a day

That I had to tighten my skirt three folds or four.

Who's seen me wear away so much ever before?

Master Zhang says:

What you say is all true, my dear Young Lady. But where are you now?

(He listens again.)

He hears her sing to the tune of *FLOWER ON BROCADE*:

We'd just completed our short union of heart

When your career tore us apart.

The long suffering for which we grieved

Had just been slightly relieved,

When we again have to endure

The never-ending thoughts of your departure.

Master Zhang says:

My Young Lady's sentiment is nothing other than mine.

How sad it is!

(He sighs and listens again.)

He hears her sing to the tune of *PETTY SONG*:

Grass purified by frost looks like waves green,

And faded leaves are dotted with dewdrops white.

The winding road goes up and down, uneven;

The wind blows furiously from left and right.

While I am hurrying up here,

Where are you resting now, my dear?

Master Zhang says:

I am here. Come in, my Young Lady!

(Suddenly wakened up) Ah! Where am I?

(Looking all around) Pooh! It is the Bridge Inn.

ACT IV

(He calls his Lute-bearer, who, being asleep, does not answer. He tries to go to sleep again, but fails and tosses about. Looking round again, he is lost in thoughts.)

He sings to the tune of CLEAR RIVER:

Dull am I in this lonely room,

With none to speak to in the gloom.

The night appears

As long as years.

He says:

I do not know what time it is now.

He continues to sing:

Do I hear evening rain fall on the willow trees

Or waning moonlight shiver in the morning breeze?

Where really am I now at night or at daybreak

From wine awake?

(He falls asleep and dreams again.)

Yingying enters, knocks at the door and says:

Open the door! Open the door!

Master Zhang says:

Who is knocking at the door? It is a female voice.

How strange! I will not open the door.

He sings to the tune of CELEBRATION OF HARMONY:

If you're a human being, make it clear!

If you're a ghost, O disappear!

Yingying says:

It is I. Open quickly!

(Master Zhang opens the door and leads Yingying in by the hand.)

Master Zhang continues to sing:

As soon as I hear

That it is you,
I take you by your fragrant sleeve.
Ah, my dear! my dear!
It's really you whom never will I leave!

Yingying says:

I thought to myself how I could live without you by my side, so I have come on purpose to accompany you.

Master Zhang says:

Where on earth can I find another heart like yours?

He sings to the tune of *PSEUDO-MEIODY*:

You're really thoroughly true.
Oh, in disorder is your raiment sweet,
Your broidered shoes covered with mud and dew,
Outworn the soles of your cold feet.

Tune: *SONG OF SWEET WATER*

When you forgot to sleep and eat,
You looked like discolored jade,
Even worse than flowers that fade.
In your cold coverlet alone,
You're like a single love-bird
Or the cloud-hidden moon.
How could your sadness be expressed in word?

Tune: *PICKING LAUREL*

I think the saddest thing to human heart
Is to be torn apart.
You pity me going afar
And all alone
O'en hill and dale, 'neath moon and star.
If I had known

ACT IV

Our love would cause such worry and regret,
I'd wish we should never have met.
I fear when wanes the moon and flowers fade,
We'd be like broken jar or jade.
You do not love a hero brave
Nor a man rich and proud,
But share with me a bed in life and a shroud
In death 'neath the same grave.

A soldier enters, and startling Master Zhang, says:

I just saw a young lady cross the river. Where is she now? Light a torch. She must have gone into the inn. Let her come out! Let her come out!

Master Zhang says:

What can be done, my Young Lady? Stand behind me and I will speak to him.

(Exit Yingying)

He sings to the tune of *SONG OF NARCISSUS*:

You once attacked the Temple with your spade and hoe;
Now you threaten my throat with sword and spear.
With brigand's heart and robber's mind, my deadly foe!

The Soldier says:

Who is that young lady? How dare you hide her?

Master Zhang continues to sing:

Silence and stand away and disappear!
Do you not know my friend is General Du?
With a mere glance he'd make mincemeat of you,
Pointing at you, he'd make of you a bloody mass,
And here he comes on his white horse from the Pu Pass.

(Exit the Soldier in fear.)

Master Zhang, embracing his Lute-bearer, says:
>You have been frightened, my dear Young Lady!

The Lute-bearer says:
>What is the matter, sir?

Master Zhang, awakened and revealing his feeling in dumb show, says:
>Ah! It was only a dream. Let me open the door and look out. All I see is a vaporous sky and a frosty ground, the morning star just rising and the waning moon still bright. The twittering of swallows on the branches heard has broken the dream of union of lonely lovebird.

He sings to the tune of WILD GEESE'S FALL:
>The wall half hidden by the green, green willow trees,
>The door is closed on silent, silent autumn night.
>Sparse leaves fall from the branches in gentle, gentle breeze,
>My window steeped in gloomy, gloomy cloud-veiled moonlight.

>**Tune: TRIUMPHANT SONG**
>The bamboo's shadow shivers, shivers like wriggling snake;
>My fancy wafts and wafts like a dreaming butterfly.
>The cricket chirps and chirps all the night long awake;
>The washerwomen's pounding spreads, spreads far and nigh.
>Acute, acute my grief at heart:
>Painful and painful from my dream to be torn apart!
>Lonely, lonely I sigh: O where,
>O where is now my charming, charming lady fair?

The Lute-bearer says:
>It is dawn now. Let us start early and have our breakfast farther on.

ACT IV

Master Zhang sings to the tune of *LOVEBIRDS' EPILOGUE*:
>My grief lasts longer than the weeping willow longs
>The rippling water sounds like my love's sobbing song.
>The waning moon and dying lamp darken the view;
>My sorrow old is aggravated by the new.
>My parting grief
>Bitter beyond belief.
>Should I not use my pen instead of my tongue,
>O how could I make known my love for my Lady Young!
>
>>(Exeunt)

To sum up the four scenes of Act IV:

>Rose helps the loves to unite.
>Madame asks what happened at night.
>The lovers drink their sad adieu.
>But they unite in dreams anew.
>
>>(The end of the Stage Version)

ACT V

ACT V

Scene 1 Report of Success

Master Zhang enters and says:
> Half a year has passed since I left my dear Young Lady last autumn. Thanks to the protection of my forefathers, I have passed the civil service examinations and am waiting for the imperial appointment now. I am afraid my Young Lady may be anxious about the result, so I hasten to write a letter and send it by my lute-boy to her and her mother lest they should feel anxiety. Now the letter is written. Where is my lute boy?

Lute-bearer says:
> Here I am at your order.

Master Zhang says:
> Take this letter to the Mid-river Prefecture without delay! When you see your young mistress, tell her that I send her this letter for fear she should be anxious.

He sings to the tune of *ENJOYING FLOWERS*:
> When we met last,
> Flowers fell fast,
> The green moss was dotted with petals red.
> After we parted,
> The broken-hearted
> Evening mist congeals into leaves dead.
> Seeing mume flower,
> I know half a year's passed.

Can I not send a letter to her bower?

He says:
Boy, when you have told her the news and get a reply, You should return without delay.

(Exit)

Lute-bearer says:
With this letter I must hasten to the Mid-river Prefecture by starlight as by daylight.

(Exit)

Yingying enters with Rose and says:
It is half a year since Master Zhang went to the capital and I have received no letter from him. I have been ill at ease in these days, reluctant to make my toilet and careless whether my waist grows slim or my skirt becomes loose. O how much I am vexed!

She sings to the tune of *GETTING TOGETHER*:
Though from my eyes I keep sorrow apart,
It still remains in my heart.
Even if my heart can get rid of it,
It would then make my eyebrows knit.
I try to forget it in vain,
Lovesickness haunts me again and again.
How can my eyebrows not be weighed down
By such a painful frown?
New sorrow comes after the old,
They mingle and become twofold.
The old looks like the high mountains perceived in dream;
The new runs onward like the endless flowing stream.

Rose says:
When my Young Mistress was out of sorts, she would recover

ACT V

after a short rest. But how much she is wasting away this time!

Yingying sings to the tune of *FREE ENJOYMENT*:

>   When previously I pined with grief,
>   I used to find relief.
>   This time it's seized on me.
>   Where could I be carefree?
>   Alone I mount to my boudoir and look,
>   Roll up and hang the curtain on its hook.
>   In vain on hills and rills I gaze;
>   Green trees are veiled in haze.
>   Withered grass blends into the skies;
>   A lonely boat along the ferry lies.

She says:

>   My clothes seem not to become me.

Rose says:

>   My Young Mistress, you are too slim and frail for your dress now.

Yingying sings to the tune of *GOLDEN CHAIN*:

>   My skirt in pomegranate hue
>   Has been slept into rouged wrinkles new.
>   My lilac-buttons more than meet
>   The button-hole in form of lotus sweet.
>   Like pearls unstrung, my tears
>   Have wet my fragrant silken sleeves.
>   My eyebrows knit like willow leaves;
>   Slimmer than golden flower my face appears.

The Lute-bearer enters and says:

>   By my Master's order, I am bringing a letter to my young mistress. I have just seen her mother in the front hall. She was very delighted and told me to come in to see my Young

Mistress in the back hall. And here I am.

(Coughing)

Rose says:

Who is there?

(Seeing the Lute-bearer and smiling)

When did you arrive? My Young Mistress is unhappy now. Have you come alone or with your master?

Lute-bearer says:

My master has won success at court, so he has told me to come first with this good news.

Rose says:

Wait a moment here. I will come in to announce you to my Young Mistress.

(Seeing Yingying and smiling)

My dear Young Mistress, good news! good news!
Master Zhang has won success at court.

Yingying says:

You little minx! Are you deceiving me to escape boredom?

Rose says:

The Lute-bearer is at the door. Having seen my Old Mistress, he is ordered to see you.

Yingying says:

At last, I need not feel shy to say he has not belied our expectation.

(The lute-bearer meets Yingying.)

Boy, When did you leave the capital?

Lute-bearer says:

About a month ago. When I left, my Master was going about the streets for merry-making.

ACT V

Yingying says:
> You silly fellow! Don't you know that the winner of laurels has to go on display around the streets for three days?

Lute-bearer says:
> You are right, my Young Lady. Here is the letter.

Yingying sings to the tune of GOLDEN CHRYSANTHEMUM'S FRAGRANCE:
> E'er since he left me ill at ease,
> I've had no heart to enjoy vernal breeze.
> How could I know now he's sent me a letter?
> Still I feel none the better.
> Has he proved true to what he said?
> In silence I hang down my head.
> Letter in hand,
> Tears lose command.

Tune: *A GOURD OF VINEGAR*
> In tears I open here the letter fair,
> Which he'd in tears have written there.
> Maybe his tears prevented him then
> From writing with his pen.
> He's sent me stains of tears
> Whose trace in the letter appears.
> The old trace still remains,
> Though drowned in my new stains.
> Our sorrow new and old
> Become twofold.

(Reading the letter)
> Zhang Gong salutes his fair sweet lady and presents her the following letter. Half a year has passed since I bade you farewell

last autumn. By the protection of my ancestors and the blessing of my worthy spouse, I have passed the civil service examinations with high honors. Now I am residing in the Hall of Worthies, awaiting appointment to my office. For fear you and your worthy mother might be anxious, I order my lute bearer to forward you this letter. Though we are far apart, my heart is always with you. I only regret we could not fly side by side like a pair of lovebirds. Please do not blame me for putting honor before love, and I will be deeply grateful to you. If you allow me to speak of my feelings for you, please wait till we meet again. Attached you will find a quatrain for your perusal at leisure:

"I've won the laurels and greet

In fairy land my lady sweet.

Soon I'll return in fine array.

Don't lean on the door for that day!"

She says:

Ah! he has won the third honor.

She sings to the tune of *THE SECOND PART*:

Then 'neath the moon he stole into the Western Bower;

Now the imperial banquet sings his glorious hour.

His feet which jumped over east wall in foremost place stand;

His heart which loves flowers wins laurels with his hand.

Nor rouge nor powder could conceal his talent fine

From now on in my boudoir his virtue will shine.

She says to the lute-bearer:

Have you had your meal yet?

Lute-bearer says:

Not yet.

ACT V

Yingying says:
> Rose, go and get something for him to eat.

Lute-bearer says:
> Will you please, my Young Mistress, write a letter in reply while I am eating? For my master told me to go back with your letter as soon as possible.

Yingying says:
> Rose, bring me pen and paper.
> (Writing a letter)
> My letter is written. How to express my feeling but send him a sweater, a girdle, a pair of stockings, a lute, a jade hair-pin and a pen of specked bamboo!
> Boy, pack up these with care! Rose, give him ten taels of silver for his traveling expenses.

Rose says:
> Now Master Zhang will be an official. How could he need these things you send him?

Yingying says:
> How can you know what is in my heart!
> Listen and I will tell you.

She sings to the tune of *PLANE LEAVES*:
> If he should sleep with this light sweater on,
> He would not feel in bed alone.
> If to his skin it's near,
> How can he not think of his dear?
> This girdle round his waist should not be kept apart
> From the left or right of his heart.
> The stockings he wears on his way
> May keep him from going astray.

Tune: **BACKYARD FLOWERS**

The lute of our first love did sing
And then united us with its string.
Could he neglect the love which lingers
In the lute which I can't forget to play with fingers?
I send him the hairpin of jade,
At the height of his fame, I am afraid,
He might forget me; then it would remind
Him not to leave his love behind.
I send him the pen of specked bamboo-
Which by the riverside in autumn grew-
So that at the sight of the empress' trace,
He might think of my tearful face.
At the foot of the Nine Mysterious Mountains
The empress' tears gushed like fountain.

Tune: **BLUE BIRDS**

Now my fragrant silk robe also appears
Like her stained bamboo wet with tears,
We have the same sentiment,
Though our causes are different.
Tears for the living as those for the dead
Are equally copiously shed.
Tell your dear master the above
Lest he should forget his first love!

Lute-bearer says:

I understand.

Yingying says:

Boy, take good care of these things!

ACT V

She sings to the tune of *A GOURD OF VINEGAR*:
>At night when you stop at an inn and rest in bed,
>Don't put on this parcel your head
>Lest the grease from your hair my gifts should stain!
>Don't rinse the parcel when it's wet with rain
>For fear the crease can't be removed when dried!
>Take good care of my gifts and don't lay them aside!
>**Tune: *GOLDEN CHRYSANTHEMUM'S FRAGRANCE***
>I would confide my letter to the wild geese,
>But I'm afraid love from his heart
>Would sooner or later be kept apart.
>I look for the capital ill at ease:
>It seems as far as the end of the sky.
>I lean on railings at the western tower's height,
>But still he's out of sight;
>In vain I see but water flowing by.

Lute-bearer says:
>I'll take leave of you, my Young Mistress, and set off now.

Yingying says:
>Boy, tell your master when you see him...

Lute-bearer says:
>What shall I say?

Yingying sings to the tune of *ROLLING WAVES*:
>He's pining for me there;
>Here for him I'm wasting away.
>When he left, his words were so fair,
>Promising to return on the ninth day
>Of the ninth moon.

Now the tenth will pass soon.
O I'm to blame.
Why should I induce him to seek for fame!

Lute-bearer says:
Now I have got the reply, I will go back by daylight as by starlight.

(Exit)

(Exeunt Yingying and Rose.)

ACT V

Scene 2 Guess

Master Zhang enters and says:
> I thought I might leave the capital after my appointment. Little did I dream I should stay in the Imperial Academy as historian. Who knows the feelings of my heart? How can I do my work well? My lute-boy has not yet come back since he left the capital. How can I sleep well and eat with relish? I have been given leave to rest in the hostel for a few days. This morning the Imperial Medical Academy sent a physician to see me and give me medicine. But my sickness is one that no doctor could ever cure. For my heart is lovesick for my dear Young Lady since I left her. So how can I feel at ease?

He sings to the tune of *PINK BUTTERFLY*:
> Since I came here,
> I have been longing for her day and night.
> In my heart lies my dear
> Dear Yingying fair and bright.
> The doctor came to see
> What's wrong with me.
> What he said was all right.
> I tried in vain to evade;
> Before an attempt was made,
> He had seen through my plight.

Tune: *INTOXICATED VERNAL WIND*

>He said that each disease
>May have its remedies,
>But that no medicine could cure
>Lovesickness, he was sure.
>O my Young Lady dear,
>If you knew how lovesick I lie,
>How willingly for you I'd die,
>For you I'd die!
>Lonely without a home,
>In foreign land I roam.
>Now it is almost half a year.

Lute-bearer enters and says:
>I was told when I came back that my Master was ill in the hostel, so I must hasten to give him the letter.
>
>(Seeing Master Zhang)

Master Zhang says:
>At last here you are!

He sings to the tune of *WELCOMING IMMORTALS*:
>On blooming branch sings the happy magpie;
>Above the curtain hangs the spider high;
>The lamp burst into sparkling flame last night:
>All seem to show a lucky foresight.
>Here comes her letter of a broken heart,
>Her verse of lovers kept far, far apart.
>When she wrote it, she must have shed copious tears.
>Otherwise, why with stains the envelope appears?
>(Reading the letter which says):

ACT V

I make bows to my dear literary talent. We have been severed for half a year, which has seemed longer than three autumns. How much have I been longing for you! Now I believe the ancient verse, "The capital is farther away than the sun." Having received the letter brought by the lute-boy, I know the success you have won and the happy state you are in. With such a lover as you, what more need I to say? As the boy has to return soon, I can express my feelings only by sending you a lute, a jade hair-pin, a specked bamboo pen, a girdle, a sweater and a pair of silk stockings. Although these articles are insignificant and unworthy of you, I hope you will accept them with pleasure. The vernal wind is keen, so take good care of yourself. Besides, I send you a quatrain in the same thyme as yours:

"Leaning on rails, my dear talent I greet.
Don't fall in love with other beauties sweet!
Knowing in the world you've made up your way,
Before my glass I try my new array."

He says:

How lovely! For such a young lady as her, I would fain give up my life!

He sings to the tune of *MOUNTING THE TOWER*:

Her handwriting like that of a calligraphist
May be inscribed on precious list.
It has the strength and power
Of the two Zhangs And the two Wangs,
Talents who had their glorious hour.
See what today my Yingying's done!
Her handwriting's second to none.

Tune: **THE SECOND PART**

As sacred book I hold,
I'd use it as a charm,
Precious as seal of gold
And valuable without harm.
If it were duly signed
And an official were made
Its messenger to come behind,
'Twould be at once obeyed.

He looks at the sweater and says:

Not to speak of her letter, just look at this sweater she has sent me.

He sings to the tune of *COURTYARD FULL OF FRAGRANCE*:

How can I not love you?
Your needlework is excellent.
It's a model in view,
In which I can perceive your sentiment.
How can you know how long my dress should be?
Imagining my waist, you had to start.
You had no one to try the dress for me
On making it, you gave it all your heart.

He says:

The articles she has sent me have all a meaning which I can guess.

He sings to the tune of *WHITE CRANE*:

The lute tells me to play within closed door,
To pay attention to the music score,
To cultivate a worthy mind
And keep my ears refined.

Tune: **THE SECOND STANZA**

The jade hair-pin

ACT V

Is long and thin
Like a shoot of bamboo
So delicate and white;
It tells me to be true
And pure and bright.

Tune: *THE THIRD STANZA*

The pen is like the branch where perch phoenixes green
With rouge and tears which stained the tree.
Emperor Shun was wept by his dear queen;
Today my mistress thinks of me.

Tune: *THE FOURTH STANZA*

The girdle's made with cotton in her hand
And needle plied by the lamplight.
It shows her grief none understand
And her heart in sad plight.

Tune: *THE FIFTH STANZA*

The stockings have stitches minute and long
And silk lining as soft as fat of goose;
They tell me to do nothing wrong
And never let my feet go loose.

He says to the lute-bearer:
> Boy, what did your Young Mistress say when you were to leave her?

Lute-bearer says:
> She said the most important thing is that you should not fall in love with another woman.

Master Zhang says:
> O my dear Young Lady, how could you not know my heart!

He sings to the tune of *HAPPY THREE*:
> The wind and rain

Do rage and reign.
How sad and drear
Is the inn here!
When I from dreams awake,
My heart is broken for your sake.

Tune: *HOMAGE TO THE EMPEROR*

I can't control my hands and feet;
To reach the monastery my heart's too fleet,
My dear Young Lady, when you see
My face, what would you say to me?
I am a prodigal son
And a romantic one.
How could I love a flower
Which has passed its fresh hour?
Since I came here, have I ever sought pleasure
Even when I had leisure?

Tune: *CONGRATULATIONS TO IMPERIAL COURT*

Is there a premier seeking for a son-in-law in view?
Could he have a daughter like you?
Could she be as tender and clever
As you are ever?
How could I not think of my Yingying deep,
Whether I'm awake or asleep!

Tune: *PLAYING THE CHILD*

Go to my study, empty a ratten box there,
And spread a few sheets of paper inside!
When you put in these things, take care
The pricks of ratten should not collide
Or tangle with the silk and cotton thread!

ACT V

If on the clothes-rack they're hung and spread,
I am afraid their color in the wind will fade.
If in a bundle they are kept pell-mell,
Their folds will be creased, I fear.
You must do as I tell
You and hold these thing dear!

Tune: *THE SECOND STANZA*

I had just won her hand
And came here to seek fame.
Can I forget the temple in the eastern land?
Peach and plum burst in flame
Last night in vernal breeze;
In autumn rain today
Leaves fall from the plane trees.
So sad am I,
Although my body's far away,
My heart to her is nigh.
It's her whom I can't quit
Whether I move or sit.

Tune: *THE THIRD STANZA*

My love fulfilling earth and sky
Will last till rocks are melted and the sea runs dry.
Could I cease to think of my dear?
Could the burnt candle shed no tear?
Could the silkworm cease to spin in ifs life?
Could I be like the fickle son
Who would desert his wife,
Severed from his dear one?

Tune: *THE FOURTH STANZA*

No yellow dog brought news to me;
No verse was sent on a red leaf.
No bloom was plucked by messenger from mume tree
On the long, long road, to my grief.
Lonely in a strange land three thousand miles away,
I think of my return twenty-four hours a day.
Upon the balustrades
I lean
To hear the river's song and see different shades
Of mountains green.

Tune: *THE LAST STANZA*

My sickness makes me sad;
Your letter makes me glad.
My soul is captured by your phoenix's song.
How much for its arrival did your lover long!

(Exeunt)

ACT V

Scene 3   Contest for the Beauty

Zheng Heng enters and says:
> I am Zheng Heng, styled Bo chang. My late father was president of the Board of Rites. While alive, he betrothed me to Cui Yingying, daughter of my paternal aunt. Unexpectedly, my uncle died and Yingying had to go into mourning, so our marriage was not carried out. My aunt along with Yingying, conveying my uncle's coffin to be buried in Boling, was stopped on the way and is staying in the Mid-river Prefecture. A few months ago she sent me a letter, telling me to go to her place. But as there was no one to look after my house, I have delayed my coming. On my arrival, I was told, to my surprise, that Sun Feihu wanted to carry Yingying off and a scholar named Zhang Junrui succeeded in making him retreat and won the hand of Yingying. I think it would be unsuitable to intrude now. So I sent for the maid Rose, on whom may depend my affair. I would tell her I have just come from the capital and dare not visit my aunt without her permission, so I ask Rose to come to my place in order that she may inform my aunt of my arrival. My messenger has been away for some time. Why has Rose not yet come?

Rose enters and says:
> Master Zheng Heng has arrived but has not come to see my Mistress. He summoned me to have a talk with him, and my

Mistress told me to come to hear what he has to say.

(Seeing Zheng Heng)

Ten thousand blessings on you, Master Zheng. My Mistress asks why you don't go to see her on your arrival.

Zheng Heng says:

I thought it unsuitable to intrude on my aunt, that is the reason why I sent for you. You remember while my uncle was alive, he had betrothed me to your Young Mistress. Now the period of mourning is over. I come here to request my aunt to select a lucky day for accomplishing our union. Then we may go together to have my uncle's coffin buried. If our union were postponed, it would be inconvenient for me to see your Young Mistress. If you can persuade my aunt to consent, I will reward you amply.

Rose says:

You must not refer to the matter again, because Yingying is already betrothed to Master Zhang.

Zheng Heng says:

Don't you know that one horse cannot have two saddles? Her father when alive betrothed her to me. Now he is dead, how can her mother go back on her father's promise? Who has ever heard anything like that?

Rose says:

The case is not as you put it. Where were you, sir, when Sun Feihu came with five thousand bandits? How could the whole family have escaped if it had not been for the rescue of Master Zhang? Now that the danger is over, you come to contend for the hand of my Young Mistress. What if the bandits had carried her off?

Zheng Heng says:

If she were betrothed to a rich lord, I would have nothing to say against it. But to a poor scholar as if I were not his better! How could he be compared with me, a man of high quality and noble family?

Rose says:

Is he not your better? Hold your tongue!

She sings to the tune of *FIGHT OF QUAILS*:

You boast of your high quality
And of your noble family.
No matter what high rank you hold,
You can't become a member of her household.
There has never been
Engaged a go-between;
Nor have betrothal gifts been sent
To ask the family's consent.
You have just come from your land
And claim my Young Mistress' hand.
How dare you thus profane her golden bower
With such a sudden shower?
How dare you dirty the coverlet spread
On her embroidered bed!

Tune: *VIOLET FLOWER*

Are you worthy of her cloud-like hair
And moon-like face?
To my Mistress tender and fair
You are but a disgrace.
How dare you bring a sudden shower
To her fragrant jade bower!
When the earth was first separated from the sky
And then divided into low and high,

> The light became the day,
> And the heavy the night.
> Between the sky and earth men stay:
> Junrui like the day is bright;
> Zheng Heng is dark like night.

Zheng Heng says:
> How could a scholar as light as a feather succeed in making the heavy bandits retreat? What you said is mere nonsense.

Rose says:
> Listen to what I'll tell you!

She singe to the tune of *CLEAR SKY OVER THE SAND*:
> Sun Feihu guarding the Bridge on the River
> Revolted east of Pu and made the people shiver;
> With five thousand men he besieged the temple's land.
> With a frost-bright sword in his hand.
> He shouted and swore by his life
> That he must have Yingying as mistress or wife.

Zheng Heng says:
> What could a single-handed scholar do against five thousand armed bandits?

Rose says:
> Then the situation was critical. My Mistress badly frightened consulted with the Abbot and told him to announce that to anyone, priest or lay man, who was able to induce the bandits away, Yingying would be made his wife. To that proposal Master Zhang responded that he had a plan to make the bandits retreat. My Mistress overdelighted asked about his plan. Master Zhang then said that he had a friend, General on the White Horse, in command of a hundred thousand soldiers

ACT V

guarding the Pu Pass. He would write a letter and send it to the general, who was sure to come to our rescue. Indeed as soon as the letter was received, the general's troops were dispatched and the critical situation was relieved.

She sings to the tune of *RED PEACH BLOSSOM*:
>The scholar of the capital was bright indeed:
>He wrote a letter at lightning speed.
>The General on the White Horse came
>And put out at once the bandits' flame.
>My Mistresses old and young were filled with delight
>To find a man who helped with main and might.
>In word and deed he's true,
>So he has won the heart of the two.

Zheng Heng says:
>I have never heard of his name before. How can I know whether what you have said is true or not? You little minx, why are you trying to bluff me by making so much of him?

Rose sings to the tune of *GOLDEN BANANA LEAVES*:
>He knows the right from wrong;
>He writes verse and prose, short or long.
>He knows what is manhood.
>How could our family
>Not act with sincerity
>And return good for good?

Zheng Heng says:
>Am I not as good as he?

Rose sings to the tune of *SONG OF FLIRTATION*:
>He is to you as a hundred to one.
>How can a firefly be compared with moon or sun?

> I will not talk about what's low and high
> Or far and nigh.
> I would compare him to a steed
> And you to a silly ass in speed.

Zheng Heng says:
> How dare you compare me to a silly ass! My family have been high officials for generations. How could I be less worthy than a poor scholar?

Rose sings to the tune of *A BALD HEAD*:
> He follows his master and friends;
> He knows the means and ends.
> You who depend on your father and brothers
> Use your influence to oppress others.
> Poor, he did not complain of poverty;
> Diligent, he attained celebrity.

Tune: *KING OF MEDICINE*
> You're prejudiced; your views are fallacies.
> You say officials come from official families.
> If it were true, how could poor sons
> Become ministers, generals and famous ones?

Zheng Heng says:
> It must be Fa Ben, son of bitch, who told you this. I shall deal with him tomorrow.

Rose sings to the tune of *A POCKMARKED FACE*:
> He is a priest who left his family
> And knows nothing but charity.
> Your eyes cannot tell good from bad;
> Your mouth will lead to something sad.

ACT V

Zheng Heng says:
> My betrothal was the dying wish of my uncle. I will choose a lucky day and bring sheep and wine to my aunt's door and see how she will deal with me.

Rose sings to the tune of *PETTY SONG*:
> You may play your abusive part.
> What do you know about a tender heart?
> You want to force her to be your wife.
> Could she be your forced companion through life?

Zheng Heng says:
> If I were rejected, I would get twenty or thirty of my men to carry her into a sedan-chair, take her to my place, disrobe her in my bed and return her a married woman.

Rose sings to the tune of *SPINNER*:
> You, a president's son,
> Look like a bandit under Flying Tiger Sun,
> You are destined to roam
> Without a home.

Zheng Heng says:
> O you little minx! It is obvious that you are serving another man's purpose. I won't talk to you any more. Tomorrow I will marry her. I will marry her.

Rose says:
> But she won't marry you, she won't marry you.

She sings to the tune of *EPILOGUE*:
> A lady's love to a handsome young man is due.
> But who could sing the praise of you?
> You are a thief to steal some grace;

No powder could embellish your face.

(Exit)

Zheng Heng says:

That minx has sided with the poor scholar. Tomorrow I'll go to see my aunt, pretending to be ignorant of the whole thing. I'll say Master Zhang has become the son-in-law of President Wei. My aunt who believes gossip will believe me. My splendid attire alone will be enough to induce her in my favor. (Singing)

While young, we lived together close,
And I was bred to verse and prose.
My uncle promised me Yingying's hand.
Who dare violate his command?
If I but put on a bold face,
Yingying could find no hiding place.
I used to oppress the good with power;
My shower will oppress the flower.

(Exit)

Madame Cui enters and says:

Zheng Heng arrived here without coming to see me but sent for Rose to inquire about the marriage. In my opinion, it would be right to give Yingying to my nephew, for my late husband, while alive, had promised to give him her hand. If I did against his wish, it would be improper for the head of a family. So let a feast be prepared, for my nephew will probably come to see me today.

Zheng Heng enters and says:

Here I am and I'll enter unannounced.

(Weeping and bowing to Madame Cui)

Madame Cui says:

Why did you not come to see me on your arrival, my dear nephew?

ACT V

Zheng Heng says:
How dare I come to see you at once, my dear aunt?

Madame Cui says:
You know Yingying was betrothed to Master Zhang who had raised the siege of Sun Feihu.

Zheng Heng says:
Which Master Zhang? Is it the one who has just passed third on the list at the civil service examinations? When I was in the capital, I saw him. He is about twenty-three or twenty-four years old, a native of Luoyang, and his name is Zhang Gong. Parading the streets for three days, he came on the second day to the residence of President Wei, whose daughter in a pavilion on the Imperial Street hit him with an embroidered ball. Looking on horse, I was almost hit. If hit, it should be I to be disengaged from Yingying. But on that day about ten maids seized Master Zhang, pulled him off the horse and dragged him into the residence of President Wei. Master Zhang cried, "I am betrothed to former Prime Minister Cui's daughter." The president would not listen but said, "My daughter has this pavilion erected by Imperial Decree, so she should be your first wife. Yingying who had surrendered to you before your marriage is only fit to be a second wife." This news spread from mouth to mouth in the capital, so I know of this Master Zhang.

Madame Cui says angrily:
I fear this student is not worthy of our family and he has indeed betrayed our trust. How could the daughter of a Prime Minister become a second wife! Since Master Zhang has deserted my daughter and made another marriage, my dear nephew, you may select a lucky day and become my son-in-

law as prearranged.

(Exit)

Zheng Heng says joyfully:
She is caught in my trap. I'll get presents and rewards ready for my marriage.

(Exit)

ACT V

Scene 4 Union

Fa Ben the Abbot enters and says:
> Yesterday I bought a list of winners at the imperial examinations and found Master Zhang's name in it. He has been appointed prefect of the Mid-river Prefecture. Who would have thought that Madame Cui has promised her daughter to Zheng Heng and would not welcome Master Zhang. What could I do but prepare a feast instead and go to welcome the new official?
>
> (Exit)

General Du enters and says:
> By imperial decree I was appointed commander at the Pu Pass in charge of military affairs in the Mid-river Prefecture. Unexpectedly my sworn brother Junrui has won high honor in civil service examinations and has been appointed prefect of the Mid-river. To be sure, he will avail himself of this opportunity to celebrate his wedding. I am going with the presents of sheep and wine to the residence of Madame Cui so as to offer her my congratulations on the one hand and to act as go-between on the other. Attendants, bring my horse here. I am going to pay a visit to the Mid-river Prefecture.
>
> (Exit)

Madame Cui enters and says:
> Who would have thought that Master Zhang has betrayed our trust and become son-in-law of President Wei? What can I do

but marry my daughter to Zheng Heng in accordance with the dying wish of my late husband? Today is a lucky date for marriage. I will get ready the wedding feast for Zheng Heng.

(Exit)

Master Zhang enters and says:

Appointed prefect of the Mid-river Prefecture by the imperial decree, I am returning in glory today. My dear Young Lady will wear her phoenix headdress and rainbow veil, which I will present to her with both hands. Who would have thought today would arrive at last!

(Singing)

My writing outshone earth and sky;
My name is well-known far and nigh.

He sings to the tune of *NEW WATER MELODY*:

Whip in hand, on proud steed I leave the capital
To be a gallant husband in Jade Hall.
Poor student yesterday,
I hold the third rank today.
By His Majesty's decree
My name is in Imperial Academy.

Tune: *HALTING THE HORSE*

Foolish as Zhang Gong looks,
He's not belied his precious sword and countless books.
Happy will Yingying be found;
To receive Five-Flowered rank and chariot she's bound.
In glory I can't forget the temple remote.
Nor the poems which in sorrow I wrote.
Since I went to the capital.
My dream has never left the temple hall.

ACT V

Master Zhang, arriving at the monastery, says:

Take my horse!

(Seeing Madame Cui and bowing)

Zhang Gong who has passed with honor the imperial examinations and has been appointed prefect of the Mid-river Prefecture makes his bows to Madame.

Madame Cui says:

Don't bow! Don't bow! You are the son-in-law of another family which has received an imperial decree. How can I be worthy of the bows from you?

Master Zhang sings to the tune of *PSEUDO-MELODY*:

After your health I have come to inquire.
What has aroused, Madame, your ire?
Maids and attendants exchange strange glances, I see.
Is there anything wrong with me?

He says:

When I left, Madame, you were delighted to give me a farewell feast. Now I have obtained office on my return, why do you look displeased unexpectedly?

Madame Cui says:

What you care about my family now? It is said in the *Book of Poetry*:
"At first they're good on earth,
But few last to the end."
At first you loved my daughter who, though not beautiful enough, had as father a prime minister. If it had not been for the siege of the bandits, how could you have gained an entry into my family? Now you have shown disregard for my daughter by becoming the son-in-law of President Wei. How can this be justified?

Master Zhang says:
>Madame, from whom did you learn this? If such be the case, may I no longer live between heaven and earth and catch a dire disease!

He sings to the tune of *WILD GEESE'S FALL*:
>'Tis said there're maidens beautiful with silken whip
>In the capital where one makes a trip.
>But my mind dwells on my Young Lady kind.
>Could I seek another hand and leave her behind?

>**Tune: *TRIUMPHANT SONG***
>
>A good man should be true from end to end.
>Could I forget the one who was my first friend?
>What rascal out of jealousy
>Has come to sever her from me?
>He could not win my lady fair and bright
>But used foul means from morn to night.
>This man must be a rogue of deepest dye;
>Sooner or later on the gallows he will die.

Madame Cui says:
>It was Zheng Heng who told me this. The embroidered ball hit your horse and you became the son-in-law of President Wei. If you don't believe, you may call Rose and ask her.

Rose enters and says:
>How anxious I am to see him! After all, he has come back, appointed to a high post. Now, we'll know right from wrong.

Master Zhang says:
>Rose, how is your Young Mistress?

Rose says:
>As you are now the son-in-law of President Wei, my Young Mistress will be married to Zheng Heng as formerly arranged.

ACT V

Master Zhang says:
> How could things turn so strange?

He sings to the tune of *CELEBRATION IN THE EASTERN PLAIN*:
> How could true lover's tree from dung heap grow?
> How could flatfish in dirty mud swim to and fro?
> Should wedding rolls be sullied by the braying donkey?
> Oh, Yingying, could you marry a mocking monkey?
> Oh, Rose, how could you serve a sooty cat?
> Oh, Zhang Gong, could you share your love with half-drowned rat?
> This would do wrong
> To our customs established long.

Rose sings to the tune of *BRUSH-WOOD*:
> I've come to pay
> Respect today,
> But try to keep down anger in my heart.
> Have you been happy since we did part?
> Where does your new bride dwell?
> How does she compare
> With my Young Mistress fair?

Master Zhang says:
> What are you talking about? How can you not know the sufferings I endured for your Young Mistress, unknown to others? How could I have a new bride other than her?

He sings to the tune of *ZITHER AND GUITAR*:
> If I had a new bride,
> May I die by your side!
> O how could I forget the waiting in moonlight
> And the lute-playing for my mistress bright!
> After I'd suffered hell on earth

And exerted myself without mirth,
We were about to become man and wife,
And she would be conferred a "Dame" for life.
I was to hand to her the patent in high glee.
How could I know a grave's opened to bury me?

Rose says to Madame Cui:
I did not believe that Master Zhang was an untrustworthy man. Will you allow me to call my Young Mistress out to question him herself?
(Calling Yingying) My Young Mistress, Master Zhang is here. Will you please come out?

Yingying enters and says:
Here I am.

(Meeting Master Zhang)

Master Zhang says:
How have you been since we parted, my dear Young Lady?

Yingying says:
Well. A thousand blessings on you, sir.

Rose says:
Haven't you anything to say to him, my Young Mistress?

Yingying, sighing, says:
What is there to be said?

She sings to the tune of *INTOXICATED EAST WIND*:
When I did not see him by night or day,
I had prepared so much to say.
But now that we have met,
O how can I forget
Everything but utter sigh on sigh!

ACT V

> He's come in haste; while I'm too shy
> To glance at him, I would unfold
> To him the sorrows of my heart.
> On meeting him, no word is told
> But to wish him blessings on my part.

She says:
> Master Zhang, has our family done you wrong? Why should you have deserted me and become the son-in-law of President Wei? How can you justify what you have done?

Master Zhang says:
> How could you believe that?

Yingying says:
> It was Zheng Heng who said that in my mother's presence.

Master Zhang says:
> My dear Young Lady, how could you believe such a rogue? But Heaven would be witness to my heart.

He sings to the tune of *MUME BLOSSOMS FALLING IN THE BREEZE*:
> Since I left Pu the eastern town
> And came to the capital of the crown,
> I've never glanced at any maiden fair.
> How could I've married President Wei's daughter there?
> If I had ever seen her lace,
> My family and I would meet disgrace.

He says:
> I think Rose was to blame. I will try to provoke her to see what she has to say.
> (To Rose) I was told you had sent for your Young Mistress a letter to Zheng Heng, telling him to come here.

Rose says:

> You fool! I ought not to have helped you to fulfill your wishes. How could you think that I could help him as I had helped you!

She sings to the tune of *SWEET WATER*:

> Master Zhang, you need
> Not worry nor take heed,
> That fellow lacks manhood;
> Our family is worthy and good.
> My Young Mistress' father was a prime minister.
> How could I've sent him a letter from her?

> **Tune: *PICKING LAURELS***

That fellow's a blockhead;
He'd tell nothing but lie.
He'd take yellow for black
And violet for red.
Though my Young Mistress' weak and shy,
Would she marry a worthless hunchback?
She loves your true manhood.
How could the Lord of Spring
Allow a cutter of wood
To catch an oriole that can sing?
It is that fellow's sole desire
To do you harm and wrong.
My heart would burst with ire
To tell you his story long.

She says to Master Zhang:

> If you have not become the son-in-law of another family, I will do my best to help you in my Mistress' presence. When that fellow comes, you should refute him face to face.

ACT V

(To Madame Cui) Madame, Master Zhang has not become the son-in-law of President wei. It was Zheng Heng who told lies. You may call them to confront each other before you.

Madame Cui says:

Since he has not, let Zheng Heng come to confront him and we shall see what is to be done.

Fa Ben enters and says:

Unexpectedly Master Zhang has won high renown after the imperial examinations and is appointed prefect of the Mid-river. Having just welcomed him, now I come to congratulate Madame Cui. As to the marriage of her daughter, I was concerned with it from the beginning. How could Madame Cui have changed her mind and prepared the wedding with Zheng Heng! If she really gives him her daughter, what could she do when the prefect comes today?

He meets all present and says to Madame Cui:

Madame, now you know I was right in saying that Master Zhang was not a student of no character. How could he forget your family? Besides, General Du was a witness to the engagement. How could you go back on your words?

He sings to the tune of *WILD GEESE'S FALL*:

General Du would look down
On ancients of renown.
He is now in command
Of Mid-river and western land.

Tune: *TRIUMPHANT SONG*

Formerly he protected your bower;
Now he is armed with power.
When he comes, he will help Master Zhang as he can

And punish the bad man,
Who cares not for relationship in life
And tries to cheat an honest man out of his wife.
If one cannot tell bad from good,
How can he boast of true manhood?

Madame Cui says to Rose:
Take your Young Mistress to her chamber.

(Exeunt Yingying and Rose)

General Du enters and says:
I have left the Pu Pass and here I am at the Salvation Monastery.

Master Zhang salutes him and says to him:
By your influence I have passed the imperial examinations. Now I have come back to be married, but a nephew of Madame Cui, named Zheng Heng, told her that I had become the son-in-law of President Wei, and Madame turned angry against me and would go back on her words and marry her daughter to Zheng Heng in spite of the motto that a chaste maiden should never marry twice.

General Du says:
Madame, it would not be right to go back on your words. My dear friend Zhang is the son of a President of the Board of Rites and has passed with honor the imperial examinations. You vowed you would have such a son-in-law. How could you cancel the marriage arrangement now?

Madame Cui says:
When my husband was alive, my daughter was betrothed to Zheng Heng. But when our lives were in danger, we were indebted to Master Zhang who requested you to drive off the bandits, so I made him my son-in-law. But recently Zheng

ACT V

Heng told me that Master Zhang had become the son-in-law of President Wei, so I wanted to marry my daughter to Zheng Heng as arranged by my late husband.

General Du says:

Zheng Heng must be a villain trying to speak ill of Master Zhang. How could you easily believe him, Madame?

Zheng Heng enters and says:

Here I am in wedding attire, ready to be the son-in-law of my aunt. Today is a lucky day. Leading sheep and carrying wine, I am coming to the house of my bride.

(Meeting all present)

Master Zhang says:

What has brought you here, Zheng Heng?

Zheng Heng says:

Woe is me! Having heard you have returned after the imperial examinations, I am coming to offer you my congratulations.

General Du says:

How dare you come to swindle an honest man out of his fiancee? I will report to the court the wrong you have done to the newly appointed prefect and have you punished.

He sings to the tune of *MUME BLOSSOMS FALLING IN THE BREEZE*:

You want to force your way into the fairylands,
Regardless of the master who there stands.
The bee's prevented by the eastern breeze.
If you do not believe, listen 'neath willow trees
To the cuckoo which will not roam
Keep on singing "Better go home!"

He says:
> If that fellow won't go away, I will have him arrested.

Zheng Heng says:
> Don't arrest me, please. I'll give up the marriage.

Madame Cui says:
> Calm your anger, General! Just turn him out!

Zheng Heng says:
> Now Yingying will be married to Master Zhang. How shamefaced I would be to go back to my house! I would dash my brains out against a tree rather than live in shame. (Singing)
> I've striven for a wife in vain;
> Only the gallant deserve the fair.
> What use to scheme with might and main?
> When I die, all will be nowhere.
>
> (He falls down dead.)

Madam Cui says:
> Though he takes his own life without being forced to, out of pity for his being fatherless and motherless, I will take charge of his burial.

General Du says:
> Please ask the Young Lady to come out. Let us hold a congratulatory feast and see the young couple united.
> (Master Zhang and Yingying bow to Madame Cui, to each other, to General Du; and Rose bows to the couple.)

Chorus sings to the tune of *BUYING SWEET WINE*:
> Four-horsed chariots crowd the gate
> Eight young dragons adorn the door.
> You marry the daughter of a prime minister late

ACT V

Who has all virtues women adore.
You have achieved your ends
Through the aid of your friends.

Tune: *A PACIFIC SONG*

Had General Du not come to save their life,
Could they become husband and wife?
Could they fulfill their wish
And be as happy as in water swim the fish?
Since olden days a worthy maid
Should be her worthy husband's aid.
 Who wins success in court above
Will win success below in love.

(Enter an imperial messenger; all bow to him.)

The messenger sings to the tune of *THE CLEAR RIVER*:

The emperor sacred and wise
Sanctions your marriage ties,
And you will never
One from the other sever.
May lovers 'neath the skies
Be united for ever and ever! (Exeunt.)

To sum up the four scenes of the Act V:

The lute-bearer reports success.
Yingying sends to Zhang Gong a vest.
Zheng Heng lost his life in distress.
The lovers' union blessed.

To sum up the five acts of the *Romance*:

The eastern talent wins his beauty.
The southern abbot does his duty.
A feast is held for northern flower.
The lovers meet in Western Bower.

许译中国经典诗文集

西厢记

【元】王实甫 著

许渊冲 许明 译

五洲传播出版社　中华书局

序

我国古代戏曲作品刊刻最多、流传最广、影响最大的应以王实甫《西厢记》为首屈一指。明末清初的戏曲理论家李渔(1611—1685)说过:"自有《西厢》以迄于今,四百余载,推《西厢》为填词第一者,不知几千万人,而能历指其所以第一之故者,独出一金圣叹(1608—1661)!"(《闲情偶寄》填词余论)。所以我们这本汉英对照《西厢记》选用了金圣叹评点的《贯华堂第六才子书西厢记》。

《圣叹外书》中说:"《西厢记》不同小可,乃是天地妙文。""今后任凭是绝代才子,切不可云此本《西厢记》我亦做得出也。便教当时作者而在,要他烧了此本重做一本,已是不可复得。""若使异时更作,亦不妨另自有其绝妙,然而无奈此番已是绝妙也。不必云异时不能更妙于此,然亦不必云异时尚将更妙于此也。"异时"另自有其绝妙"的作品,是三百年后英国莎士比亚的《罗密欧与朱丽叶》。

为什么说《西厢记》"此番已是绝妙"呢?以主题而论,金圣叹认为《西厢记》写的是莺莺和张生"不辞千死万死,而几几乎各愿以其两死并为一死"的"必至之情"。以人物而论,金圣叹说:"《西厢记》只写得三个人,一个是双文(莺莺),一个是张生,一个是红娘。其余如夫人,如法本,如白马将军,如欢郎,如法聪,如孙飞虎,如琴童,如店小二,他俱不曾着一笔半笔写,俱是写三个人时所忽然应用之家伙耳。""譬如文字,则双文是题目,张生是文字,红娘是文字之起承转合。有此许多起承转合,便令题目透出文字,文字透入题目也。其余如夫人等,

西厢记

算只是文字中间所用之乎者也等字。""譬如药,则张生是病,双文是药,红娘是药之炮制。有此许多炮制,便令药往就病,病来就药也。其余如夫人等,算只是炮制时所用之姜醋酒蜜等物。""《西厢记》前半是张生文字,后半是双文文字,中间是红娘文字。""《西厢记》必须与美人并坐读之。与美人并坐读之者,验其缠绵多情也。"

以结构而论,金圣叹说:"若夫《西厢》之为文……有'生'有'扫'。'生'如生叶生花,'扫'如扫花扫叶……最前《惊艳》一篇谓之'生',最后《哭宴》一篇谓之'扫'……而后于其中间,则有'此来彼来'。何谓'此来'?如《借厢》一篇是张生来,谓之'此来'。何谓'彼来'?如《酬韵》一篇是莺莺来,谓之'彼来'……设使张生不借厢,是张生不来;张生不来,此事不生。即使张生借厢,而莺莺不酬韵,是莺莺不来;莺莺不来,此事亦不生。今既张生慕色而来,莺莺又慕才而来,如是谓之'两来'……而后则有'三渐'。何谓'三渐'?《闹斋》第一渐,《寺警》第二渐,《后候》第三渐。第一渐者,莺莺始见张生也;第二渐者,莺莺始与张生相关也;第三渐者,莺莺始许张生定情也。此'三渐',又谓之'三得'。何谓'三得'?自非《闹斋》之一篇,则莺莺不得而见张生也;自非《寺警》之一篇,则莺莺不得而与张生相关也;自非《后候》之一篇,则莺莺不得而许张生定情也……而后则又有'二近'、'三纵'。何谓'二近'?《请宴》一近,《前候》一近。盖'近'之为言,几几乎如将得之也……'三纵'者,《赖婚》一纵,《赖简》一纵,《拷艳》一纵……'纵'之为言,几几乎如将失之也……而后则有'两不得不然'。何谓'两不得不然'?《听琴》不得不然,《闹简》不得不然。听琴者,红娘不得不然;闹简者,莺莺不得不然……而后则有'实写'一篇……《酬简》之一篇是也。又有'空写'一篇……《惊梦》之一篇是也。"总而言之,"两来","三渐","三得","二近","三纵","两不得不然","实写","空写",这就是《西厢记》的结构。以笔法而论,金圣叹说:"子弟欲看《西厢记》,须教其先看《国风》。盖《西厢记》所写事,便全是《国风》所写事。然《西厢记》写事,曾无一笔不雅驯,便全学《国风》写事,曾无一笔不雅驯;《西厢记》写事,曾无一笔不透脱,便全学《国风》写事,曾无一笔不透脱。敢疗子弟笔下雅驯不透脱、透脱不雅驯之病。"

今天看来,《西厢记》与《国风》是继承与发展的关系。所谓"雅驯",就是文字高雅,遵守规范;所谓"透脱",就是深刻透彻,洒脱自如。用孔子的话来说,就是"从心所欲不逾矩"。"从心所欲"是"透脱","不逾矩"是"雅驯"。例如《国风》第一篇《关雎》就是"从心所欲不逾矩"的典范。

关关雎鸠,在河之洲;窈窕淑女,君子好逑。
参差荇菜,左右流之;窈窕淑女,寤寐求之。
求之不得,寤寐思服;悠哉悠哉,辗转反侧。
参差荇菜,左右采之;窈窕淑女,琴瑟友之。
参差荇菜,左右芼之;窈窕淑女,钟鼓乐之。

西厢记

君子在河之洲,听到雎鸠叫春,就对"窈窕淑女,寤寐求之",这是"发乎情"。后来订婚结婚,"琴瑟友之","钟鼓乐之",这是止乎礼乐。换句话说,这也是"从心所欲不逾矩"。《西厢记》中《惊艳》一折"发乎情",《衣锦荣归》一折是止乎礼乐,这是《西厢记》对《国风》的继承。但是两书相差两千年,其间自然大有发展。《国风》中的"关关雎鸠,在河之洲",都是客观地写鸟、写河。《西厢记·哭宴》一折中的"拆鸳鸯坐两下里","伯劳东去燕西飞",说的是鸟,指的却是张生和莺莺。又如"泪添九曲黄河溢",写的是"九曲黄河",象征的却是莺莺的柔肠九转,传达的却是主观的离愁别恨。再如《关雎》中的"求之不得,辗转反侧",也只是客观的描写;而《哭宴》中的"归家怕看罗帏里,昨宵是绣衾奇暖留春住,今日是翠被生寒有梦知",对莺莺的内心世界作了细致的刻画,传达的相思之情也就更加深刻透彻、洒脱自如了。再又如《关雎》中谈到的食物,只有"参差荇菜"四个字。而在《哭宴》中莺莺说:"将来的酒共食,尝着似土和泥,假如便是土和泥,也有些土气息,泥滋味。暖溶溶玉醅,白泠泠似水,多半是相思泪。面前茶饭不待吃,恨塞满愁肠胃。"金圣叹批道:"此节是说酒,是说泪,不可得辨也。李后主云'此中日夕只以眼泪洗面',便是如出一口说话也。"由此可见,《西厢记》中的客观世界和人物的内心世界已经融成一片,难解难分。早在三百年前,金圣叹就已经"能历指其所以第一之故"了。

其实,《西厢记》"所以第一之故",不但是继承、发展了

序

《国风》,而且是超越了"发乎情,止乎礼"的限制。《国风》中有一篇著名的情诗《野有死麕》,全诗如下:

野有死麕,白茅包之。有女怀春,吉士诱之。

林有朴樕,野有死鹿,白茅纯束,有女如玉。

"舒而脱脱兮!无感我帨兮!无使尨也吠!"

最后三句是怀春的少女对求欢的猎人说的话,余冠英语体译文是:"慢慢儿来啊,悄悄地来啊!我的围裙可别动!别惹得狗儿叫起来啊!"这里说的是"别动围裙",暗示的却是猎人已经解开了少女的围裙和衣带。再比较《西厢记·酬简》中张生的唱词:

我将你纽扣儿松,我将你罗带儿解,

兰麝散幽斋,不良会把人禁害。

哈!怎不回过脸儿来?软玉温香抱满怀。

呀!刘阮到天台!春至人间花弄色。

柳腰款摆,花心轻折,露滴牡丹开。

金圣叹批语说:"双文之面虽终不得而看,而双文之扣,双文之带,则趁势已解矣。夫双文之扣,双文之带,此真非轻易可得而解也。今用明修栈道、暗度陈仓之法,轻轻遂已解得。世间真乃无第二手也。"描写情爱,从《国风》的暗示"别动围裙",到《酬简》的明说"纽扣儿松","罗带儿解"(这是"明修栈道"),再到"露滴牡丹开"的象征写法(这是"暗度陈仓"),真是很大的发展,不但在中国,就是在全世界,恐怕也"无第二手了"。中国诗歌从《国风》发展到《西厢记》,中

229

西厢记

间还有唐宋诗词的影响。如《哭宴》中莺莺的唱词:
> 我见她蹙愁眉,死临侵地。
> 阁泪汪汪不敢垂,恐怕人知。
> 猛然见了把头低,长吁气,推整素罗衣。
> ……知他今宵宿在哪里?有梦也难寻觅。

在唐人韦庄(836—910)的《女冠子》词中,已有类似的描写:
> 忍泪佯低面,含羞半敛眉。
> 不知魂已断,空有梦相随。

忍泪,低头,敛眉,寻梦,两词都有描写,但唐词精练、高雅,元曲铺陈、细腻。比较一下,既可以看出唐词对元曲的影响,也可以看到元曲对唐词的发展。又如《哭宴》中的《收尾》:
> 四围山色中,一鞭残照里。
> 将遍人间烦恼填胸臆,
> 量这般大小车儿,如何载得起!

试比较宋代女词人李清照(1084—1151)的《武陵春》下半片:
> 闻说双溪春尚好,也拟泛轻舟。
> 只恐双溪舴艋舟,载不动许多愁。

李清照说轻舟载不动愁,《西厢记》说车儿载不起烦恼。元曲对宋词的继承和发展,在这里看得更清楚了。有了这两千年的文化积累,《西厢记》描写离情别恨,可以说是达到了新的高峰;而描写男女情爱,则在中国文学史上,简直是前无古人。李政道教授说得好:"艺术,例如诗歌、绘画、雕塑、音乐等等,用创新的手法去唤起每个人的意识或潜意识中深藏着的已经存在的情感,情感越珍贵,唤起越强烈,反响越普遍,艺术就越优秀。"(《光明日报》,1996年6月24日)。《西厢记》非常强烈地唤起了千百万人深藏心头的爱情,这是人类最珍贵的情感,反响持续了几个世纪,真是世界上不可多得的艺术珍品。

三百年后,莎士比亚的《罗密欧与朱丽叶》在西方流传很广,影响很大,可以和《西厢记》先后媲美。如果比较一下东西方的爱情故事,可以说东方的情人更加含蓄婉转,西方的情人更加直截了当。如《酬韵》中的张生和莺莺的唱和:

张生:月色溶溶夜,花阴寂寂春。
　　　如何临皓魄,不见月中人。
莺莺:兰闺深寂寞,无计度芳春。
　　　料得高吟者,应怜长叹人。

张生不说自己爱慕莺莺,却婉转地说他见月思人;莺莺也不说自己怜才,却含蓄地要才子怜惜佳人。而罗密欧和朱丽叶却大不相同,开门见山,握手吻嘴。请看曹禺的译文:

罗密欧:神不也有嘴唇,香客也有?
朱丽叶:进香的朋友,嘴唇是用来祈祷。
罗密欧:哦,我的神,让嘴唇也学学手,
　　　　答应了吧,不然,信念就化成苦恼。

他们说的是神、香客、祈祷,指的却是朱、罗、亲吻,并且说到做到,立刻见于行动。这是东西方不同的一点:东方发乎情,止乎礼;西方却一见钟情,甚至借宗教之名,来行情爱之

实。但东西方情人也有相同之处，如《酬韵》后，
> 张生：你若共小生厮觑定，
> 　　　隔墙儿酬和到天明，
> 　　　便是惺惺惜惺惺。

这和罗密欧离开朱丽叶时的对话，大同小异。请看曹禺译的罗密欧和朱生豪译的朱丽叶：
> 罗：爱去找爱，就像逃学的孩子躲开书房；
> 　　两个分开，好比垂头丧气赶回到学堂。
> 朱：晚安！晚安！离别是这样甜蜜的凄清，
> 　　我真要向你道晚安直到天明。

张生说的"惺惺惜惺惺"和罗密欧说的"爱去找爱"，张、崔"酬和到天明"和罗、朱道晚安直到天明，不但内容相似，而且形式和词语都有相同之处，真可以说是"诗人所见略同"了。

张生说话和罗、朱有相同之处，莺莺和朱丽叶却有所不同，这从红娘和奶妈口中，可以听得出来，奶妈在二幕五场中对朱丽叶说：
> 那就去吧，去吧，快到神父那儿去吧，
> 那儿新郎官等着你来做新娘子呢？　　（曹译）

奶妈说话直截了当，也说明了朱丽叶直截了当的性格。红娘说话有时转弯抹角，既说明了她自己聪明伶俐，又衬托莺莺的含蓄婉转。如红娘在《闹简》中说到莺莺：
> 几曾见，寄书的颠倒瞒着鱼雁？
> 小则小，心肠儿转关，

序

教你跳东墙，女字边干。
原来五言包得三更枣，四句埋得九里山。
你赤紧将人慢，你要会云雨闹中取静，
却教我寄音书忙里偷闲！

金圣叹说："《西厢记》只为要写此一个人（双文），便不得不又写一个人。一个人者，红娘是也。若使不写红娘，却如何写双文？然而《西厢记》写红娘，当知正是出力写双文。"可见中国评论家早就知道"烘云托月"的写法了。

总而言之，以《西厢记》和莎剧的主题而论，都是写爱情与家庭的矛盾。《西厢记》以"金榜题名"为家庭赢得了荣誉，以"洞房花烛"为双方赢得了爱情，这是中国典型的大团圆结局。莎剧却以儿女的死亡为代价，使两家世仇化敌为友，这是西方爱情与荣誉冲突的典型悲剧。换句话说，解决矛盾，东方用的是文化，西方用的是暴力。以结构而论，两剧情节都很曲折，但《西厢记》的曲折多是内心的，莎剧却多是外界的。以人物而论，《西厢记》描写外在形象，更加生动；莎剧描写内在情感，更加深刻。以笔法而论，《西厢记》善用抽象迭词，历史典故；莎剧善用具体形象，双关文字。两剧各有千秋。

《西厢记》在西方，远不如莎剧广为人知。直到1935年，英国才出版了熊式一的散体译本，本书英文前言中有所摘引，以见一斑。林语堂认为熊译准确有余，诗意不足。后来香港出版了新译本，还是译成散文。到了20世纪90年代，美国又出了加州大学韦斯特教授的散体译本。1992年，我国外文出版社才出了我译的

西厢记

韵文本；但我根据金圣叹的评论，只译了四本十六折，译到《惊梦》为止。直到现在这本英译，才把五本二十折完全译出；其中唱词全部译成韵文，说白则译成散文，和莎剧中抒情多用诗体，叙事多用散体，有相似之处。

早在20世纪初，英国哲学家罗素就说过，中国文化在三方面优于西方文化。第一，在艺术方面，象形文字高于拼音文字；第二，在哲学方面，儒家的人本主义优于宗教的神权思想；第三，在政治方面，"学而优则仕"高于贵族世袭制。这三方面的优势，在《西厢记》中都有所表现；具体说来，不用暴力，而用文化来解决家族之间的矛盾，就是一个例子。

许渊冲
2009年3月1日
北京大学畅春园

第一本

西厢记

第一折 惊 艳

（夫人引莺莺、红娘、欢郎上云）老身姓郑，夫主姓崔，官拜当朝相国，不幸病薨。只生这个女儿，小字莺莺，年方一十九岁，针黹女工，诗词书算，无有不能。相公在日，曾许下老身侄儿，郑尚书长子郑恒为妻，因丧服未满，不曾成合。这小妮子，是自幼伏侍女儿的，唤做红娘。这小厮儿，唤做欢郎，是俺相公讨来压子息的。相公弃世，老身与女儿扶柩往博陵安葬，因途路有阻，不能前进，来到河中府，将灵柩寄在普救寺内。这寺乃是天册金轮武则天娘娘敕赐盖造的功德院。长老法本，是俺相公剃度的和尚。因此上有这寺西边一座另造宅子，足可安下。一壁写书附京师，唤郑恒来，相扶回博陵去。俺想相公在日，食前方丈，从者数百，今日至亲只这三四口儿，好生伤感人也呵。

【仙吕·赏花时】（夫人唱）夫主京师禄命终，子母孤孀途路穷，旅榇在梵王宫[1]。盼不到博陵旧冢[2]，血泪洒杜鹃红。

今日暮春天气，好生困人红娘，你看前边庭院无人，和小姐闲散心，立一回去。（红娘云）晓得。

【后】（莺莺唱）可正是人值残春蒲郡东，门掩重关萧寺中，花落水流红。 闲愁万种无语怨东风。

（夫人引莺莺、红娘、欢郎下）（张生引琴童上云）小生姓张名珙，字君瑞，本贯西洛人也。先人拜礼部尚书。小生功名未遂，游于四方。即今贞元十七年二月上旬，欲往上朝取应。路经河中府，有一故人，姓杜名确，字君实，与小生同郡同学，曾为八拜之交，后弃文就武，遂得武举状元，官拜征西大元帅，统领十万大军，现今镇守蒲关。小生就探望哥哥一道，却往京师未迟。暗想小生，萤窗雪案，学成满腹文章，尚在湖海飘零，未知何日得遂大志也呵。正是：万金宝剑藏秋水，满马春愁压绣鞍。

【仙吕·点绛唇】（张生唱）游艺中原，脚根无线，如蓬转。望眼连天，日近长安远。

【混江龙】向诗书经传，蠹鱼似不出费钻研[3]。棘围呵守暖[4]，铁砚呵磨穿。投至得云路鹏程九万里，先受了雪窗萤火十余年。才高难入俗人机，时乖不遂男儿愿。怕你不雕虫篆刻，断简残篇。

行路之间，早到黄河这边，你看好形势也呵。

【油葫芦】九曲风涛何处险？正是此地偏。带齐梁，分秦晋，隘幽燕。雪浪拍长空，天际秋云卷。竹索缆浮桥，水上苍龙偃。东西贯九州，南北串百川。归舟紧不紧，如何见，似弩箭乍离弦。

【天下乐】疑是银河落九天，高源云外悬，入东洋不离此径穿。滋洛阳千种花，润梁园万顷田。我便要浮槎到日月边[5]。

说话间，早到城中。这里好一座店儿。琴童接了马者。店小二哥那里？（店小二云）自家是状元坊店小二哥。官人要下呵，俺这里有干净店房。（张生云）便在头房里下。小二哥，你来，这里有甚么闲散心处。（小二云）俺这里有座普救寺，是天册金轮武则天娘娘敕建的功德院,盖造非常,南北往来过者,无不瞻仰,只此处可以游玩。(张生云)琴童,安顿行李,撒和了马。我到那里走一遭。(琴童云)理会得。(俱下)(法聪上云)小僧法聪,是这普救寺法本长老的徒弟。今日师父赴斋去了,著俺在寺中,但有探望的,便记著,待师父回来报知。山门下立地,看有甚么人来。(张生上云)"曲径通幽处,禅房花木深。"却早来到也。(相见科)(聪云)先生从何处来?(张生云)小生西洛至此,闻上刹清幽,一来瞻礼佛像,二来拜谒长老。(聪云)俺师父不在,小僧是弟子法聪的便是,请先生方丈拜茶。(张生云)既然长老不在呵,不必赐茶,敢烦和尚相引,瞻仰一遭。(聪云)理会得。(张生云)是盖造得好也。

【村里迓鼓】随喜了上方佛殿,又来到下方僧院。厨房近西,法堂北,钟楼前面。游洞房,登宝塔,将回廊绕遍。我数毕罗汉,参过菩萨,拜罢圣贤。那里又好一座大院子,却是何处?待小生一发随喜去。

(聪拖住云)那里须去不得,先生请住者,里面是崔国家眷寓宅。(张生见莺莺红娘科)蓦然见五百年风流业冤[6]。

【元和令】颠不剌的见了万千,这般可喜娘罕曾见。我眼花缭乱口难言,魂灵儿飞去半天。尽人调戏,𠣞著香肩[7],只将花笑拈。

【上马娇】是兜率宫,是离恨天?我谁想这里遇神仙。宜嗔宜喜春风面。偏、宜贴翠花钿。

【胜葫芦】宫样眉儿新月偃[8],侵入鬓云边。未语人前先腼腆，樱桃红破，玉粳白露[9]，半晌，恰方言。

【后】似呖呖莺声花外啭。

（莺莺云）红娘，我看母亲去。

解舞腰肢娇又软，千般袅娜，万般旖旎，似垂柳在晚风前。（莺莺引红娘下）

【后庭花】你看衬残红，芳径软，步香尘底印儿浅。休题眼角留情处，只这脚踪儿将心事传。慢俄延[10]，投至到栊门前面，只有那一步远。分明打个照面，风魔了张解元。神仙归洞天，空余杨柳烟，只闻鸟雀喧。

【柳叶儿】门掩了梨花深院，粉墙儿高似青天。恨天不与人方便，难消遣，怎留连？有几个意马心猿。

【寄生草】兰麝香仍在，珮环声渐远[11]。东风摇曳垂杨线，游丝牵惹桃花片，珠帘掩映芙蓉面。这边是河中开府相公家，那边是南海水月观音院。

【赚煞尾】望将穿，涎空咽。我明日透骨髓相思病缠，怎当他临去秋波那一转[12]，我便铁石人也意惹情牵！近庭轩，花柳依然，日午当天塔影圆。春光在眼前，奈玉人不见。将一座梵王宫，化作武陵源。

西厢记

注释

[1] 旅榇(chèn)：尚未入祖茔前暂时寄放他处的棺木。

[2] 冢(zhǒng)：原义指坟茔，因祖茔在家乡，故以"旧冢"指代故乡。

[3] 蠹(dù)鱼：即衣鱼，蛀食衣服、书籍等的小虫。

[4] 棘围：指考场。旧时科举考试，常在试院围墙之上插满荆棘，以防人们捣乱或作弊。

[5] 槎(chá)：木筏、竹排。

[6] 业冤：即所谓前世冤家。冤家，本系佛家用语，后用以指仇家，也常用为对情人的爱称，是爱至极处的反语。

[7] 軃(duò)：下垂。

[8] 官样眉：按照宫中流行式样描画的眉毛。

[9] 玉粳(jīng)：光洁似玉的粳米，喻指洁白齐整的牙齿。

[10] 俄延：拖延。

[11] 珮环：玉环。

[12] 秋波：如秋水般明澈的眼睛。

第二折 借厢

（夫人上云）红娘，你传着我的言语，去寺里问他长老，几时好与老相公做好事。问的当了，来回我话者。（红娘云）理会得。（下）（法本上云）老僧法本，在这普救寺内住持做长老。夜来老僧赴个村斋，不知曾有何人来探望？（唤法聪问科）（法聪云）夜来有一秀才，自西洛而来，特谒我师，不遇而返。（法本云）山门外觑者，倘再来时，报我知道。（法聪云）理会得。（张生上云）自夜来见了那小姐，着小生一夜无眠。今日再到寺中，访他长老，小生别有话说。（与法聪拱手科）

【中吕·粉蝶儿】（张生唱）不做周方[1]，埋怨杀你个法聪和尚！

（聪云）先生来了，小僧不解先生话哩。

你借与我半间儿客舍僧房，与我那可憎才居止处，门儿相向。虽不得窃玉偷香，且将这盼行云眼睛打当。

（聪云）小僧不解先生话。

【醉春风】我往常见傅粉的委实着[2]，画眉的敢是谎。今番不是在先，人心儿里早痒，痒。撩拨得心慌，断送得眼乱，轮转得肠忙。

（聪云）小僧不解先生话也。师父久待，小僧通报去。

（张生见法本科）

【迎仙客】我只见头似雪,鬓如霜,面如少年得内养。貌堂堂,声朗朗,只少个圆光,便是捏塑的僧伽像[3]。

（法本云）请先生方丈内坐。夜来老僧不在,有失迎迓,望先生恕罪!（张生云）小生久闻清誉,欲来座下听讲,不期昨日相左。今得一见、三生有幸矣。（本云）敢问先生,世家何郡?上姓大名?因甚至此?（张生云）小生西洛人氏,姓张,名珙,字君瑞。因上京应举,经过此处。

【石榴花】大师一一问行藏,小生仔细诉衷肠。自来西洛是吾乡,宦游在四方[4],寄居在咸阳。先人礼部尚书多名望,五旬上因病身亡。平身正直无偏向,至今留四海一空囊。

【斗鹌鹑】闻你浑俗和光[5],果是风清月朗。小生呵,无意求官,有心听讲。

小生途路无可申意,聊具白金一两,与常住公用,伏望笑留。

秀才人情从来是纸半张,他不晓七青八黄[6]。任凭人说短论长,他不怕掂斤播两。

【上小楼】我是特来参访,你竟无须推让。这钱也难买柴薪,不够斋粮,略备茶汤。你若有主张,对艳妆,将言词说上,还要把你来生死难忘。

（本云）先生客中,何故如此?先生必有甚见教。（张生云）小生不揣有恳[7],因恶旅邸繁冗,难以温习经史。欲暂借一室,晨昏听讲,房金按月任凭多少。（本云）敝寺颇有空房,任凭拣择,不呵,就与老僧同榻何如?

【后】不要香积厨,不要枯木堂,不要南轩,不要东墙。只近西厢，靠主廊，过耳房，方暂停当。快休题长老方丈。

（红娘上云）俺夫人着俺问长老，几时好与老相公做好事，问的当了回话。（见本科）长老万福。夫人使侍妾来问，几时可与老相公做好事？（张生云）好个女子也呵！

【脱布衫】大人家举止端详，全不见半点轻狂。大师行深深拜了，启朱唇语言的当。

【小梁州】可喜庞儿浅淡妆，穿一套缟素衣裳[8]。鹘伶渌老不寻常[9]，偷睛望，眼挫里抹张郎[10]。

【幺】我共你多情小姐同鸳帐，我不教你叠被铺床。将小姐央，夫人央，他不令许放，我自写与你从良。

（本云）先生少坐，待老僧同小娘子到佛殿上一看便来。（张生云）小生便同行如何？（本云）使得。（张生云）著小娘子先行，我靠后些。

【快活三】崔家女艳妆，莫不演撒上老洁郎。既不是睃趁放毫光[11]，为甚打扮着特来晃。

【朝天子】曲廊洞房，你好事从天降。

（本发怒云）先生好模好样，说那里话！（张生云）你须怪不得我说。

好模好样忒莽戆，烦恼耶唐三藏。偌大个宅堂，岂没个儿郎？要梅香来说勾当[12]。你在我行口强，你硬着头皮上。

（本云）这是崔相国小姐孝心，与他父亲亡过老相国追荐做好事，一点志诚，不遣别人，特遣自己贴身的侍妾红娘来问日期。（本对红娘云）这斋供道场都完备了，十五日是佛受供日，请老夫人、小姐拈香。（张生哭云）"哀哀父母，生我劬劳[13]，欲报深思，昊天罔极!"小姐是一女子,尚思报本,望和尚慈悲,小生亦备钱五千,怎生带得一分儿斋,追荐我父母,以尽人子之心。便夫人知道,料也不妨。(本云)不妨。法聪,与先生带一分斋者。(张生私问聪云)那小姐是必来么?(聪云)小姐是他父亲的事,如何不来!(张生喜云)这五千钱使得着也。

【四边静】人间天上,看莺莺强如做道场[14]。软玉温香,休言偎傍,若能够汤他一汤,早与人消灾障。

(本云)都到方丈吃茶。(张生云)小生更衣咱。(张生先出,云)那小娘子一定出来也,我只在这里等候他者。(红娘辞本云)我不吃茶了,恐夫人怪迟,我回话去也。(红出,张生迎揖云)小娘子拜揖。(红云)先生万福。(张生云)小娘子莫非莺莺小姐的侍妾红娘乎?(红云)我便是,何劳动问?(张生云)小生有句话敢说么?(红云)言出如箭,不可乱发,一入人耳,有力难拔。有话但说不妨。(张生云)小生姓张,名珙,字君瑞,本贯西洛人氏。年方二十三岁,正月十七日子时建生,并不曾娶妻。(红云)谁问你来?我又不是算命先生,要你那生年月日何用?(张生云)再问红娘,小姐常出来么?(红怒云)出来便怎么?先生是读书君子,道不得个"非礼勿言,非礼勿动"。俺老夫人治家严肃,凛若冰霜,即三尺童子,非奉呼唤,不敢辄入中堂。先生绝无瓜葛,何得如此?早是妾前可以容恕,若夫人知道,岂便干休?今后当问的便问,不当问的休得胡问!(红娘下)(张生良久良久,云)这相思索是害杀我也。

【哨遍】听说罢,心怀怏怏,把一天愁,都撮在眉尖上!说夫人节操凛冰霜,不召呼,不可辄入中堂。自思量,假如你心中畏惧老母威严,你不合临去也回头望。待飏下[15],教人怎飏?赤紧的深沁了肺腑[16],牢染在肝肠。若今生你不是并头莲,难道前世我烧了断头香?我定要手掌儿上奇擎[17],心坎儿上温存,眼皮儿上供养。

【耍孩儿】只闻巫山远隔如天样,听说罢又在巫山那厢。我这业身虽是立回廊[18],魂灵儿实在他行。莫不他安排心事正要传幽客[19],只怕是漏泄春光与乃堂。春心荡,他见黄莺作对,粉蝶成双。

【五煞】红娘你自年纪小,性气刚。张郎倘去相偎傍,他遭逢一见何郎粉,我邂逅偷将韩寿香。风流况,成就我温存娇婿,管甚么拘束亲娘。

【四煞】红娘你忒虑过,空算长。郎才女貌年相仿,定要到眉儿浅淡思张敞,春色飘零忆阮郎。非夸奖,他正德言工貌[20],小生正恭俭温良。

【三煞】红娘他眉儿是浅浅描,他脸儿是淡淡妆,他粉香腻玉搓咽项[21]。下边是翠裙鸳绣金莲小,上边是红袖鸾销玉笋长[22]。不想呵,其实强,你也掉下半天风韵,我也去万种思量。

(张生转身见本云)却忘了辞长老。小生敢问长老房舍何如?(本云)塔院西厢有一间房,甚是潇洒,正可先生安下,随先生早晚来。(张生云)小生便回店中搬行李来。(本云)先生是必来者。(法本下)(张生云)搬则搬来,怎生捱这凄凉也呵!

【二煞】红娘,我院宇深,枕簟凉[23],一灯孤影摇书幌[24]。

245

纵然酬得今生志,着甚支吾此夜长[25]?**睡不着,如翻掌,少呵,有一万声长吁短叹,五千遍捣枕捶床。**

【尾声】娇羞花解语,温柔玉有香。乍相逢,记不真娇模样。尽无眠,手抵着牙儿慢慢地想[26]。

注 释

[1]周方:即周旋方便,意谓与人方便、成全他人。

[2]傅粉:傅,涂抹,傅粉即搽抹妆粉。

[3]僧伽:梵文音译,佛教称四个或以上的出家人聚结一处为僧伽,即僧团之意。后来单个出家人也称僧伽。

[4]宦游:外出为官或因求仕进而四方游历。

[5]浑俗和光:混同于世俗而不露锋芒,意为与世无争。

[6]七青八黄:指黄金。

[7]不揣(chuǎi):不自量而冒昧。

[8]缟素:白色衣服,指丧服。

[9]鹘伶渌老:形容聪明伶俐的眼睛。鹘伶,一种猛禽,目光敏锐;《知新录》:"渌老,谓眼也。"

[10]眼挫:眼角。

[11]睃(suō)趁:看;趁是无实际意义的语音助词。

[12]勾当:泛指事情。

[13]劬(qú)劳:劳累、辛苦。

[14]道场:梵文意译,可指修行所据之佛法,奉佛祭祀之所、寺院、为逝者追福以超度亡灵而举行的佛事及修行习道之地等。

[15]飏(yáng)：抛开、丢下。

[16]赤紧的：当真的、真个的。

[17]奇擎(qíng)：即擎，捧护。

[18]业身：造孽之身，多为自怨自责之语。

[19]幽客：这里指深闺女儿。

[20]德言工貌：封建时代要求女子具有德言工容四种美德。德，贞顺；言，择词而语；工，专纺织、洁酒食、奉宾客；貌，即容，身无垢辱。

[21]腻玉：形容肌肤细润光洁。

[22]玉笋：比喻女子手指纤细光润。

[23]簟(diàn)：竹席。

[24]摇书幌：谓灯影下书斋中晃动的身影。书幌、书斋、书帷。

[25]支吾：支撑、应付。

[26]手抵着牙儿：即以手托腮。

第三折　酬　韵

（莺莺上云）母亲使红娘问长老修斋日期，去了多时，不见来回话。（红娘上云）回夫人话了，去回小姐话去。（莺莺云）使你问长老几时做好事？（红云）恰回夫人话也，正待回小姐话。二月十五，佛什么供日，请夫人小姐拈香。（红笑云）小姐，我对你说一件好笑的事。咱前日庭院前瞥见的秀才，今日也在方丈里坐地。他先出门外等着红娘，深深唱喏道[1]："小娘子莫非莺莺小姐侍妾红娘乎？"又道："小生姓张，名珙，字君瑞，本贯西洛人氏，年方二十三岁，正月十七日子时建生，并不曾娶妻。"（莺莺云）谁着你去问他？（红云）却是谁问他来？他还呼着小姐名字说："常出来么？"被红娘一顿抢白[2]，回来了。（莺莺云）你不抢白他也罢。（红云）小姐，我不知他想甚么哩。世间有这等傻角[3]，我不抢白他？（莺莺云）你曾告夫人知道也不？（红云）我不曾告夫人知道。（莺莺云）你已后不告夫人知道罢。天色晚也，安排香案，咱花园里烧香去来。正是，无端春色关心事，闲倚熏笼待月华。（莺莺、红娘下）（张生上云）搬至寺中，正得西厢居住。我问和尚，知道小姐每夜花园内烧香。恰好花园便是隔墙，比及小姐出来，我先在太湖石畔墙角儿头等待，饱看他一回，却不是好。且喜夜深人静，月朗风清，是好天气也呵！闲寻方丈高僧坐，闷对西厢皓月吟。

【越调·斗鹌鹑】（张生唱）玉宇无尘，银河泻影，月色横空，花阴满庭。罗袂生寒，芳心自警。侧著耳朵儿听，蹑著脚步儿行，悄悄冥冥[4]，潜潜等等。

【紫花儿序】等我那齐齐整整，袅袅婷婷，姐姐莺莺。一更之后，万籁无声[5]。我便直至莺庭，到回廊下，没揣的见你那可憎[6]，定要我紧紧搂定，问你个：会少离多，有影无形。

（莺莺上云）红娘，开了角门，将香案出去者！

【金蕉叶】猛听得角儿门呀的一声，风过处衣香细生。踮着脚尖儿仔细定睛：比那初见时，庞儿越整。

【调笑令】我今夜甫能[7]，见娉婷，便是月殿姐娥，不恁般撑[8]。

料想春娇厌拘束，等闲飞出广寒宫。容分一脸，体露半襟，弹长袖以无言，垂湘裙而不动。似湘陵妃子，斜偎舜庙朱扉；如洛水神人，欲入陈王丽赋。是好女子也呵！

遮遮掩掩穿芳径，料应他小脚儿难行。行近前来百媚生，兀的不引了人魂灵。

（莺莺云）将香来。（张生云）我听小姐祝告甚么。

（莺莺云）此一炷香，愿亡过父亲，早升天界！此一炷香，愿中堂老母，百年长寿！此一炷香……（莺莺良久不语科）（红云）小姐，为何此一炷香每夜无语？红娘替小姐祷告：咱愿配得姐夫，冠世才学，状元及第，风流人物，温柔性格，与小姐百年成对波！（莺莺添香拜科）世间无限伤心事，尽在深深一拜中。（长吁科）

（张生云）小姐，你心中如何有此倚栏长叹也！

【小桃红】夜深香霭散空庭，帘幕东风静。拜罢也，斜将曲栏凭,长吁了两三声。剔团圞明月如圆镜[9],又不见轻云薄雾,都只是香烟人气,两般儿氤氲得不分明[10]。小生仔细想来:小姐此叹,必有所感。我虽不及司马相如,小姐你莫非倒是一位文君?小生试高吟一绝,看他说甚的。月色溶溶夜[11],花阴寂寂春。如何临皓魄,不见月中人?

　　(莺莺云)有人在墙角吟诗。(红云)这声音便是那二十三岁,不曾娶妻的那傻角。(莺莺云)好清新之诗。红娘,我依韵和一首。(红云)小姐试和一首,红娘听波。(莺莺吟云)兰闺深寂寞,无计度芳春。料得高吟者,应怜长叹人!(张生惊喜云)是好应酬得快也呵。

【秃厮儿】早是那脸儿上扑堆着可憎,更堪那心儿里埋没着聪明。他把我新诗和得忒应声,一字字,诉衷情,堪听。

【圣药王】语句又轻,音律又清,你小名儿真不枉唤做莺莺。你若共小生厮觑定[12],隔墙儿酬和到天明。便是惺惺惜惺惺[13]。我撞过去,看小姐怎么?

【麻郎儿】我拽起罗衫欲行,他可陪着笑脸相迎?不做美的红娘莫浅情,你便道"谨依来命"!

【幺】忽听一声猛惊。

　　(红云)小姐,咱家去来,怕夫人嗔责。(莺莺、红娘关角门下)扑剌剌宿鸟飞腾,颤巍巍花梢弄影,乱纷纷落红满径。

【络丝娘】碧澄澄苍苔露冷,明皎皎花筛月影。白日相思枉耽病,今夜我去把相思投正。

【东原乐】帘垂下,户已扃[14]。我试悄悄相问,你便低低应。月朗风清恰二更,厮觑幸[15]。如今是你无缘,小生薄命。

【绵搭絮】恰寻归路,伫立空庭。竹梢风摆,斗柄云横。呀!今夜凄凉有四星,他不偢人待怎生?何须眉眼传情,你不言,我已省。

只是今夜,甚么睡魔到得我眼里呵!

【拙鲁速】碧荧荧是短檠灯[16],冷清清是旧围屏。灯儿是不明,梦儿是不成。淅泠泠是风透疏棂,忒楞楞是纸条儿鸣。枕头是孤零,被窝是寂静。便是铁石人不动情。

【后】也坐不成,睡不能。有一日,柳遮花映,雾幛云屏,夜阑人静,海誓山盟,风流嘉庆,锦片前程,美满恩情,咱两个画堂春自生。

【尾】我一天好事今宵定,两首诗分明互证。再不要青琐闼梦儿中寻[17],只索去碧桃花树儿下等。

西厢记

注 释

[1] 唱喏(rě)：旧时礼节，边作揖边发声致敬。

[2] 抢白：训斥、责备。

[3] 傻角：痴子、呆人。

[4] 冥冥：意为暗地里。

[5] 万籁：自然界万物发出的声音。

[6] 没揣的：意外的、含侥幸之意。

[7] 甫能：刚刚、方才。

[8] 撑：美丽、漂亮。

[9] 剔：极、很；团圞(luán)：圆。

[10] 氤氲(yīn yūn)：云烟蒸腾缭绕。

[11] 溶溶：形容水流潺湲，也用以形容如水的月色。

[12] 厮觑(qù)定：互相对视，注目良久。

[13] 惺惺惜惺惺：惺惺，聪明机敏。形容才智格调相近的人相互敬重、爱慕，也指同病相怜。

[14] 扃(jiōng)：关门。

[15] 徯(xī)幸：无着落，怅然失落。

[16] 短檠(qíng)灯：意指寒门读书人夜读时照明的灯。

[17] 青琐闼(tà)：宫门，代指朝廷。

第一本

第四折 闹斋

（张生上云）今日二月十五日，和尚请拈香，须索走一遭。云晴雨湿天花乱，海涌风翻贝叶轻。

【双调·新水令】（张生唱）梵王宫殿月轮高，碧琉璃瑞烟笼罩。

（法本引僧众上云）今日是二月十五，释迦牟尼佛入大涅槃日[1]，纯陀长者与文殊菩萨，修斋供佛，若是善男信女今日做好事，必获大福利。张先生早已在也。大众动法器者，待天明了，请夫人小姐拈香。

行香云盖结，讽咒海波潮[2]。幡影飘飖，诸檀越尽来到[3]。

【驻马听】法鼓金铙，二月春雷响殿角。钟声佛号，半天风雨洒松梢。侯门不许老僧敲，纱窗也没有红娘报。我是馋眼脑，见他时，要看个十分饱。

（本见张生科，本云）先生先拈香，若夫人问呵，只说是老僧的亲。（张生拈香拜科）

【沉醉东风】惟愿存在的人间寿高，亡过的天上逍遥，我真正为先灵礼三宝[4]。再焚香暗中祷告：只愿红娘休劣，夫人休觉，犬儿休恶，佛啰，成就了幽期密约！

（夫人引莺莺、红娘上云）长老请拈香，咱走一遭。

【雁儿落】我只道玉天仙离碧霄，原来是可意种来清醮。我是个多愁多病身，怎当你倾国倾城貌？

【得胜令】你看檀口点樱桃，粉鼻倚琼瑶[5]。淡白梨花面，轻盈杨柳腰。妖娆,满面儿堆著俏。苗条,一团儿真是娇。

　　（法本云）老僧一句话敬禀夫人:有敝亲,是上京秀才,父母亡后,无可相报,央老僧带一分斋。老僧一时应允了,恐夫人见责。（夫人云）追荐父母,有何见责?请来相见咱。（张生见夫人毕）

【乔牌儿】大师年纪老,高座上**也**凝眺。举名[6]的班首真呆僗[7],将法聪头做磬敲。

【甜水令】老的少的,村的俏的,没颠没倒,胜似闹元宵。稔色人儿,可意冤家,怕人知道,看人将泪眼偷瞧。

【折桂令】著小生心痒难挠。哭声儿似莺啭乔林,**泪珠儿似露滴花梢**。大师难学,**把个慈悲脸儿朦着**。点烛的头陀可恼[8],烧香的行者堪焦。烛影红摇,香霭云飘,贪看莺莺,烛灭香消。

【碧玉箫】我情引眉梢,心绪他知道。他愁种心苗,情思我猜着。畅懊恼,响珰珰云板敲[9],行者又嚎,沙弥又哨[10],你须不夺人之好!

【鸳鸯煞】你有心争似无心好,我有情早被无情恼。

　　（本宣疏烧纸科,云）天明了也,请夫人小姐回宅。

　　（夫人、莺莺、红娘下）（张生云）再做一日也好!哪里发付小生?

劳攘了一宵,月儿早沉,钟儿早响,鸡儿早叫。玉人儿归去得疾,好事儿收拾得早。道场散了,酩子里各回家[11],葫芦提已到晓[12]。

　　题目　老夫人开春院　崔莺莺烧夜香
　　正名　小红娘传好事　张君瑞闹道场

注 释

[1] 涅槃(pán)：佛教用语，本指超脱生死的境界，后用以指代佛或僧人的去世。
[2] 讽咒：诵念佛经。
[3] 檀越：佛教僧人称向寺院施舍财物饮食的世俗信徒为檀越，或称施主。
[4] 三宝：即佛、法、僧。
[5] 琼瑶：美玉。
[6] 举名：佛教做佛事时的呼令。
[7] 呆佬(láo)：方言，呆痴懵懂。
[8] 头陀：梵语，涤除烦恼意，此处泛指僧人。
[9] 云板：铁铸成的用于佛事的云状法器，也用于报时。
[10] 沙弥：梵语为行善息恶之意，佛教指刚刚剃度受戒的僧人。
[11] 酪子里：犹言暗地里。
[12] 葫芦提：俗语，糊里糊涂。

西厢记

第二本

第一折 寺 警

（孙飞虎领卒子上云）自家孙飞虎的便是。方今天下扰攘[1]，主将丁文雅失政，俺分统五千人马，镇守河桥。探知相国崔珏之女莺莺，眉黛青颦，莲脸生春，有倾国倾城之容，西子、太真之色。现在河中府普救寺停丧借居。前日二月十五，做好事追荐父亲，多曾有人看见。俺心中想来，首将尚然不正，俺独何为哉？大小三军，听吾号令：人尽衔枚[2]，马皆勒口，连夜进兵河中府，掳掠莺莺为妻，是我平生愿足。（法本慌上云）祸事到！谁想孙飞虎领半万贼兵，围住寺门，犹如铁桶，鸣锣击鼓，呐喊摇旗，要掳小姐为妻。老僧不敢违误，只索报知与夫人小姐。（夫人慌上云）如此却怎了，怎了？长老，俺便同到小姐房前商议去。（俱下）（莺莺引红娘上云）前日道场亲见张生，神魂荡漾，茶饭少进，况值暮春天气，好生伤感也呵！正是：好句有情怜皓月，落花无语怨东风。

【仙吕·八声甘州】（莺莺唱）恹恹瘦损，早是多愁，那更残春。罗衣宽褪[3]，能消几个黄昏？我只是风袅香烟不卷帘，雨打梨花深闭门。莫去倚阑干，极目行云。

【混江龙】况是落红成阵，风飘万点正愁人。昨夜池塘梦晓，今朝阑槛辞春。蝶粉乍沾飞絮雪，燕泥已尽落花尘。系春情短柳丝长，隔花人远天涯近。有几多六朝金粉，三楚精神。

（红娘云）小姐情思不快，我将这被儿熏得香香的，小姐睡些则个。

【油葫芦】翠被生寒压绣裀，休将兰麝熏，便将兰麝熏尽，我不解自温存。分明锦囊佳句来勾引，为何玉堂人物难亲近？这些时坐又不安，立又不稳，登临又不快[4]，闲行又困，镇日价情思睡昏昏。

【天下乐】我依你搭伏定[5]，鲛绡枕头上儿盹。我但出闺门，你是影儿似不离身。这些时他恁般堤备人，小梅香服侍得勤，老夫人拘系得紧，不信俺女儿家折了气分[6]。

【那吒令】你知道我但见个客人，愠的早噷，便见个亲人，厌的倒褪[7]。独见了那人，兜的便亲[8]。我前夜诗依前韵，酬和他清新。

【鹊踏枝】不但字儿真，不但句儿匀，我两首新诗，便是一合回文。谁做针儿将线引，向东墙通个殷勤？

【寄生草】风流客，蕴藉人，相你脸儿清秀身儿韵，一定性儿温克情儿定[9]，不由人不口儿作念心儿印。我便知你一天星斗焕文章，谁可怜你十年窗下无人问。

（夫人、法本同上，敲门科）（红云）小姐，夫人为何请长老直来到房门外？（莺莺见夫人科）（夫人云）我的孩儿，你知道么？如今孙飞虎领半万贼兵，围住寺门。道你眉黛青颦，莲脸生春，有倾国倾城之容，西子，太真之色，要掳你去做压寨夫人[10]，我的孩儿，怎生是了也？

【六幺序】我魂离壳，这祸灭身，袖梢儿扭不住啼痕。一时去住无因，进退无门，教我那埚儿人急偎亲。孤孀母子无投奔，赤紧的先亡了我的有福之人。耳边金鼓连天震[11]，征云冉冉，土雨纷纷。

【后】风闻，胡云：道我眉黛青颦，莲脸生春，倾国倾城，西子太真。把三百僧人，他半万贼军，半霎儿便待翦草除根。那厮于家于国无忠信，恣情的掳掠人民。他将这天宫般盖造谁偢问？便做出诸葛孔明博望烧屯。

（夫人云）老身年纪五旬，死不为夭，奈孩儿年少，未得从夫，早罹此难，如之奈何？（莺莺云）孩儿想来，只是将我献与贼汉，庶可免一家性命！（夫人哭云）俺家无犯法之男，再婚之女，怎舍得你献与贼汉，却不辱没了俺家谱？（莺莺云）母亲休要爱惜孩儿，还是献与贼汉，其便有五：

【元和令带后庭花】第一来，免摧残国太君。第二来，免堂殿作灰尘。第三来，诸僧无事得安存。第四来，先公的灵柩稳。第五来，欢郎虽是未成人，也算崔家后代儿孙。若莺莺惜己身，不行从乱军：伽蓝火内焚[12]，诸僧血污痕，先灵为细尘。可怜爱弟亲，痛哉慈母恩。

【柳叶儿】俺一家儿不留龁龅[13]。待从军，果然辱没家门。俺不如白练套头，寻个自尽，将尸榇献贼人，你们得远害全身。

（法本云）咱每同到法堂上，问两廊下僧俗，有高见的，同商议个长策。（同到科）（夫人云）我的孩儿，却是怎的是？你母亲有一句话，本不舍得你，却是出于无奈！如今两廊下众人，不问僧俗，但能退得贼兵的，你母亲做主，倒陪房奁，便欲把你送与为妻。虽不门当户对，还强如陷于贼人。（夫人哭云）长老，便在法堂上,将此言与我高叫者!我的孩儿,只是苦了你也!(本云)此计较可。

【青哥儿】母亲,你都为了莺莺身分,你对人一言难尽,你更莫惜莺莺这一身,不拣何人,建立功勋,杀退贼军,扫荡烟尘,倒陪家门[14]。愿与英雄结婚姻,为秦晋。

（法本叫科）（张生鼓掌上云）我有退兵之计,何不问我?（见夫人科）（本云）禀夫人,这秀才便是前十五日附斋的敝亲。（夫人云）计将安在?（张生云）禀夫人,重赏之下,必有勇夫,赏罚若明,其计必成。（夫人云）恰才与长老说下,但有退得贼兵的,便将小女与他为妻。（张生云）既是恁的,小生有计,先用着长老。（本云）老僧不会厮杀,请先生别换一个!（张生云）休慌!不要你厮杀。你出去与贼头说,夫人钧命:小姐孝服在身,将军要做女婿呵,可按甲束兵,退一箭之地,等三日功德圆满,拜别相国灵柩,改换礼服,然后方好送与将军。不争便送来呵,一来孝服在身,二来于军不利。你去说来。（本云）三日后如何?（张生云）小生有一故人,姓杜,名确,号为白马将军,见统十万大军,镇守蒲关。小生与他八拜至交,我修书去,必来救我。（本云）禀夫人,若果得白马将军肯来时,何虑有一百孙飞虎?夫人请放心者!（夫人云）如此多谢先生!红娘,你服侍小姐回去者!（莺莺云）红娘,真难得他也!

【赚煞尾】诸僧伴,各逃生,众家眷,谁偢问?他不相识横枝儿著紧,非是他书生叨议论,也自防玉石俱焚。甚姻亲,可怜咱命在逡巡,济不济,权将这秀才来尽。他真有出师的表文,下燕的书信,只他这笔尖儿敢横扫五千人。

（莺莺引红娘下）（法本叫云）请将军打话[15]。（虎引卒子上云）快送莺莺上来！（本云）将军息怒！有夫人钧命，使老僧来与将军说，（云云。）（虎云）既然如此，限你三日，若不送来，我着你人人皆死，个个不存。你对夫人说去，恁般好性儿的女婿，教他招了者！

（虎引卒子下）（法本云）贼兵退了也，先生作速修书者。（张生云）书已先修在此，只是要一个人送去。（本云）俺这厨房下，有一个徒弟，唤做惠明，最要吃酒厮打。若央他去，他便必不肯。若把言语激着他，他却偏要去。只有他可以去得。（张生叫云）我有书送与白马将军，只除厨房下惠明不许他去，其余僧众谁敢去得？（惠明上云）惠明定要去，定要去！

【正宫·端正好】（惠明唱）不念《法华经》，不礼梁皇忏。飏了僧帽[16]，袒下了偏衫[17]。杀人心斗起英雄胆，我便将乌龙尾钢椽撼。

【滚绣球】非是我搀[18]，不是我揽，知道他怎生唤做打参[19]？大踏步，只晓得杀入虎窟龙潭。非是我贪，不是我敢，这些时吃菜馒头委实口淡。五千人也不索炙煿煎燣[20]，腔子里热血权消渴，肺腑内生心先解馋，有甚腌臜[21]？

【叨叨令】你们的浮沙羹、宽片粉添杂糁，酸黄齑[22]、臭豆腐真调淡，我万斤墨面从教暗，我把五千人做一顿馒头馅。你休误我也么哥，休误我也么哥！包残余肉，旋教青盐蘸。

（本云）惠明呵，张解元不用你去，你偏生要去，你真个敢去不敢去？

【倘秀才】你休问小僧敢去也那不敢，我要问：大师真个用咱也不用咱？你道飞虎声名赛虎般，那厮能淫欲，会贪婪，诚何以堪？

（张生云）你出家人，怎不诵经持咒，与众师随堂修行，却要与我送书？

【滚绣球】我经怕谈，禅懒参，戒刀[23]，新蘸，无半星儿土渍尘淹。别的女不女，男不男，大白昼把僧房门胡掩，那里管焚烧了七宝伽蓝？你真有个善文能武人千里，要下这济困扶危书一缄，我便有勇无惭。

（张生云）你独自去，还是要人帮扶着？

【白鹤子】着几个小沙弥，把幢幡宝盖擎，病行者，将面杖火叉担。你自立定脚把众僧安，我撞钉子将贼兵探[24]。

（张生云）他若不放你过去，却待如何？

（惠云）他敢不放我过去？你宽心！

我瞅一瞅古都都翻海波，喊一喊厮琅琅振山岩。脚踏得赤力力地轴摇，手攀得忽剌剌天关撼。远的，破一步将铁棒彤。近的，顺着手把戒刀钐。小的，提起来将脚尖撞。大的，扳过来把骷髅砍。

（张生云）我今将书与你，你却到几时可去？

【耍孩儿煞】我从来驳驳劣劣[25]，世不曾忐忐忑忑，打熬成不厌，天生是敢。我从来斩钉截铁常居一，不学那惹草拈花没掂三[26]，就死也无憾。便提刀仗剑，谁勒马停骖[27]？我从来欺硬怕软，吃苦辞甘，我休只因亲事胡扑掩。若杜将军不把干戈退，你张解元也干将风月担。便是言辞赚，一时纰缪剔[28]，半世羞惭！

我去也！

【收尾】你助威神，擂三通鼓，仗佛力，呐一声喊，绣幡开，遥见英雄俺。你看半万贼兵先吓破胆。

（张生云）老夫人吩咐小姐放心，此书一到，雄兵即来。

第二本

鲤鱼连夜飞驰去，白马从天降下来。

（杜将军引卒子上云）自家姓杜，名确，字君实，本贯西洛人也。幼与张君瑞同学儒业，后弃文就武。当年武状元及第，官拜征西大将军，正授管军元帅，统领十万之众，镇守蒲关。有人自河中府来，探知君瑞兄弟在普救寺中，不来看我，不知甚意？近日丁文雅失政，纵军劫掠人民，即当兴师，剪而朝食，奈虚实未的，不敢造次[29]。好。昨又差探子去了。好。今日升帐，看有甚军情来报者。（开辕门坐科）（惠明上云）俺离了普救寺，早至蒲关，这里杜将军辕门，俺闯入去。（卒捉住报科）（杜云）着他入来。（惠进跪科）（杜云）兀那和尚，你是那里做奸细者？（惠云）俺不是奸细，俺是普救寺僧人。今有孙飞虎作乱，将半万贼兵围住寺门，欲劫故臣崔相国女为妻。有游客张君瑞奉书，使俺递至麾下，望大人速解倒悬之危[30]！（杜云）左右的，放了这和尚者。张君瑞是我兄弟，快将他的书来。（惠叩头递书科）（杜拆念云）"同学小弟张珙顿首再拜，奉书君实仁兄大人大元帅麾下：自违国表，寒暄再隔，风雨之夕，念不能忘。辞家赴京，便道河中，即拟觐谒，以叙间阔。路途疲顿，忽遘采薪[31]，昨已初愈，不为忧也。轻装小顿，乃在萧寺。几席之下，忽值弄兵。故臣崔公，身后多累，持丧闻戒，暂僦安居。何期暴客，见其粲者，拥众五千，将逞无礼。谁无弱息，遽见狼狈，不胜愤懑，便当甘心。自恨生平，手无缚鸡，区区微命，真反不计。伏惟仁兄，仰受节钺，专制一方，咄叱所临，风云变色。夙承古人，方叔召虎，信如仁兄，实乃不愧。今弟危逼，不及转烛，仰望垂手，非可言喻。万祈招摇，前指河中，譬如疾雷，朝发夕到。使我涸鲋[32]，不恨西江。崔公九原，亦当衔结。伏乞台照，不宣。张珙再顿首拜。二月十六日书。"既然如此，我就传令。和尚你先回去，我星夜便来，比及你到寺里时[33]，多敢我已捉了这贼子也。（惠云）寺中十分紧急，大人是必疾来者。（下）（杜传令云）大小三军，听我号令，就点中权五千人马，星夜起发，直指河中府普救寺，救我兄弟去走一遭！（众应云）得令！（俱下）（孙引卒奔上云）白马爷爷来了，怎么了？怎么了？我们都下马卸甲，投戈跪倒，悉凭爷爷发落也！（杜引卒上云）你们做甚么都下马卸甲，投戈跪倒？你指望我饶你们也。也罢，止将孙飞虎一人砍首号令，其余不愿的，都归农去，愿的，开报花名，我与你安插者！（贼众下）（夫人、法本上云）下书已两日，不见回音。（张生上云）山门外暴雷似声，喏，敢是我哥哥到也。（杜与生相见拜科）（张生云）自别台颜，久失德教，今日见面，乃如梦中。（杜云）正闻行旌，近在邻治，不及过访[34]，万乞恕罪！（杜与夫人相见，拜科）（夫人云）孤寡穷途，自分必死，今日之命，实蒙再造。（杜云）狂贼跳梁，有失防御，致累受惊，敢辞万死！敢问贤弟，因甚不至我处？（张生云）小弟贱恙偶作，所以失谒。今日便应随仁兄去，却又为夫人昨日许以爱女相配，不敢仰劳仁兄执柯。小弟意思，成过大礼，弥月后便叩谢[35]。（杜云）恭喜贺喜，老夫人，下官自当作伐[36]。（夫人云）老身尚有处分。安排茶饭者。（杜云）适间投诚五千人，下官尚须料理，异日却来拜贺。（张生云）不敢久留仁兄，恐妨军政。（杜起马科）马离普救敲金镫，人望蒲关唱凯歌。（下）（夫人云）先生大恩，不可忘也！自今先生休在寺里下，便移来家下书院内安歇。明日略备草酌[37]，着红娘来请，先生是必来者。（夫人下）（张生别法本云）小生收拾行李，去书院里去也。无端豪客传烽火，巧为襄王送雨云。孙飞虎，小生感谢你不尽也！（法本云）先生得闲，仍旧来老僧方丈里攀话者！（张生下，法本下）

注释

[1]扰攘：动荡、混乱。

[2]衔枚：古时行军、狩猎或行丧礼时，口中含物以禁喧哗。

[3]宽褪：宽松。

[4]登临：登高临水。泛指游玩。

[5]搭伏定：伏在某物之上。

[6]折了气分：丢了颜面、失了光彩。

[7]厌的：猛的、突然。

[8]兜(dōu)的：猛的、突然。

[9]温(yùn)克：温良谦恭。

[10]压寨夫人：旧时戏曲小说里指占山为王的寇盗首领之妻。

[11]金鼓：钟鼓，古时用以指挥军队进退，击鼓而进，鸣金则退。

[12]伽(qié)蓝：本指修筑僧舍之基地，转而用为佛寺总称。

[13]韶龀(tiáo chèn)：指童年或儿童。

[14]倒陪家门：家门指家私财物，倒陪家门指不仅不索取财礼，反陪送家产。

[15]打话：对话。
[16]飑(diū)：甩、抛掷。
[17]偏衫：僧人法衣，开脊接领，斜披于左肩上。
[18]撺：争、抢。
[19]打参：即打坐，佛教徒跏趺（盘腿）而坐，摒除杂念而入定。
[20]炙煿(bó)煎爁(lǎn)：都是烹饪之法，即烤、爆、炒、炖。
[21]腌臜(ā zā)：肮脏，不洁净。
[22]酸黄齑(jī)：即酸菜。
[23]戒刀：僧人所带的月头小刀，按律只许用以割衣物。
[24]撞钉子：比喻自己将如尖钉直楔入物体般向敌阵冲去。
[25]驳驳劣劣：莽撞、蛮憨。
[26]没掂三：形容做事不果断、不着调。
[27]骖(cān)：古时四马驾车，中间驾辕的马称服，两边的马叫骖。
[28]纰缪(pī miù)：差错、纰漏。
[29]造次：仓猝、轻率、鲁莽。
[30]倒悬：比喻处境危急险恶。
[31]采薪：此处是生病的婉称。
[32]涸鲋(hé fù)：身陷干涸车辙里的鲋鱼，比喻处于困境急待救援的人。
[33]比及：等到。
[34]过访：访问、拜访。
[35]弥月：满一个月，整月。
[36]作伐：即做媒。
[37]草酌：自谦准备的是粗茶淡饭。酌，酒饭。

第二本

第二折 请 宴

（张生上云）夜来老夫人说，使红娘来请我。天未明便起身，直等至这早晚不见来，我的红娘也呵！（红娘上云）老夫人着俺请张生，须索早去者。

【中吕·粉蝶儿】（红娘唱）半万贼兵，卷浮云，片时扫净。俺一家儿死里重生。只据舒心的列仙灵，陈水陆，张君瑞便当钦敬。前日所望无成，倒是一缄书，为了媒证[1]。

【醉春风】今日东阁带烟开，再不要西厢和月等。薄衾单枕有人温[2]，你早则不冷，冷。你好宝鼎香浓，绣帘风细，绿窗人静。

可早到书院里也。

【脱布衫】幽僻处，可有人行，点苍苔，白露泠泠[3]。隔窗儿咳嗽一声，

（张生云）是谁？（红云）是我。（张生开门相见科）
只见启朱扉，疾忙开问。

【小梁州】叉手[4]，躬身礼数迎，我道不及万福先生！乌纱小帽耀人明，白襕净，角带闹黄鞓[5]。

【幺】衣冠济楚，那更庞儿整。休说引动莺莺，据相貌，凭才性，我从来心硬，一见了也留情。

（红云）奉夫人严命……（张生云）小生便去。

【上小楼】我不曾出声，他连忙答应。早飞去莺莺跟前，姐姐呼之，喏喏连声。秀才们闻道请，似得了将军令，先是五脏

神愿随鞭镫[6]。

（张生云）敢问红娘姐，此席为何？可有别客？

【后】第一来为压惊，第二来因谢承。不请街坊，不会诸亲，不受人情。避众僧，请贵人，和莺莺匹聘。见他谨依来命。

【满庭芳】又来回，顾影。文魔[7]，秀士，风欠酸丁[8]。下功夫把头颅挣，已滑倒苍蝇，光油油耀花人眼睛，酸溜溜螫得人牙疼。安排定，封锁过陈米数升，盖好过七八瓮蔓菁。

【快活三】这人一事精，百事精，不比一无成百无成。世间草木是无情，犹有相兼并。

【朝天子】这生后生，怎免相思病？天生聪俊，打扮又素净，夜夜教他孤另。曾闻才子多情，若遇佳人薄幸，常要耽搁了人性命。他的信行，他的志诚，你今夜亲折证[9]。

【四边静】只是今宵欢庆，软弱莺莺，那惯经，你索款款轻轻。灯前交颈，端详可憎，好煞人无干净。

（张生云）敢问红娘姐，那边今日如何铺设？小生岂好轻造。

【耍孩儿】俺那边落花满地胭脂冷，一霎良辰美景。夫人遣妾莫消停，请先生切勿推称[10]。正中是鸳鸯夜月销金帐，两行是孔雀春风软玉屏。下边是合欢令，一对对凤箫象板，雁瑟鸾笙。

（张生云）敢问红娘姐，小生客中无点点财礼，却是怎生好见夫人？

【四煞】聘不见争，亲立便成，新婚燕尔天教定。你生成是一双跨凤乘鸾客，怕他不卧看牵牛织女星？真徯幸，不费半丝红线[11]，已就一世前程。

【三煞】想是灭寇功，举将能，你两般功效如红定。先是莺娘心下十分顺，总为君瑞胸中百万兵。自古文风盛，那见珠围翠绕，不出黄卷青灯[12]。

【二煞】夫人只一家，先生无伴等，并无繁冗真幽静。立等你有恩有义心中客，回避他无是无非廊下僧。夫人命，不须推托，即便同行。

（张生云）既如此，红娘姐请先行一步，小生随后便来。

【收尾】先生休作谦，夫人专意等。自古恭敬不如从命，休使红娘再来请。

（张生云）红娘去了，小生拽上书院门者。比及我到得夫人那里，夫人道："张生，你来了也，与俺莺莺做一对儿，饮两杯酒便去卧房内做亲。"（笑科）孙飞虎，你真是我大恩人也！多亏了他，我改日空闲，索破十千贯足钱，央法本做好事超荐他。惟愿龙天施法雨，暗酬虎将起朝云。（下）

西厢记

注释

[1]媒证:媒人。

[2]衾(qīn):被子。

[3]泠泠(líng líng):形容露珠晶莹剔透的样子。

[4]叉手:自唐以来的一种施礼方式;身体拱立,双手抱拳或左手握右手拇指拱抱于胸前,略屈身以示恭敬。

[5]鞓(tīng):带状衣饰。

[6]愿随鞭镫:愿意跟从的意思。

[7]文魔:读书着魔的人,即书呆子、书痴。

[8]风欠酸丁:指迂腐作态、咬文嚼字的书呆子。

[9]亲折证:当面对质、当面分辩。

[10]推称:寻找借口以推托。

[11]红线:旧时男方给女家财礼,多以红绡红线缠裹,故以红线代指财礼。

[12]黄卷青灯:黄卷喻书籍,青灯指幽昏的灯光。黄卷青灯,代指读书人的清寒生活。

第三折 赖 婚

（夫人上云）红娘去请张生，如何不见来？（红娘见夫人云）张生着红娘先行、随后便来也。（张生上，拜夫人科）（夫人云）前日若非先生，焉有今日？我一家之命，皆先生所活。聊备小酌，非为报礼，勿嫌轻意。（张生云）"一人有庆，兆民赖之。"此贼之败，皆夫人之福。此为往事，不足挂齿。（夫人云）将酒来，先生满饮此杯。（张生云）"长者赐，不敢辞。"（立饮科，张生把夫人酒科）（夫人云）先生请坐。（张生云）小生礼当侍立，焉敢与夫人对坐？（夫人云）道不得个恭敬不如从命[1]。（张生告坐科）（夫人唤红娘请小姐科）（莺莺上云）迅扫风烟还净土，双悬日月照华筵。

【双调•五供养】（莺莺唱）若不是张解元识人多，别一个怎退干戈？排酒果，列笙歌，篆烟微，花香细，卷起东风帘幕。他救了咱全家祸，殷勤呵正礼，钦敬呵当合[2]。

（红娘云）小姐今日起得早也。

【新水令】恰才向碧纱窗下画了双蛾，拂绰了罗衣上粉香浮涴[3]，将指尖儿轻轻的贴个钿窝[4]。若不是惊觉人呵，犹压着绣衾卧。

（红云）小姐梳妆早毕也。小姐洗手咱。我觑小姐脸儿吹弹得破，张生你好有福也。小姐真乃天生就一位夫人！

【后】你看没查没例谎偻科,道我宜梳妆的脸儿吹弹得破。你那里休聒,不当一个信口开合。知他命福如何,我做夫人便做得过。

【乔木查】除非说我相思为他,他相思为我,今日相思都较可。这酬贺,当酬贺。母亲你好心多。

【搅筝琶】我虽是赔钱货,亦不到两当一弄成合。况他举将除贼,便消得你家缘过活。你费甚么便结丝萝[5]。休波,省钱的奶奶忒虑过,恐怕张罗。

【庆宣和】门外帘前,末将小脚儿挪,我先目转秋波。(张生云)小生更衣咱。

(做撞见莺莺科)谁想他识空便的灵心儿早瞧破[6],慌得我倒躲,倒躲!(夫人云)小姐近前来,拜了哥哥者!(张生云)呀!这声息不好也!(莺莺云)呀!俺娘变了卦也!(红娘云)呀!这相思今番害也!

【雁儿落】只见他荆棘剌怎动挪!死憎腾无同互[7],措支剌不对答[8],软兀剌难蹲坐[9]。

【得胜令】真是积世老婆婆,甚妹妹拜哥哥?白茫茫溢起蓝桥水,扑腾腾点着祆庙火[10]。碧澄澄清波,扑剌剌把比目鱼分破。急攘攘因何?扢搭地把双眉锁纳合。

【甜水令】粉颈低垂,烟鬟全堕,芳心无那[11],还有甚相见话偏多?星眼朦胧,檀口嗟咨,撅窨不过[12],这席面真乃乌合。

(夫人云)红娘,看热酒来,小姐与哥哥把盏者。(莺莺把盏科)(张生云)小生量窄。(莺莺云)红娘,接了台盏去者!

【折桂令】他其实咽不下玉液金波。他谁道月底西厢,变做梦里南柯？泪眼偷淹，他酩子里都韫湿衫罗。他眼倦开，软瘫做一垛。他手难抬，称不起肩窝。病染沉疴，他断难又活。母亲！你送了人呵，还使甚喽啰！（夫人云）小姐，你是必把哥哥一盏者！（莺莺把盏科）（张生云）说过小生量窄。（莺莺云）张生，你接这台盏者。

【月上海棠】一杯闷酒尊前过，你低首无言只自摧挫[13]，你不甚醉颜酡[14]。你嫌玻璃盏大，你从依我，你酒上心来较可。【后】你而今烦恼犹闲可，你久后思量怎奈何？我有意诉衷肠，怎奈母亲侧坐，与你成抛躲，咫尺间天样阔。

（张生饮酒科）（莺莺入席科）（夫人云）红娘，再斟上酒者，先生满饮此杯，（张生不答科）

【乔牌儿】转关儿虽是你定夺，哑谜儿早已人猜破。还要把甜话儿将人和，越教人不快活。

【清江引】女人自然多命薄，秀才又从来懦。闷杀没头鹅[15]，撇下赔钱货，不知他那答儿发付我。（张生冷笑科）

【殿前催】你道他笑呵呵，这是肚肠阁落泪珠多。若不是一封书把贼兵破，俺一家怎得存活？他不想姻缘想甚么？难捉摸，你说谎天来大，成也是你母亲，败也是你萧何！

【离亭宴带歇拍煞】从今后，我也玉容寂寞梨花朵，朱唇浅淡樱桃颗。如何是可？昏邓邓黑海来深，白茫茫陆地来厚，碧悠悠青天来阔。前日将他太行山般仰望，东洋海般饥渴，如今毒害得恁么[16]！把嫩巍巍双头花蕊搓，香馥馥同心缕带割，长挽挽连理琼枝挫[17]。只道白头难负荷，谁料青春有耽搁，将锦片前程已蹬脱。一边甜句儿落空他，一边虚名儿误赚我。

（夫人云）红娘，送小姐卧房里去者。（莺莺辞张生下）（张生云）小生醉也，告退。夫人跟前，欲一言尽意，未知可否？前者狂贼思逞，变在仓卒，夫人有言："能退贼者，以莺莺妻之。"是曾有此语否。（夫人云）有之。（张生云）当此之时，是谁挺身而出？（夫人云）先生实有活命之恩，奈先相国在日……（张生云）夫人却请住者！当时小生疾忙作书，请得杜将军来，徒为今日铺啜地乎[18]？今早红娘传命相呼，将谓永践诺金，快成倚玉。不知夫人何见，忽以"兄妹"二字，兜头一盖。请问：小姐何用小生为兄？若小生真不用小姐为妹。常言：算错非迟，还请夫人三思！（夫人云）这个小女，先相国在日，实已许下老身侄儿郑恒。前日发书曾去唤他，此子若至，将如之何？如今情愿多以金帛奉酬，愿先生别拣豪门贵宅之女，各谐秦晋，似为两便。（张生云）原来夫人如此，只不知杜将军若是不来，孙飞虎公然无礼，此时夫人又有何说？小生何用金帛？今日便索告别。（夫人云）先生住者，你今日有酒了也[19]。红娘，扶哥哥去书房中歇息，到明日，咱别有话说。（夫人下）（红娘扶张生云）张先生，少吃一盏，却不是好？（张生云）哎呀，红娘姐，你也糊涂，我吃甚么酒来？小生自从瞥见小姐，忘餐废寝，直到如今，受无限苦楚，不可告诉他人，须不敢瞒你。前日之事，小生这一封书，本何足道？只是夫人堂堂一品太君，金口玉言，许以婚姻之约。红娘姐，这不是你我二人独听见的，两廊下无数僧俗，乃至上有佛天，下有护法，莫不共闻。不料如今忽然变卦，使小生心尽计穷，更无出路。此事几时是了？就小娘子跟前，只索解下腰带，寻个自尽。可怜闭户悬梁客[20]，真作离乡背井魂。（解带科）（红娘云）先生休慌。先生之于小姐，妾已窥之深矣。其在前日，真为素昧平生，突如其来，难怪妾之得罪。至于今日，夫人实有成言，况是以德报德，妾当尽心谋之！（张生云）如此，小生生死不忘。只是计将安出？（红娘云）妾见先生有囊琴一张，必善于此。俺小姐酷好琴音，今夕妾与小姐，少不得花园烧香。妾以咳嗽为号，先生听见，便可一弹。看小姐说甚言语，便好将先生衷曲禀知。若有说话，明日早来回报。这早晚怕夫人呼唤，我只索回去。（下）（张生云）依旧夜来萧寺寡，何曾今夕洞房春？

西厢记

注释

[1] 道不得个：旧时引俗语、成语等时多用此开头，相当于说"常言道""岂不闻"。

[2] 当合：应该、合当。

[3] 浮涴(wò)：浮尘、浮土。

[4] 钿窝：衣服上的饰物。

[5] 丝萝：丝，菟丝，蔓生植物；萝指女萝，地衣类植物，二者均须依附他物生长，后即以丝萝喻婚姻。

[6] 识空(kòng)便：见机行事，识相。

[7] 死懵腾：呆滞而了无生气的模样。

[8] 措支刺：慌张失态，手足无措。

[9] 软兀刺：软瘫无力的样子。

[10] 袄庙火：使恋人离散的大火。袄，袄教，即拜火教，南北朝时自伊朗一带传入中国，称天神为袄，所建庙宇称袄庙、袄祠。

[11] 无那：无奈。

[12] 撖窨(diān yìn)：形容愤懑无奈而忍气吞声。撖，顿足。

[13] 摧挫：忧伤，受折磨。

[14] 醉颜酡(tuó)：酒后面红耳赤之态。

[15] 没头鹅：鹅群中有领头鹅，若失去头鹅，则群鹅茫然无首。形容不知所措。

[16] 恁(nèn)么：这么、如此、这样。

[17] 长挣挣：长长的样子。

[18] 馎啜(bǔ chuò)：即吃喝。

[19] 有酒：喝多了酒。

[20] 悬梁客：悬梁，典出《战国策》，苏秦头悬梁、锥刺股以发奋攻读。形容身在异乡的刻苦读书人。

第二本

第四折 琴 心

（张生上云）红娘教我今夜花园中，待小姐烧香时，把琴心探听他。寻思此言，深有至理。天色晚也，月儿你于我分上，不能早些出来呵。呀，恰早发擂也[1]。呀，恰早撞钟也。（理琴科云）琴呵，小生与足下湖海相随，今日这场大功，都只在你身上！天那，你于我分上，怎生借得一阵轻风，将小生这琴声，送到我那小姐的玉琢成、粉捏就、知音俊俏耳朵里去者！（莺莺引红娘上，红云）小姐，烧香去来，好明月也。（莺莺云）红娘，我有甚心情烧香来？月儿呵，你出来做甚那！

【越调·斗鹌鹑】（莺莺唱）云敛晴空，冰轮乍涌[2]。风扫残红，香阶乱拥。离恨千端，闲愁万种。娘呵！靡不初，鲜有终。他做会影里情郎，我做会画中爱宠。

【紫花儿序】只许心儿空想，口儿闲题，梦儿相逢。昨日个大开东阁，我只道怎生般炮凤烹龙[3]。朦胧，却教我"翠袖殷勤捧玉钟"。要算主人情重。将我雁字排连，着他鱼水难同。

（红云）小姐，你看月阑[4]，明日敢有风也？（莺莺云）呀，果然一个月阑呵。

【小桃红】人间玉容，深锁绣帏中，是怕人搬弄。想嫦娥，西没东生有谁共？怨天公，裴航不作游仙梦。劳你罗帏数重，愁他心动，围住广寒宫。

（红轻咳嗽科）（张生云）是红娘姐咳嗽，小姐来了也！（弹琴科）（莺莺云）红娘，这是甚么响？（红云）小姐，你猜咱！

【天净沙】是步摇得宝髻玲珑，是裙拖得环珮玎琤。是铁马儿檐前骤风[5]，是金钩双动，吉丁当敲响帘栊。

【调笑令】是花宫夜撞钟，是疏竹潇潇曲槛中。是牙尺剪刀声相送[6]，是漏声长滴响壶铜。我潜身再听，在墙角东，元来西厢理结丝桐。

【秃厮儿】其声壮，似铁骑刀枪冗冗。其声幽，似落花流水溶溶。其声高，似清风月朗鹤唳空。其声低，似儿女语小窗中喁喁[7]。

【圣药王】他思已穷，恨不穷，是为娇鸾雏凤失雌雄。他曲未通，我意已通，分明伯劳飞燕各西东。尽在不言中。

（红云）小姐，你住这里听者，我瞧夫人便来。（假下）

【麻郎儿】不是我他人耳聪，知你自己情衷。知音者芳心自同，感怀者断肠悲痛！

（张生云）窗外微有声息，定是小姐，我今试弹一曲。

（莺莺云）我近这窗儿边者。（张生叹云）琴呵，昔日司马相如求卓文君，曾有一曲，名曰《文凤求凰》。小生岂敢自称相如，只是小姐呵，教文君将甚来比得你？我今便将此曲依谱弹之。琴曰：

有美一人兮，见之不忘。一日不见兮，思之如狂！凤飞翱翔兮，四海求凰。无奈佳人兮，不在东墙。张琴代语兮，欲诉衷肠。何时见许兮，慰我彷徨[8]！愿言配德兮，携手相将。不得于飞兮，使我沦亡[9]！

（莺莺云）是弹得好也呵！其音哀，其节苦，使妾闻之，不觉泪下！

【后】 本宫，始终，不同。这不是清夜闻钟，这不是黄鹤醉翁，这不是泣麟悲凤。

【络丝娘】 一字字是更长漏永，一声声是衣宽带松。别恨离愁做这一弄[10]，越教人知重[11]。

（张生推琴云）夫人忘恩负义，只是小姐，你却不宜说谎！（红娘掩上科）（莺莺云）你错怨了也！

【东原乐】 那是娘机变[12]，如何妾脱空[13]？他由得俺乞求效鸾凤？他无夜无明并女工，无有些儿空。他那管人把妾身咒诵？

【绵搭絮】 外边疏帘风细，里边幽室灯青，中间一层红纸，几眼疏棂[14]，不是云山几万重，怎得个人来信息通？便道十二巫峰，也有高唐来梦中。

（红娘突出云）小姐，甚么"梦中"？那夫人知道怎了？

【拙鲁连】 走将来气冲冲，不管人恨匆匆，吓得人来怕恐。我又不曾转动，女孩儿家怎响喉咙。我待紧磨砦，将他拦纵[15]，怕他去夫人行把人葬送。

（红云）适才闻得张先生要去也，小姐，却是怎处？

（莺莺云）红娘，你便与他说，再住两三日儿。

【尾】 只说道，夫人时下有些唧哝[16]，好和歹你不脱空。我那口不应的狠毒娘，你定要别离了这志诚种！

（红娘云）小姐不必吩咐，我知道了也，明日我看他去。（莺莺红娘下）（张生云）小姐去了也。红娘姐呵，你便迟不得一步儿，今夜便回覆小生波？没奈何，

且只得睡去！（张生下）

题目　张君瑞破贼计　莽和尚杀人心
正名　小红娘昼请客　崔莺莺夜听琴

注释

[1] 发擂：敲鼓。

[2] 冰轮：形容皎洁的月亮。

[3] 炮凤烹龙：比喻珍馐佳馔，丰盛的筵席。

[4] 月阑：月亮四周的光圈，也称月晕，常为将起风的征兆。

[5] 铁马：悬于屋檐下的铁片或铃铛，即风铃。

[6] 牙尺：镶饰着象牙的尺子，是对尺子的美称。

[7] 喁喁(yú yú)：形容低声说话。

[8] 彷徨：走来踱去，犹豫不决。

[9] 沦亡：陷入困境、没落。

[10] 一弄：即一曲。

[11] 知重：相敬相知。

[12] 机变：机巧奸诈。

[13] 脱空：无着落，撒谎。

[14] 疏棂：疏，窗户；疏棂即窗棂。

[15] 拦纵：阻拦、阻挡。

[16] 唧哝：小声说话，嘀咕。

第三本

第一折　前　候

（莺莺引红娘上云）自昨夜听琴，今日身子这般不快呵。红娘，你左则闲着，你到书院中看张生一遭，看他说甚么，你来回我话者。（红云）我不去，夫人知道呵，不是耍。（莺莺云）我不说，夫人怎得知道，你便去咱。（红云）我便去了，单说张生你害病，俺的小姐也不弱。春昼不曾双劝酒，夜寒无那又听琴。

【仙吕·赏花时】（红娘唱）针线无心不待拈[1]，脂粉香消懒去添，春恨压眉尖。灵犀一点，医可病恹恹[2]。

（红娘下）（莺莺云）红娘去了，看他回来说甚么。十分心事一分语，尽夜相思尽日眠。（莺莺下）（张生上云）害杀小生也！我央长老说将去，道我病体沉重，却怎生不着人来看我？因思上来，我睡些儿咱。（睡科）

（红娘上云）奉小姐言语，著俺看张生[3]，须索走一遭。俺想来，若非张生，怎还有俺一家儿性命呵！

【仙吕·点绛唇】（红娘唱）相国行祠，寄居萧寺。遭横事[4]，幼女孤儿，将欲从军死。

【混江龙】谢张生伸致，一封书到便兴师，真是文章有用，何干天地无私？若不剪草除根了半万贼，怕不灭门绝户了一家儿。莺莺君瑞，许配雄雌。夫人失信，推托别辞，婚姻打灭，兄妹为之。而今搁起成亲事。一个糊涂了胸中锦绣，一个淹渍了脸上胭脂。

【油葫芦】一个憔悴潘郎鬓有丝，一个杜韦娘不似旧时，带围宽过了瘦腰肢。一个睡昏昏不待观经史，一个意悬悬[5]懒去拈针黹[6]。一个丝桐上调弄出离恨谱，一个花笺上删抹成断肠诗。笔下幽情，弦上的心事，一样是相思。

【天下乐】这叫做才子佳人信有之。红娘自思：乖性儿，何必有情不遂皆似此？他自恁抹媚[7]，我却没三思[8]，一纳头只去憔悴死。

却早来到也。俺把唾津儿湿破窗纸，看他在书房里做甚么那？

【村里迓鼓】我将这纸窗儿湿破，悄声儿窥视。多管是和衣儿睡起，你看罗衫上前襟褶裢[9]。孤眠况味，凄凉情绪，涩滞气色，微弱声息，黄瘦脸儿。张生呵，你不病死多应闷死。

【元和令】我将金钗敲门扇儿，

（张生云）是谁。（红娘上云）我是散相思的五瘟使。（张生开门，红娘入科）（张生云）夜来多谢红娘姐指教，小生铭心不忘。只是不知小姐可曾有甚言语？（红掩口笑云）俺小姐么，俺可要说与你——他昨夜风清月朗夜深时，使红娘来探尔。他至今胭粉未曾施，念到有一千番张殿试。（张生云）小姐既有见怜之心，红娘姐，小生有一简[10]，可敢寄得去？意便欲烦红娘姐带回。

【上马娇】他若见甚诗，看甚词，他敢颠倒费神思。

他拽扎起面皮[11]，道红娘："这是谁的言语，你将来！"

这妮子，怎敢胡行事？嗤，扯做了纸条儿。

（张生云）小姐决不如此，只是红娘姐不肯与小生将去。小生多以金帛拜酬红娘姐。

【胜葫芦】你个挽弓酸俫,没意儿,卖弄你有家私[12]。我图谋你东西来到此?把你做先生的钱物,与红娘为赏赐,我果然爱你金赍[13]?

【幺】你看人似桃李春风墙外枝,卖笑倚门儿。我虽是女孩儿,有志气,你只合道,可怜见小子只身独自,我还有个寻思。

　　(张生云)依著红娘姐,"可怜见小子只身独自",这如何?(红云)兀的不是也。你写波,俺与你将去。(张生写科)(红云)写得好呵,念与我听!(张生念云)张珙百拜,奉书双文小姐阁下:昨尊慈以怨报德,小生虽生犹死。筵散之后,不复成寐。曾托樵梧,自鸣情抱,亦见自今以后,人琴俱去矣。因红娘来,又奉数字,意者宋玉东邻之墙,尚有庄周西江之水。人命至重,或蒙矜恤!珙不胜悚仄,待命之至。附五言诗一首,伏惟赐览。

相思恨转添,漫把瑶琴弄。乐事又逢春,芳心尔亦动。此情不可违,虚誉何须奉。莫负月华明,且怜花影重。

　　张珙再百拜。

【后庭花】我只道拂花笺打稿儿,元来是走霜毫不构思[14]。先写下几句寒温序,后题著五言八句诗。不多时,翻来覆去,叠做个同心方胜儿[15]。你忒聪明,忒煞思,忒风流,忒浪子。虽是些假意儿,小可的难到此。

【青哥儿】又颠倒写鸳鸯二字,方信道在心为志。喜怒其间我觑意儿。放心波学士,我愿为之,并不推辞,自有言辞。我只说昨夜弹琴那人教传示。

这简帖儿，我与你将去。只是先生当以功名为念，休堕了志气者！

【寄生草】你偷香手，还准备折桂枝。休教淫词污了龙蛇字，藕丝缚定鹍鹏翅，黄莺夺了鸿鹄志。休为翠帏锦帐一佳人，惧你玉堂金马三学士！

【赚煞尾】弄得沈约病多般，宋玉愁无二，清减做相思样子。

（张生云）红娘姐好话，小生终身敬佩！只是方才简帖，我的红娘姐，是必在意者！（红云）先生放心！若是眉眼传情未了时，我中心日夜图之。怎因而有美玉于斯，我定教发落这张纸。我将舌尖上说辞，传你简帖里心事，管教那人来探你一遭儿！（红娘下）（张生云）红娘将简帖去了，不是小生夸口，这是一道会亲的符箓。他明日回话，必有好处！若无好赋因风去，岂有仙云入梦来？（张生下）

西厢记

注释

[1]不待：不想、没心思。

[2]恹恹(yān yān)：形容体弱多病而精神萎靡。

[3]著(zhuó)：派遣。

[4]横(hèng)事：灾祸、凶事。

[5]悬悬：思念、牵挂。

[6]针黹(zhǐ)：针线。

[7]抹媚：深深迷恋、迷惑。

[8]没三思：即没心思、无心。

[9]褶裥(zhě zhì)：衣物上的褶皱。

[10]简：书信。

[11]拽扎：原意为绷紧，此处即板起面孔的意思。

[12]家私：家产、家财。

[13]赀(zī)：计算，也指钱财、费用。

[14]霜毫：本指秋时的兽毛，最为细密，适合制笔。这里代指毛笔。

[15]方胜儿：本是古时妇女用丝织品编织而成的装饰物，此处指折叠成方或菱形的信笺。

第二折 闹 简

（莺莺上云）红娘这早晚敢待来也！起得早了些儿，俺如今再睡些。（睡科）（红娘上云）奉小姐言语，去看张生，取得一封书来，回他话去。呀！不听得小姐声音，敢又睡哩，俺便入去看他。绿窗一带迟迟日，紫燕双飞寂寂春。

【中吕·粉蝶儿】（红娘唱）风静帘闲，绕窗纱麝兰香散，启朱扉摇响双环。绛台高[1]，金荷小[2]，银釭犹烂[3]。我将他暖帐轻弹，揭起海红罗软帘偷看。

【醉春风】只见他钗軃玉斜横，髻偏云乱挽。日高犹自不明眸，你好懒，懒。

（莺莺起身，欠身长叹科）半晌抬身，几回搔耳，一声长叹。是便是，只是这简帖儿，俺那好递与小姐？俺不如放在妆盒儿里，等他自见。（放科）（莺莺整妆，红娘偷觑科）

【普天乐】晚妆残，乌云軃，轻匀了粉脸，乱挽起云鬟。将简帖儿拈，把妆盒儿按，拆开封皮孜孜看[4]，颠来倒去不害心烦。只见他厌的挖皱了黛眉[5]，忽的低垂了粉颈，氲的改变了朱颜。

（红做意科，云）呀！决撒了也[6]！（莺莺怒科，云）红娘过来。（红云）有！（莺莺云）红娘，这东西哪里来的？我是相国的小姐，谁敢将这简帖儿来戏弄我？我几曾惯看这样东西来？我告过夫人，打下你个小贱人下截来。（红云）小姐使我去，他着我将来。小姐不使我去，我敢问他讨来？我又不识字，知他写的是些甚么？

【快活三】分明是你过犯[7]，没来由把我摧残。教别人颠倒恶心烦！你不惯，谁曾惯？

小姐休闹，比及你对夫人说科，我将这简帖儿，先到夫人行出首去[8]。（莺莺怒云）你到夫人行却出首谁来？（红云）我出首张生。（莺莺做意云）红娘，也罢，且饶他这一次。（红云）小姐，怕不打下他下截来！（莺莺云）我正不曾问你，张生病体如何？（红云）我只不说。（莺莺云）红娘，你便说咱！

【朝天子】近间面颜，瘦得实难看。不思量茶饭，怕动弹。

（莺莺云）请一位好太医，看他证候咱！（红云）他也无甚证候，他自家说来：

我是晓夜将佳期盼，废寝忘餐。黄昏清旦，望东墙淹泪眼。我这病患要安，只除是出点风流汗。

（莺莺云）红娘，早是你口稳来，若别人知道呵，成何家法？今后他这般的言语，你再也休题。我和张生，只是兄妹之情，有何别事？（红云）是好话也呵！

【四边静】怕人家调犯[9]，早晚怕夫人行破绽，只是你我何安？又问甚他危难？你只撺掇上竿[10]，拔了梯儿看。

（莺莺云）虽是我家亏他，他岂得如此？你将纸笔过来，我写将去回他，着他下次休得这般。（红云）小姐，你写甚的那？你何苦如此？（莺莺云）红娘，你不知道！（写科）（莺莺云）红娘，你将去对他说，小姐遭看先生，乃兄妹之礼，非有他意。再一道儿是这般呵，必告俺夫人知道。红娘，和你小贱人，都有话说也！（红云）小姐，你又来！这帖儿我不将去，你何苦如此？（莺莺掷书地下云）这妮子，好没分晓！（莺莺下）（红娘拾书叹云）咳，小姐，你将这个性儿那里使也。

【脱布衫】小孩儿口没遮拦，一味的将言语摧残。把似你使性子，休思量秀才，做多少好人家风范[11]。

【小梁州】我为你梦里成双觉后单，废寝忘餐。罗衣不耐五更寒，愁无限，寂寞泪阑干[12]。

【换头】似等辰勾[13]，空把佳期盼。我将角门儿更不牢拴，愿你做夫妻无危难。你向筵席头上整扮，我做个缝了口的撮合山[14]。

【石榴花】你晚妆楼上杏花残，犹自怯衣单。那一夜听琴时，露重月明间，为甚向晚不怕春寒？几乎险被先生馈。那其间岂不胡颜？为他不酸不醋风魔汉，隔窗儿险化做望夫山。

【斗鹌鹑】你既用心儿拨雨撩云，我便好意儿传书递简。不肯搜自己狂为，只待觅别人破绽。受艾焙[15]，我权时忍这番。畅好是奸。对别人巧语花言，背地里愁眉泪眼。

俺若不去来，道俺违拗他。张生又等俺回话，只得再到书房。（推门科）（张生上云）红娘姐来了，简帖儿如何？（红云）不济事了！先生休傻。（张生云）小生简帖儿、是一道会亲的符篆，只是红娘姐不肯用心，故致如此。（红云）是我不用心？哦！先生，头上有天哩，你那个简帖儿里面好听也！

【上小楼】这是先生命悭，不是红娘违慢。那的做了你的招状[16]，他的勾头[17]，我的公案！若不觑面颜，厮顾盼，担饶轻慢,争些儿把奴拖犯[18]。

【后】从今后我相会少,你见面难。月暗西厢,便如凤去秦楼,云敛巫山。你也赸[19],我也赸,请先生休讪[20],早寻个酒阑人散。

只此,足下再也不必申诉肺腑。怕夫人寻我,我回去也。(张生云)红娘姐。(定科)(良久,张生哭云)红娘姐,你一去呵,更望谁与小生分剖?(张生跪云)红娘姐!红娘姐!你是必做个道理,方可救得小生一命!(红娘云)先生,你是读书才子,岂不知此意?

【满庭芳】你休呆里撒奸[21]。你待恩情美满,苦我骨肉摧残。他只少手搭棍儿摩娑看,我粗麻线怎过针关?定要我挂着拐帮闲钻懒,缝合口送暖偷寒,前已是踏着犯!

(张生跪不起,哭云)小生更无别路,一条性命都只在红娘姐身上,红娘姐!我没来由只管分说,小姐回你的书,你自看者。(递书科)(张生拆书,读毕,起立笑云)呀!红娘姐!(又读毕云)红娘姐,今日有这场喜事!(又读毕云)早知小姐书至,理合应接,接待不及,切勿见罪!红娘姐,和你也欢喜。(红云)却是怎么?(张生笑云)小姐骂我都是假,书中之意,"哩也波哩也啰哩[22]"。(红云)怎么?(张生云)书中约我今夜花园里去。(红云)约你花园里去怎么?(张生云)约我后花园里去相会。(红云)相会怎么?(张生笑云)红娘姐,你道相会怎么哩?(红云)我只不信。(张生云)不信由你。(红云)你试读与我听。(张生云)是五言诗四句哩,妙也!待月西厢下,迎风户半开。拂墙花影动,疑是玉人来。红娘姐,你不信?

（红云）此是甚么解？（张生云）有甚么解？（红云）我真个不解。（张生云）我便解波："待月西厢下"，着我待月上而来。"迎风户半开"，他开门等我。"拂墙花影动"，着我跳过墙来。"疑是玉人来"，这句没有解，是说我至矣。（红云）真个如此解？（张生云）不是这般解，红娘姐你来解！不敢欺红娘姐，小生乃猜诗谜的社家[23]，风流隋何，浪子陆贾。不是这般解，怎解？（红云）真个如此写？（张生云）现在，（红定科，良久）（张生又读科）（红云）真个如此写？（张生笑云）红娘姐好笑也！如今现在，（红怒云）你看我小姐，原来在我行使乖道儿[24]！

【耍孩儿】几曾见，寄书的颠倒瞒着鱼雁？小则小，心肠儿转关，教你跳东墙，女字边干。原来五言包得三更枣，四句埋将九里山。你赤紧将人慢[25]，你要会云雨闹中取静，却教我寄音书忙里偷闲！

【四煞】纸光明玉版，字香渍麝兰，行儿边湮透非娇汗。是他一缄情泪红犹湿，满纸春愁墨未干。我也休疑难，放着个玉堂学士，任从你金雀鸦鬓。

【三煞】将他来别样亲，把俺来取次看，是几时孟光接了梁鸿案？将他来甜言媚你三冬暖，把俺来恶语伤人六月寒。今日为头看，看你个离魂倩女，怎生的掷果潘安？（张生云）只是小生读书人，怎生跳得花园墙过？

【二煞】拂墙花又低，迎风户半拴，偷香手段今番按。你怕墙高怎把龙门跳？嫌花密难将仙桂攀。疾忙去，休辞惮！他望穿了盈盈秋水，蹙损了淡淡春山[26]。

（张生云）小生曾见花园，已经两遭。

西厢记

【煞尾】虽是去两遭,敢不如这番。你当初隔墙酬和都胡侃,证果是他今朝这一简。

> (红娘下)(张生云)叹万事自有分定。适才红娘来,千不欢喜,万不欢喜,谁想小姐有此一场好事?小生实是猜诗谜的社家,风流隋何,浪子陆贾,此四句诗,不是这般解,又怎解?"待月西厢下",是必须待得月上。"迎风户半开",门方开了。"拂墙花影动,疑是玉人来",墙上有花影,小生方好去。今日这颏天,偏百般的难得晚。天那,你有万物于人,何苦争此一日?疾下去波。

快书快友快谈论,不觉开西立又昏。今日碧桃花有约,鳔胶黏了又生根。

> 呀!才向午也。再等一等,又看咱,今日百般的难得下去呵。

空青万里无云,悠然扇作微薰。何处缩天有术,便教逐日西沉。

> 呵,初倒西也。再等一等咱。

谁将三足乌[27],来向天上阁?安得后羿弓,射此一轮落。

> 谢天谢地, 日光菩萨,你也有下去之日。呀!却早上灯也。呀,却早发擂也。呀!却早撞钟也。拽上书房门,到得那里,手挽着垂杨,滴溜扑碌跳过墙去,抱住小姐。咦!小姐,我只替你愁哩,

二十颗珠藏简帖,三千年果在花园。(张生下)

注释

[1] 绛台：红色的蜡烛台。

[2] 金荷：烛台上部承接融化烛液的荷叶形铜盘，亦称铜荷。

[3] 银釭(gāng)：灯。

[4] 孜孜看：细细看、认真看。

[5] 扢(gē)皱：紧皱、皱起（眉）。

[6] 决撒：坏事了，败露了。

[7] 过犯：罪过。

[8] 出首：自首。

[9] 调犯：说长道短，嘲讽。

[10] 撺掇(cuān duo)：从旁鼓动他人，怂恿。

[11] 好人家：犹言有身份的人家。

[12] 泪阑干：涕泪横流。

[13] 辰勾：即水星。

[14] 撮合山：媒人。

[15] 艾焙(bèi)：原是指以艾绒卷炙烤经穴处以驱病，此处意为受训斥、被责备。

[16] 招状：犯人招认罪行的供词。

[17] 勾头：抓捕人犯时的拘票。

[18] 争些儿：差点儿、险些个。

[19] 赸(shàn)：离开、散伙。

[20] 讪(shàn)：抱怨。

[21] 呆里撒奸：表面诚实厚道而内藏奸狡。

[22] 这句没有什么具体意思，等于说"如此这般"。

[23] 社家：行家。

[24] 道儿：圈套。

[25] 幔：同瞒，欺骗。

[26] 春山：形容女子美丽的眉形。

[27] 三足乌：传说太阳里有三只脚爪的乌鸦，即以三足乌代指太阳。

西厢记

第三折 赖 简

（红娘上云）今日小姐着俺寄书与张生，当面偌多假意儿，诗内却暗约着他来。小姐既不对俺说，俺也不要说破他，只请他烧香，看他到其间怎生瞒俺。（红娘请云）小姐，俺烧香去来。（莺莺上云）花香重叠晚风细，庭院深沉早月明。

【双调·新水令】（红娘唱）晚风寒峭透窗纱，控金钩绣帘不挂。门阑凝暮霭，楼阁抹残霞。恰对菱花[1]，楼上晚妆罢。

【驻马听】不近喧哗，嫩绿池塘藏睡鸭。自然幽雅，淡黄杨柳带栖鸦。金莲蹴损牡丹芽，玉簪儿抓住荼蘼架[2]。早苔径滑，露珠儿湿透凌波袜。

俺看我小姐和张生，巴不得到晚哩。

【乔牌儿】自从那日初时，想月华，捱一刻，似一夏。见柳梢斜日迟迟下，道好教贤圣打。

【搅筝琶】打扮得身子儿乍[3]，准备来云雨会巫峡。为那燕侣莺俦，扯杀心猿意马。他水米不沾牙，越越的闭月羞花。真假，这其间性儿难按捺，我一地胡拿[4]。

小姐，这湖山下立地，我闭了角门儿，怕有人听咱说话。（红娘瞧门外科）（张生上云）此时正好过去也。
（张生瞧门内科）

【沉醉东风】是槐影风摇暮鸦，是玉人帽侧乌纱[5]。你且潜身曲槛边，他今背立湖山下。那里叙寒温打话。

（张生搂红娘云）我的小姐。（红云）是俺也。早是差到俺，若是差到夫人，怎了也？

便做道搂得慌，也索觑咱，多管是饿得你穷神眼花。

我且问你，真个着你来么？（张生云）小生是猜诗谜社家，风流隋何，浪子陆贾，准定扢扢帮便倒地。

（红云）你却休从门里去，只道我接你来，你跳过这墙去！张生，你见么？今夜一弄儿风景，分明助你两个成亲也！

【乔牌儿】你看淡云笼月华，便是红纸护银蜡。柳丝花朵便是垂帘下，绿莎便是宽绣榻。

【甜水令】良夜又迢遥，闲庭又寂静，花枝又低亚[6]。只是他女孩儿家，你索意儿温存，话儿摩弄，性儿浃洽[7]。休猜做路柳墙花。

【折桂令】他娇滴滴美玉无瑕，莫单看粉脸生春，云鬓堆鸦。我也不去受怕担惊，我也不图浪酒闲茶。是你夹被儿时当奋发，指头儿告了消乏。打叠起嗟呀，毕罢了牵挂，收拾过忧愁，准备著撑达。

（张生跳墙科）（莺莺云）是谁？（张生云）是小生。

（莺莺唤云）红娘。（红娘不应科）（莺莺怒云）哎哟！张生，你是何等之人？我在这里烧香，你无故至此，你有何说？（张生云）哎哟！

【锦上花】为甚媒人心无惊怕，赤紧夫妻意不争差。我蹑足潜踪去悄地听他，一个羞惭，一个怒发。

【后】一个无一言，一个变了卦。一个悄悄冥冥，一个絮絮答答。（红娘远立低叫云）张生，你背地里硬嘴那里去了？你向前呵！告到官司，怕羞了你？为甚进定隋何，禁住陆贾，叉手躬身,如聋似哑。

【清江引】你无人处且会闲嗑牙[8],就里空奸诈。怎想湖山边,不似西厢下?

　　(莺莺云)红娘,有贼!(红云)小姐,是谁?(张生云)红娘,是小生。(红云)张生,这是谁着你来?你来此有甚的勾当?(张生不语科)(莺莺云)快扯去夫人那里去!(张生不语科)(红云)扯去夫人那里,便坏了他行止,我与小姐处分罢。张生,你过来跪者!你既读孔圣之书,必达周公之礼,你夤夜来此何干[9]?
香美娘处分花木瓜。

【雁儿落】不是一家儿乔坐衙,要说一句儿衷肠话。只道你文学海样深,谁道你色胆天来大。

【得胜令】你夤夜入人家,我非奸做盗拿。你折桂客做了偷花汉,不去跳龙门,来学骗马。

　　小姐,且看红娘面,饶过这生者!(莺莺云)先生活命之恩,恩则当报。既为兄妹,何生此心?万一夫人知之,先生何以自安?今看红娘面,便饶过这次,若更如此,扯去夫人那里,决不干休!谢小姐贤达,看我面,做情罢。若到官司详察,先生整备精皮肤一顿打[10]!

　　(莺莺云)红娘,收了香桌儿,你进来波!(莺莺下)

　　(红娘羞张生云)羞也波!羞也波!却不道猜诗谜社家,风流隋何,浪子陆贾,今日便早死心塌地也!

【离亭宴带歇拍煞】再休题"春宵一刻千金价",准备去"寒窗重守十年寡"。猜诗谜的社家,巧拍了"迎风户半开",山障了"隔墙花影动",云𩅦了"待月西厢下"。一任你将何郎粉去搽,他已自把张敞眉来画。强风情措大,晴干了尤云殢雨心[11]，忏悔了窃玉偷香胆，涂抹了倚翠偎红话。淫词儿早则休，简帖儿从今罢。犹古自参不透风流调法。小姐，你息怒嗔波卓文君，张生，你游学去波汉司马[12]！

注释

[1]菱花：古代人使用铜镜，镜背往往刻有菱形花纹，所以用菱花代指铜镜。

[2]荼蘼(tú mí)：即荼蘼，蔷薇科属植物，开白色重瓣花朵。

[3]乍：体面、美丽。

[4]胡拿：乱来、胡闹。

[5]乌纱：旧时当官者所戴官帽以黑色纱织物制成，故以乌纱代指做官。

[6]低亚：低垂。

[7]浃洽：和善，与人合得来。

[8]闲嗑牙：说闲话。

[9]夤(yín)夜：深夜。

[10]整备：整理备办。

[11]殢(tì)：滞留。

[12]汉司马：汉代的司马相如，借指张生。

第四折 后 候

（夫人上云）早间长老使人来说，张生病重。俺着人去请太医，一壁分付红娘看去，问太医下什么药，是何证候，脉息如何，便来回话者。（夫人下）（红娘上云）夫人使俺去看张生。夫人呵，你只知张生病重，那知他昨夜受这场气呵，怕不送了性命也！（红娘下）（莺莺上云）张生病重，俺写一简，只说道药方，着红娘将去，与他做个道理。（唤红娘科）（红应云）小姐，红娘来也。（莺莺云）张生病重，我有一个好药方儿，与我将去咱！（红云）小姐呵，你又来也。也罢，夫人正使我去，我就与你将去波！（莺莺云）我专等你回话者。（莺莺下，红娘下）（张生上云）昨夜花园中，我吃这场气，投着旧证候[1]，眼见得休了也！夫人着长老请太医来看我，我这恶证候，非是太医所治，除非小姐有甚好药方儿，这病便可了。（红娘上云）俺小姐害得人一病郎当，如今又着俺送甚药方儿。俺去则去，只恐越着他沉重也！异乡最有离愁病，妙药难医肠断人。

【越调·斗鹌鹑】（红娘唱）先是你彩笔题诗，回文织锦，引得人卧枕着床，忘餐废寝。到如今鬓似愁潘，腰如病沈。恨已深，病已沉。多谢你热劫儿对面抢白，冷句儿将人厮侵[2]。

【紫花儿序】你倚着桃门儿待月，依着韵脚儿联诗，侧着耳

朵儿听琴。昨夜忽然撇假偌多,说:"张生,我与你兄妹之礼,甚么勾当?"忽把个书生来跌窨,

今日又是:"红娘,我有个好药方儿,你将去与了他!"又将我侍妾来逼凌。难禁,倒教俺似线脚儿般殷勤,不离了针。从今后由他一任。甚么义海恩山,无非远水遥岑。(见张生问云)先生,可怜呵!你今日病体如何?(张生云)害杀小生也!我若是死呵,红娘姐,阎罗王殿前,少不得你是干连人。(红云)普天下害相思,不像你害得忒煞也。小姐,你那里知道呵?

【天净沙】你心不存学海文林[3],梦不离柳影花阴,只去窃玉偷香上用心。又不曾有甚,我见你海棠开想到如今。

你因甚便害到这般了?(张生云)你行,我敢说谎?我只因小姐来。昨夜回书房,一气一个死。我救了人,反被人害。古云:"痴心女子负心汉。"今日反其事了。

(红云)这个与他无干。

【调笑令】你自审这邪淫,看尸骨岩岩是鬼病侵。便道秀才们从来恁,似这般单相思好教撒唔[4]。功名早则不遂心,婚姻又反吟伏吟。

夫人着俺来看先生,吃甚么汤药。这另是一个甚么好药方儿,送来与先生。(张生云)在那里?(红授简云)在这里。(张生开读,立起笑云)我好喜也!是一首诗。(揖云)早知小姐诗来,礼合跪接。红娘姐!小生贱体不觉顿好也!(红云)你又来也,不要又差了一些儿!(张生云)我那有差的事?前日原不得差,得失亦事之偶然耳。(红云)我不信,你念与我听呵。(张生云)你欲闻好语,必须致诚敛衽而前。(张生整冠带,

双手执简科)(念诗云)休将闲事苦萦怀,取次摧残天赋才。不意当时完妾行,岂防今日作君灾?仰酬厚德难从礼,谨奉新诗可当媒。寄语高唐休咏赋,今宵端的雨云来。红娘姐,此诗又非前日之比。(红低头沉吟云)哦,有之,我知之矣。小姐,你真个好药方儿也!

【小桃红】桂花摇影夜深沉,酸醋当归浸。紧靠湖山背阴,里窨最难寻。一服两服令人恁。忌的是知母未寝,怕的是红娘撒沁[5]。这其间使君子一星儿参。

【鬼三台】只是你其实啉[6],休妆唔。真是风魔翰林,无投处问佳音,向简帖上计禀。得了个纸条儿恁般绵里针,若见了玉天仙,怎生软厮禁。俺小姐正合忘恩,偻人负心[7]。

【秃厮儿】你身卧一条布衾,头枕三尺瑶琴,他来怎生一处寝?冻得他战兢兢。知音。

【圣药王】果若你有心,他有心,昨宵秋千院宇夜深沉。花有阴,月有阴,便该春宵一刻抵千金,何须又诗对会家吟?

【东原乐】我有鸳鸯枕,翡翠衾,便遂杀人心,只是如何赁?你便不脱和衣更待甚,不强如指头儿恁。你成亲已大福荫。

先生,不瞒你说,俺的小姐呵,你道怎么来?

【绵搭絮】他眉是远山浮翠,眼是秋水无尘,肤是凝酥[8],腰是弱柳,俊是庞儿俏是心,体态是温柔性格是沉[9]。他不用法灸神针,他是一尊救苦难观世音。

然虽如此,我终是不敢信来。

【后】我慢沉吟[10],你再思寻。

(张生云)红娘姐,今日不比往日。(红云)呀!先生不然!

你往事已沉,我只言目今。

不信小姐今夜却来。今夜三更他来恁。（张生云）红娘姐，小生吩咐你，来与不来，你不要管，总之其间望你用心。

我是不曾不用心，怎说白璧黄金，满头花，拖地锦[11]。

【煞尾】夫人若是将门禁，早共晚，我能教称心。

先生，我也要吩咐你，总之其间你自用心，来与不来，我都不管。

来时节，肯不肯怎由他，见时节，亲不亲尽在您。

题目 张君瑞寄情诗 小红娘递密约
正名 崔莺莺乔坐衙 老夫人问医药

注释

[1]投着：应合，正中。

[2]厮侵：此处为关切亲近之意。

[3]学海文林：形容学问渊博，文章深奥。

[4]撒唔(tūn)：装傻充愣。

[5]撒沁(qìn)：胡说。

[6]啉(lín)：傻、呆的样子。

[7]佞人：指巧言善辩而不诚实的人。

[8]凝酥：形容肌肤白嫩细腻。酥，牛羊奶所制奶酪。

[9]沉：稳重。

[10]慢沉吟：念叨个不停。

[11]拖地锦：成婚时所穿的服饰，或指曳地长裙。

西厢记

第四本

第四本

第一折 酬 简

（莺莺上云）红娘传简帖儿去，约张生今夕与他相会，等红娘来，做个商量。（红娘上云）小姐着俺送简帖儿与张生，约他今夕相会，俺怕又变卦，送了他性命不是耍。俺见小姐去，看他说甚的。（莺莺云）红娘，收拾卧房，我去睡。（红云）不争你睡呵，那里发付那人？（莺莺云）甚么那人？（红云）小姐，你又来也，送了人性命不是耍。你若又翻悔，我出首与夫人："小姐着我将简帖儿，约下张生来！"（莺莺云）这小妮子倒会放刁！（红云）不是红娘放刁，其实小姐切不可又如此！（莺莺云）只是羞人答答的！（红云）谁见来？除却红娘，并无第三个人。（红娘催云）去来，去来！（莺莺不语科）（红娘催云）小姐，没奈何，去来，去来！（莺莺不语，做意科）（红娘催云）小姐，我们去来，去来！（莺莺不语，行又住科）（红娘催云）小姐，又立住怎么？去来，去来！（莺莺不语，行科）（红娘云）我小姐语言虽是强，脚步儿早已行也。

【正宫•端正好】（红娘唱）因小姐玉精神，花模样，无倒断晓夜思量[1]。今夜出个至诚心，盖抹咱瞒天谎[2]。出画阁，向书房；离楚岫，赴高唐。学窃玉，试偷香。巫娥女，楚襄王。楚襄王敢先在阳台上。

（莺莺随红娘下）（张生上云）小姐着红娘，将简帖儿约小生,今夕相会,这早晚初更尽呵,怎不见来。人间良夜静复静,天上美人来不来?

【仙吕·点绛唇】(张生唱)伫立闲阶,夜深香霭横金界。潇洒书斋[3],闷杀读书客。

【混江龙】彩云何在,月明如水浸楼台。僧居禅室,鸦噪庭槐。风弄竹声,只道金珮响。月移花影,疑是玉人来。意悬悬业眼,急攘攘情怀。身心一片,无处安排。呆打孩[4],倚定门儿待。越越的青鸾信杳[5],黄犬音乖。

【油葫芦】我情思昏昏眼倦开,单枕侧,梦魂几入楚阳台。早知恁无明无夜因他害,想当初"不如不遇倾城色"。人有过,必自责,勿惮改。我却待"贤贤易色"将心戒,怎当他兜的上心来?

【天下乐】我倚定门儿手托腮。好着我难猜:来也那不来?夫人行料应难离侧。望得人眼欲穿,想得人心越窄。多管是冤家不自在。偌早晚不来,莫不又是谎?

【那吒令】他若是肯来,早身离贵宅。他若是到来,便春生敝斋。他若是不来,似石沉大海。数着他脚步儿行,靠着这窗棂儿待。寄语多才[6]。

【鹊踏枝】恁的般恶抢白,并不曾记心怀。博得个意转心回,许我夜去明来。调眼色已经半载,这其间委实难捱。

【寄生草】安排着害,准备着抬[7]。想着这异乡身,强把茶汤捱。只为你可憎才,熬定心肠耐。办一片至诚心,留得形骸在。试教司天台,打算半年愁,端的太平车,敢有十余载。

(红娘上云)小姐,我过去,你只在这里。(敲门科)

(张生云)小姐来也。(红云)小姐来也,你接了衾枕者。(张生揖云)红娘姐,小生此时一言难尽,惟天可表。（红云）你放轻者，休谎了他。你只在这里，我迎他去。（红娘推莺莺上云）小姐，你进去，我在窗儿外等你。（张生见莺莺跪抱云）张珙有多少福，敢劳小姐下降。

【村里迓鼓】猛见了可憎模样，早医可九分不快。先前见责，谁承望今宵相待？教小姐这般用心，不才珙，合跪拜。小生无宋玉般情，潘安般貌，子建般才。小姐，你只可怜我为人在客。（莺莺不语）（张生起，揎莺莺坐科）

【元和令】绣鞋儿刚半拆[8]，柳腰儿恰一搦[9]，羞答答不肯把头抬，只将鸳枕捱。云鬟仿佛坠金钗，偏宜鬓髻儿歪。

【上马娇】我将你纽扣儿松，我将你罗带儿解，兰麝散幽斋，不良会把人禁害。哈[10]！怎不回过脸儿来？（张生抱莺莺，莺莺不语科）

【胜葫芦】软玉温香抱满怀。呀，刘阮到天台，春至人间花弄色。柳腰款摆，花心轻拆，露滴牡丹开。

【后】蘸着些儿麻上来，鱼水得和谐。嫩蕊娇香蝶恣采。你半推半就，我又惊又爱。檀口揾香腮。

【柳叶儿】我把你做心肝般看待，点污了小姐清白。我忘餐废寝舒心害，若不真心耐，至心捱，怎能勾这相思苦尽甘来。

【青歌儿】成就了今宵欢爱，魂飞在九霄云外。投至得见你个多情小弥妹，你看憔悴形骸，瘦似麻秸。今夜和谐，犹是疑猜。露滴香埃，风静闲阶，月射书斋，云锁阳台。我审视明白：难道是昨夜梦中来？（张生起，跪谢云）张珙今夕得侍小姐，终身犬马之报。（莺莺不语科）（红娘请云）小姐，回去波，怕夫人觉来。（莺莺起行，不语科）（张生携莺莺手再看科）愁无奈。

【寄生草】多丰韵，忒稔色，乍时相见教人害，霎时不见教人怪，些时得见教人爱。今宵同会碧纱橱[11]，何时重解香罗带。

　　（红娘催云）小姐，快回去波，怕夫人觉来。（莺莺不语，行下阶科）（张生双携莺莺手再看科）

【赚煞尾】春意透酥胸，春色横眉黛，贱却那人间玉帛。杏脸桃腮，乘月色，娇滴滴越显红白。下香阶，懒步苍苔，非关弓鞋凤头窄。叹鲰生不才[12]，谢多娇错爱。你破工夫今夜早些来。

注释

[1]无倒断：没完没了，无休止。
[2]盖抹：改正、遮掩。
[3]潇洒：此处为凄清、萧疏之意。
[4]呆打孩：愣怔呆滞的样子。
[5]越越的：静悄悄的。
[6]寄语：转告，传话。
[7]抬：意为因害相思而致病亡被人抬走。
[8]拆：计一拃的长短，"半拆"言女子的脚十分小巧。
[9]一搦(nuò)：一握、一把。
[10]咍(hāi)：招呼声，如哎、喂。
[11]碧纱橱：蒙覆着绿纱床幔的床。
[12]鲰(zōu)生：小子、小人。

第四本

第二折 拷艳

（夫人引欢郎上，云）这几日见莺莺语言恍惚，神思加倍，腰肢体态别又不同，心中甚是委决不下。（欢云）前日晚夕，夫人睡了，我见小姐和红娘去花园里烧香，半夜等不得回来。（夫人云）你去唤红娘来。（欢唤红娘科）（红云）哥儿，唤我怎么？（欢云）夫人知道你和小姐花园里去，如今要问你哩。（红惊云）呀，小姐，你连累我也。哥儿，你先去，我便来也。金塘水满鸳鸯睡，绣户风开鹦鹉知。

【越调·斗鹌鹑】（红娘唱）只若是夜去明来，倒有个天长地久。不争你握雨携云，常使我提心在口。你只合戴月披星，谁许你停眠整宿？夫人他心数多，情性仇[1]，还要巧语花言，将没作有。

【紫花儿序】猜他穷酸做了新婿，猜你小姐做了娇妻，猜我红娘做的牵头。况你这春山低翠，秋水凝眸，都休。只把你裙带儿拴，纽门儿扣，比旧时肥瘦，出落得精神，别样的风流。

我算将来，我到夫人那里，夫人必问道，兀那小贱人，

【金蕉叶】我着你但去处，行监坐守[2]，谁教你迤逗他，胡行乱走。这般问，如何诉休[3]？

我便只道，夫人在上，红娘自幼不敢欺心。

便与他个知情的犯由。只是我图着什么来？

【调笑令】他并头效绸缪，倒凤颠鸾百事有。我独在窗儿

外,几曾敢轻咳嗽?立苍苔直把绣鞋儿冰透。如今嫩皮肤,去受粗棍儿抽,我这通殷勤的着甚来由。

　　咳,小姐,我过去呵,说得过,你休欢喜,说不过,你休烦恼,你只在这里打听波。(红娘见夫人科)(夫人云)小贱人,怎么不跪下?你知罪么?(红云)红娘不知罪。(夫人云)你还自口强哩,若实说呵,饶你,若不实说呵,我只打死你个小贱人。(说科)谁着你和小姐半夜花园里去……(红云)不曾去,谁见来。(夫人云)欢郎见来,尚兀自推哩。(打科)(红云)夫人,不要闪了贵手,且请息怒,听红娘说。

【鬼三台】夜坐时停了针绣,和小姐闲穷究[4]。说哥哥病久,咱两个背着夫人,向书房问候。

　　(夫人云)问候呵,他说什么?他说,夫人近来恩做仇,教小生半途喜变忧。他说,红娘你且先行,他说,小姐权时落后。(夫人云)哎哟,小贱人,他是个女孩儿家,著他落后怎么?

【秃厮儿】定然是神针法灸,难道是燕侣莺俦?他两个经今月余,只是一处宿。何须你一一搜缘由。

【圣乐王】他们不识忧,不识愁,一双心意两相投。夫人你得好休,便好休,其间何必苦追求。

　　(夫人云)这事,都是你个小贱人。(红云)非干张生、小姐、红娘之事,乃夫人之过也。(夫人云)这小贱人,倒拖下我来,怎么是我之过。(红云)信者人之根本,人而无信,大不可也。当日军围普救,夫人许退得军者,以女妻之。张生非慕小姐颜色,何故无干建策?夫人兵退身安,悔却前言,岂不为失信乎?既不允其亲事，便当酬以金帛，令其舍此远去。却不合留于书院，相近咫尺，使怨女旷夫[5]，各相窥伺，因而有此一端。夫人若不遮盖此事，一来，辱没相国家谱。二来，张生施恩于人，反受其辱。三来，告到官司，夫人先有治家不严之罪。依红娘愚见，莫若恕其小过，完其大事，实为长便。常言女大不中留。

【麻郎儿】又是一个文章魁首，一个仕女班头。一个通彻三教九流，一个晓尽描鸾刺绣。

【后】世有，便休，罢手。大恩人怎做敌头？启白马将军故友，斩飞虎么么草寇。

【络丝娘】不争和张解元参辰卯酉，便是与崔相国出乖弄丑[6]，到底干连着自己皮肉。夫人，你休究！

（夫人云）这小贱人，倒也说得是，我不合养了这个不肖之女，经官呵，其实辱没家门。罢，罢！俺家无犯法之男、再婚之女，便与了这禽兽罢。红娘，先与我唤那贱人过来。（红娘请云）小姐，那棍子儿只是滴溜溜在我身上转，吃我直说过了，如今夫人请你过去。（莺莺云）羞人答答的，怎么见我母亲？（红云）哎哟，小姐你又来，娘跟前有什么羞，羞时，休做！

【小桃红】你个月明才上柳梢头，却早人约黄昏后。羞得我脑背后，将牙儿衬着衫儿袖。怎凝眸，只见你鞋底尖儿瘦，一个恣情的不休，一个哑声儿厮耨[7]。那时不曾害半星儿羞。

（莺莺见夫人科）（夫人云）我的孩儿。（夫人哭科，莺莺哭科，红娘哭科）（夫人云）我的孩儿，你今日被人欺负，做下这等之事，都是我的业障[8]，待怨谁来！我待经官呵，辱没了你父亲，这等事，不是俺相国人家做出来的。（莺莺大哭科）（夫人云）红娘，你扶住小姐。罢，罢！都是俺养女儿不长进，你去书房里，唤那禽兽来。（红娘唤张生科）（张生云）谁唤小生？（红云）你的事发了也，夫人唤你哩。（张生云）红娘姐，没奈何，你与我遮盖些。不知谁在夫人行说来？小生惶恐，怎好过去？（红云）你休佯小心，老着脸儿，快些过去。

【后】既然泄漏怎干休？是我先投首[9]。他如今赔酒赔茶倒搁就，你反担忧。何须定约通媒媾，我担着个部署不周。你元来苗而不秀，呸，一个银样镴枪头。

（张生见夫人科）（夫人云）好秀才，岂不闻"非先王之德行，不敢行"。我便待送你到官府去，只辱没了我家门。我没奈何，把莺莺便配与你为妻。只是俺家三辈不招白衣女婿[10]，你明日便上朝取应去，俺与你养着媳妇儿。得官呵，来见我，剥落呵，休来见我。（张生无语，跪拜科）（红云）谢天谢地，谢我夫人。

【东原乐】相思事，一笔勾，早则展放从前眉儿皱，密爱幽欢恰动头。谁能够，兀的般可喜娘庞儿也要人消受。

（夫人云）红娘，你分付收拾行装，安排酒肴果盒，明日送张生到十里长亭[11]，饯行去者。寄语西河堤畔柳，安排青眼送行人。（夫人引莺莺下）（红云）张生，你还是喜也，还是闷也？

【收尾】直要到归来时，画堂箫鼓鸣春昼，方是一对儿鸾交凤友。如今还不受你说媒红，吃你谢亲酒。

注释

[1]㑇(zhòu)：脾气固执，刚愎自用。

[2]行监坐守：一举一动都要看守监视。

[3]如何诉休：如何诉说。

[4]穷究：原意为追根究底，此处意为聊天、说闲话儿。

[5]怨女旷夫：成年而未嫁之女称怨女，成年而未娶的男子为旷夫。

[6]出乖弄丑：做出错事、丑事而丢人现眼。

[7]厮耨(nòu)：戏弄纠缠。

[8]业障：佛教语称行恶业（坏事）则障阻正道。

[9]投首：自首。

[10]白衣：古时未为官者着白衣，白衣即指没有功名的人。

[11]长亭：古代设于道路旁供行人歇宿、休息的公用屋舍。

第三折 哭 宴

（夫人上云）今日送张生赴京，红娘，快催小姐同去十里长亭。我已吩咐人安排下筵席，一面去请张生，想亦必定收拾了也。（莺莺、红娘上云）今日送行，早则离人多感，况值暮秋时候，好烦恼人也呵。（张生上云）夫人夜来，逼我上朝取应，得官回来，方把小姐配我。没奈何，只得去走一遭。我今先往十里长亭，等候小姐，与他作别呵。（张生先行科）（莺莺云）悲欢离合一杯酒，南北东西四马蹄。（悲科）

【正宫·端正好】（莺莺唱）碧云天，黄花地，西风紧，北雁南飞。晓来谁染霜林醉？总是离人泪！

【滚绣球】恨成就得迟，怨分去得疾。柳丝长，玉骢难系[1]。倩疏林[2]，你与我挂住斜晖。马儿慢慢行，车儿快快随。恰告了相思回避，破题儿又早别离。猛听得一声去也，松了金钏。遥望见十里长亭，减了玉肌。

（红云）小姐，你今日竟不曾梳裹呵。（莺莺云）红娘，你那知我的心来！此恨谁知？

【叨叨令】见安排车儿马儿，不由不熬熬煎煎的气！甚心情花儿靥儿[3]，打扮得娇娇滴滴的媚？眼看着衾儿枕儿，只索要昏昏沉沉的睡。谁管他衫儿袖儿，湿透了重重叠叠的泪。兀的不闷杀人也么哥，闷杀人也么哥！谁思量书儿信儿，还望他恓恓惶惶的寄。

（夫人、莺莺、红娘作到科）（张生拜见夫人科）（莺莺背转科）（夫人云）张生你近前来，自家骨肉，不须回避。孩儿，你过来见了呵。（张生、莺莺相见科）

（夫人云）张生这壁坐，老身这壁坐，孩儿这壁坐。红娘斟酒来。张生，你满饮此杯。我今既把莺莺许配于你，你到京师，休辱没了我孩儿，你挣扎个状元回来者。（张生云）张珙才疏学浅，凭仗先相国及老夫人恩荫，好歹要夺个状元回来，封拜小姐。（各坐科）（莺莺吁科）

【脱布衫】下西风黄叶纷飞，染寒烟衰草凄迷。酒席上斜签着坐的。我见他蹙愁眉，死临侵地[4]。

【小梁州】阁泪汪汪不敢垂，恐怕人知。猛然见了把头低，长吁气，推整素罗衣。

【幺】虽然久后成佳配，这时节怎不悲啼？意似痴，心如醉，只是昨宵、今日清减了小腰围。

【上小楼】我只为合欢未已，离愁相继，前暮私情，昨夜分明，今日别离。我恰知那几日相思滋味，谁想那别离情更增十倍？

（夫人云）红娘，服侍小姐把盏者。（莺莺把盏科）（张生吁科）（莺莺低云）你向我手里吃一盏酒者。

【幺】你轻远别，便相掷，全不想腿儿相压，脸儿相偎，手儿相持。你与崔相国做女婿，妻荣夫贵，这般并头莲，不强如状元及第。（重入席科，吁科）

【满庭芳】供食太急，你眼见须臾对面，顷刻别离。若不是席间子母当回避，有心待举案齐眉。虽是厮守得一时半刻，也合教俺夫妻每共桌而食。眼底空留意，寻思就里，险化做望夫石。

（夫人云）红娘把盏者。（红娘把张生盏毕，把莺莺盏云）小姐，你今早不曾用早饭，随意饮一口儿汤波。

【快活三】将来的酒共食，尝着似土和泥，假若便是土和泥，也有些土气息，泥滋味。

【朝天子】暖溶溶玉醅[5]，白泠泠似水，多半是相思泪。面前茶饭不待吃，恨塞满愁肠胃。只为蜗角虚名[6]、蝇头微利，拆鸳鸯坐两下里。一个这壁，一个那壁，一递一声长吁气。

【四边静】霎时间杯盘狼藉，还要车儿投东，马儿向西，两处徘徊，大家是落日山横翠。知他今宵宿在那里？有梦也难寻觅。

（夫人云）红娘，吩付辆起车儿，请张生上马，我和小姐回去。（各起身科）（张生拜夫人科）（夫人云）别无他嘱，愿以功名为念，疾早回来者。（张生谢云）谨遵夫人严命。（张生、莺莺拜科）（莺莺云）此一行，得官不得官，疾便回来者。（张生云）小姐放心，状元不是小姐家的，是谁家的？小生就此告别。（莺莺云）住者，君行别无所赠，口占一绝[7]，为君送行："弃掷今何道，当时且自亲。还将旧来意，怜取眼前人！"

（张生云）小姐差矣！张珙更敢怜谁？此诗——一来小生此时方寸已乱，二来小姐心中到底不信。且等即日状元及第回来，那时敬和小姐。

【般涉·耍孩儿】淋漓红袖淹情泪，知你的青衫更湿。伯劳东去燕西飞，未登程先问归期。分明眼底人千里，已过尊前酒一杯。我未饮心先醉，眼中流血，心内成灰。

【五煞】到京师，服水土[8]，趁程途，节饮食，顺时[9]，自保千金体。荒村雨露眠宜早,野店风霜起要迟。鞍马秋风里,无人调护,自去扶持。

【四煞】忧愁诉与谁?相思只自知,老天不管人憔悴。泪添九曲黄河溢,恨压三峰华岳低。到晚西楼倚,看那夕阳古道,衰柳长堤。

【三煞】方才还是一处来,如今竟是独自归。归家怕看罗帏里,昨宵是绣衾奇暖留春住,今日是翠被生寒有梦知。留恋应无计,一个据鞍上马[10],两个泪眼愁眉。

【二煞】不忧文齐福不齐[11],只忧停妻再娶妻。河鱼天雁多消息。我这里青鸾有信频须寄,你切莫金榜无名誓不归!君须记,若见些异乡花草,再休似此处栖迟[12]。

(张生云)小姐金玉之言,小生一一铭之肺腑。相见不远,不须过悲,小生去也。忍泪佯低面,含情假放眉。

(莺莺云)不知魂已断,那有梦相随。(张生下)(莺莺吁科)

【一煞】青山隔送行,疏林不做美,淡烟暮霭相遮蔽。夕阳古道无人语,禾黍秋风尚马嘶。懒上车儿内,来时甚急,去后何迟。(夫人云)红娘,扶小姐上车,天色已晚,快回去波。终然宛转从娇女,算是端严做老娘。

(夫人下)(红娘云)前车夫人已远,小姐只索快回去波。(莺莺云)红娘,你看他在那里?

【收尾】四围山色中,一鞭残照里。将遍人间烦恼填胸臆,量这般大小车儿[13],如何载得起?

西厢记

注 释

[1] 玉骢:青白色的骏马。

[2] 倩(qìng):请人代自己做事。

[3] 花儿靥儿:指头上所戴或饰于面部的饰物。

[4] 死临侵地:木呆呆地、无精打采的样子。

[5] 玉醅(pēi):美酒。

[6] 蜗角虚名:比喻极微小的浮名。

[7] 口占:随口吟出。

[8] 服:习惯、适应。

[9] 顺时:顺应四时之变化。

[10] 据鞍:跨上马鞍。

[11] 文齐福不齐:才华横溢而少有福分;暗喻不能考中。

[12] 栖迟:逗留、留连。

[13] 量(liàng):度量、估量。

第四本

第四折 惊 梦

（张生引琴童上云）离了蒲东，早二十里也。兀的前面是草桥店，宿一宵，明日早行。这马百般的不肯走呵。

【双调·新水令】（张生唱）望蒲东萧寺暮云遮，惨离情半林黄叶！马迟人意懒，风急雁行斜。愁恨重叠，破题儿第一夜。

【步步娇】昨宵个翠被香浓熏兰麝，欹枕把身躯儿趄[1]。脸儿厮揾者，仔细端详，可憎得别！云鬟玉梳斜，恰似半吐的初生月。

早至也，店小二哥那里？（店小二云）官人，俺这里有名的草桥店，官人头房里下者。（张生云）琴童，撒和了马者。点上灯来，我诸般不要吃，只要睡些儿。（琴童云）小人也辛苦，待歇息也，就在床前打铺。（琴童先睡着科）（张生云）今夜甚睡魔到得我眼里来？

【落梅风】旅馆欹单枕，乱蛩鸣四野[2]，助人愁，纸窗风裂。乍孤眠，被儿薄又怯，冷清清几时温热？

（张生睡科，反覆睡不着科，又睡科，睡熟科，入梦科，自问科，云）这是小姐的声音，呀，我如今却在那里？待我立起身来听咱。（内唱，张生听科）

【乔木查】走荒郊旷野，把不住心娇怯，喘吁吁难将两气接。疾忙赶上者。

（张生云）呀，这明明是我小姐的声音，他待赶上谁来?待小生再听咱。他打草惊蛇。

【搅筝琶】把俺心肠撧,因此不避路途赊[3],瞒过夫人,稳住侍妾。

（张生云）分明是小姐也。再听咱——

见他临上马,痛伤嗟,哭得我似痴呆。不是心邪,自别离已后,到西日初斜,愁得陡峻,瘦得咤嗻[4]。半个日头,早掩过翠裙三四褶,我曾经这般磨灭。

（张生云）然也,我的小姐,只是你如今在那里呵?

（又听科）

【锦上花】有限姻缘,方才宁贴,无奈功名,使人离缺。害不倒愁怀,恰才较些,掉不下思量,如今又也。

（张生云）小姐的心,分明便是我的心,好不伤感呵!

（吁科,再听科）

【后】清霜净碧波,白露下黄叶。下下高高,道路坳折。四野风来,左右乱趷[5]。俺这里奔驰,你何处困歇?

（张生云）小姐,我在这里也,你进来波。（忽醒云）哎呀,这里却是那里?（看科）呸!原来却是草桥店。

（唤琴童,童睡熟不应科,仍复睡科,睡不着,反覆科,再看科。想科）

【清江引】（张生唱）呆打孩店房里没话说,闷对如年夜。

竟不知此时,是甚时候了。

是暮雨催寒蛩,是晓风吹残月,真个今宵酒醒何处也?（睡着科,重入梦科）（莺莺上,敲门云）开门!开门!（张生云）谁敲门哩,是一个女子声音,作怪也,我不要开门呵。

【庆宣和】是人呵,疾忙快分说,是鬼呵,速灭!

（莺莺云）是我,快开门咱!（张生开门科,携莺莺入科）听说，将香罗袖儿拽，原来是小姐，小姐！（莺莺云）我想你去了呵，我怎得过日子，特来和你同去波。

（张生云）难得小姐的心肠也！

【乔牌儿】你为人真为彻，将衣袂不藉[6]。绣鞋儿被露水泥沾惹，脚心儿管踏破也。

【甜水令】你当初废寝忘餐，香消玉减，比花开花谢犹自较争些。又便枕冷衾寒，凤只鸾孤，月圆云遮，寻思怎不伤嗟！

【折桂令】想人生最苦是离别，你怜我千里关山，独自跋涉，似这般挂肚牵肠，倒不如义断恩绝。这一番花残月缺，怕便是瓶坠簪折。你不恋豪杰，不羡骄奢，只要生则同衾，死则同穴！

（辛子上）（张生惊科）（辛子云）方才见一女子渡河，不知那里去了，打起火把者，走入这店里去了，将出来！将出来！（张生云）却怎生了也，小姐，你靠后些，我自与他说话。（莺莺下）

【水仙子】你硬围着普救下锹撅，强当住我咽喉仗剑钺，贼心贼脑天生劣！

（辛云）他是谁家女子？你敢藏着？

休言语，靠后些，杜将军你知道是英杰，觑觑着你化为齑酱[7]，指指教他变做胔血[8]，骑着匹白马来也。

（辛子怕科，辛子下）（张生抱琴童云）小姐，你受惊也。（童云）官人！怎么？（张生醒科，做意科）

呀，元来是一场大梦。且将门儿推开看，只见一天露气，满地霜华，晓星初上，残月犹明。无端燕雀高枝上，一枕鸳鸯梦不成！

【雁儿落】绿依依墙高柳半遮，静悄悄门掩清秋夜。疏剌剌林梢落叶风，惨离离云际穿窗月。

【得胜令】颤巍巍竹影走龙蛇，虚飘飘庄生梦蝴蝶。絮叨叨促织儿无休歇[9]，韵悠悠砧声儿不断绝[10]。痛煞煞伤别，急煎煎好梦儿应难舍。冷清清咨嗟，娇滴滴玉人儿何处也！

（童云）天明也，早行一程儿，前面打火去。

【鸳鸯煞】柳丝长咫尺情牵惹，水声幽仿佛人呜咽。斜月残灯半明不灭，旧恨新愁连绵郁结。别恨离愁，满肺腑难淘泻[11]。除纸笔代喉舌，千种相思对谁说？

　　题目　小红娘成好事　老夫人问由情
　　正名　短长亭斟别酒　草桥店梦莺莺

（舞台剧终）

注释

[1]赸(qiè)：歪斜着。

[2]蛩(qióng)：古书上指蟋蟀。

[3]赊：远。

[4]咗嚤：厉害，了不起。

[5]趣(xué)：盘旋。

[6]将衣袂(mèi)不藉(jiè)：不顾惜衣衫。

[7]醯(xī)酱：醯，醋。醯酱意如肉酱。

[8]膋(liáo)血：血水。

[9]促织儿：蟋蟀。

[10]砧声：在捣衣石上以槌棒敲打洗衣发出的声音。

[11]淘泻：抒发，排遣。

第五本

第一折 捷 报

（张生上云）自去秋与小姐相别，倏经半载[1]。托赖祖宗福荫，一举及第，目今听候御笔亲除。惟恐小姐望念，特地修书一封，着琴童赍去，报知夫人和小姐，使知小生得中，以安其心。书写就了，琴童何在？（童云）有何吩咐？（张生云）你将这封书，星夜送到河中府去，见小姐时，说官人怕小姐担忧，特地先着小人送书来。

【仙吕·赏花时】（张生唱）相见时红雨纷纷点绿苔[2]，别离后黄叶萧萧凝暮霭。今日见梅开，忽惊半载，特地寄书来。琴童，你报知了，索得回书，疾忙来者。

（张生下）（童云）得了这书，星夜往河中府走一遭。

（琴童下）（莺莺引红娘上云）自张生上京，恰早半年，到今杳无音信。这些时神思不安，妆镜慵临，腰肢瘦损，茜裙宽褪，好生烦恼人也呵！

【商调·集贤宾】虽离了眼前，闷却在我心上有，不甫能离了心上，又早眉头。忘了时依然还又，恶思量无了无休[3]。大都来一寸眉心[4]，怎容得许多颦皱？新愁近来接着旧愁，厮混了难分新旧。旧愁是太行山隐隐，新愁是天堑水悠悠。

（红娘云）小姐往常也曾不快，将息便好，不似这番清减得十分利害也。

【逍遥乐】曾经消瘦，每遍犹闲[5]，这番最陡。何处忘忧，独上妆楼。手卷珠帘上玉钩，空目断山明水秀，苍烟迷树，衰草连天，野渡横舟。

红娘，我这衣裳，这些时都不是我穿的。（红云）小姐，正是腰细不胜衣。

【挂金索】裙染榴花，睡损胭脂皱。纽结丁香，掩过芙蓉扣。线脱珍珠，泪湿香罗袖。杨柳眉颦，人比黄花瘦。

（琴童上云）俺奉官人言语，特赍书来与小姐。恰才前厅上见了夫人，夫人好生欢喜，着入来见小姐，早至后堂。（童咳嗽科）（红云）是谁？（红见童笑云）你几时来？小姐正烦恼哩。你自来？和官人同来？（童云）官人得了官也，先着我送书来报喜。（红云）你只在这里等，我对小姐说了，你入来。（红见莺莺笑云）小姐，喜也，喜也！张生得了官了。（莺莺云）这妮子见我闷呵，特来哄我。（红云）琴童在门首，见了夫人，使他入来见小姐。（莺莺云）惭愧，我也有盼着他的日头。（童见莺莺科）（莺莺云）琴童，你几时离京师？

（童云）一月来也，我来时，官人游街耍子去了。（莺莺云）这禽兽不省得，中了状元，唤做夸官，游街三日。（童云）小姐说得是，有书在此。

【金菊香】早是我因他去后，减了风流，不争你寄得书来，又与我添些证候。说来的话儿不应口，无语低头，书在手，泪盈眸。

【醋葫芦】我这里开时和泪开，他那里修时和泪修，多管是阁着笔儿未写泪先流，寄将来泪点儿兀自有。我这新痕把旧痕湮透，这的是一重愁，翻做两重愁。

（念书云）张珙再拜，奉书芳卿可人妆次：伏自去秋拜违,倏尔半载。上赖祖宗之荫,下托贤妻之德,叨中鼎甲。目今寄迹招贤馆[6],听候除授[7]。惟恐夫人与贤妻忧念,特令琴童赍书驰报。小生身遥心迩,恨不得鹣鹣比翼,蛩蛩并驱,幸勿以重功名而薄恩情,深加谴责。感荷良深,如许阔私,统容面悉。后缀一绝,以奉清照。

"玉京仙府探花郎,寄语蒲东窈窕娘。指日拜恩衣昼锦,是须休作倚门妆!"

（莺莺云）惭愧!探花郎是第三名也呵!

【后】当日向西厢月底潜,今日在琼林宴上挡[8]。跳东墙脚儿占了鳌头,惜花心养成折桂手,脂粉丛里包藏着锦绣。从今后,晚妆楼改做至公楼。

（问童云）你吃饭不曾。（童云）不曾吃。（莺莺云）红娘,你快去取饭与他吃。（童云）小人一壁吃饭,小姐上紧写书。官人吩咐小人,索了回书,快回去哩。

（莺莺云）红娘,将纸笔来。（写书毕科）（莺莺云）书写了,无可表意,有汗衫一领[9],裹肚一条,袜儿一双,瑶琴一张,玉簪一枝,斑管一枚,琴童,收拾得好者。红娘,取十两银来,与他做盘缠。（红云）张生做了官,岂无这几件东西?寄与他有甚缘故?（莺莺云）你怎么知得我心中事,听我说与你者:

【梧叶儿】这汗衫,若是和衣卧,便是和我一处宿,贴着他皮肉,不信不想我温柔。这裹肚儿,常不要离了前后,守着左右,系在心头。这袜儿,拘管他胡行乱走。

【后庭花】这琴,当初五言诗紧趁逐[10],后来七弦琴成配偶。他怎肯冷落了诗中意,我只怕生疏了弦上手。这玉簪儿,我须有缘由,他如今功名成就,只怕撇人在脑背后。这斑管儿，湘江两岸秋，当日娥皇因虞舜愁，今日莺莺为君瑞忧。这九嶷山下竹，共香罗衫袖口。

【青哥儿】都一般啼痕湮透，并泪斑宛然依旧，万种情缘一样愁。涕泪交流，怨慕难收。对学士叮咛说缘由，是**必休忘旧**！

（琴童云）理会得。（莺莺云）琴童，这东西收拾得好者。

【醋葫芦】你逐宵野店上宿，休将包袱做枕头，怕油脂沾污急难酬[11]。倘或水浸雨湿休便扭，只怕干时节熨不开摺皱。一桩桩，一件件，细收留。

【金菊香】书封雁足此时修，情系人心早晚休。长安望来天际头，倚遍西楼，人不见，水空流。

（童云）小人拜辞了小姐，即便去也。（莺莺云）琴童，你去见官人，对他说……（童云）又说甚么？

【浪里来煞】他那里为我愁，我这里因他瘦。临行啜赚人的巧舌头[12]。他归期约定九月九，已过了小春时候。到如今悔教夫婿觅封侯。

（童云）得了回书，星夜回话去。（琴童下）（莺莺、红娘下）

注释

[1] 倏:倏忽,极快。

[2] 红雨:喻落花。

[3] 恶思量:相思得厉害。

[4] 大都来:只不过。

[5] 每遍犹闲:每每都还平常。

[6] 寄迹:寄身。

[7] 除授:拜官授职。

[8] 挡(chōu):搀扶。

[9] 汗衫:穿在朝服里面的中衣,又叫中单。

[10] 趁逐:追随、追逐。

[11] 酬:此处为洗涤之意。

[12] 啜赚:哄弄诳骗。

第二折 猜　寄

（张生上云）小生满望除授后，便可出京，不想奉圣旨着在翰林院编修国史。谁知我的心事，什么文章做得成？琴童去了，又不见回来。这几日睡卧不安，饮食无味，给假在邮亭中将息。早间太医院差医士来看视下药，我这病，便是卢扁也医不得，自离了小姐，无一日心宽也呵！

【中吕·粉蝶儿】从到京师，思量心，旦夕如是，向心头横躺着我那莺儿。请医师看诊罢，一星星说是[1]。本意待推辞，早被他察虚实，不须看视。

【醉春风】他道是医杂证有方术，治相思无药饵。小姐呵，你若知我害相思，我甘心儿为你死，死！四海无家，一身客寄，半年将至。

（琴童上云）俺回来，闻说官人在驿中抱病，须索送回书去咱。（见张生科）（张生云）琴童，你回来也。

【迎仙客】噪花枝灵鹊儿，垂帘幕喜蛛儿，短檠夜来灯爆时。若不是断肠词，定是断肠诗。写时管情泪如丝，既不呵，怎生泪点儿封皮上渍。

（念书云）薄命妾崔氏，拜覆君瑞才郎文儿：别逾半载，奚啻三秋？思慕之心，未尝少怠[2]。昔云"日近长安远"，妾今信斯言矣。琴童至，接来书，知君置身青云，且悉佳况，得君如此，妾复何言。琴童促回，无以达意，聊具瑶琴一张，玉簪一枝，斑管一枚，裹肚一

条，汗衫一领，绢袜一双，物虽微鄙，愿君详纳。春风
　　多厉，千万珍重，复依来韵，敬和一绝：
阑干倚遍盼才郎，莫恋宸京黄四娘。病里得书知及第，窗前览镜试新妆。

　　我那风流的小姐，似这等女子，张珙死也死得着了。

【上小楼】 堪为字史，当为款识[3]。有柳骨颜筋，张旭张颠，羲之献之。此一时，彼一时，佳人才思，俺莺莺，世间无二。

【后】 俺做经咒般持，符篆般使[4]。高似金章，重似金帛，贵似金赀。这上面若签个押字，使个令史，差个勾使，是一张不及印赴期的咨示。

　　（看汗衫科云）休说文字，只看他这汗衫，

【满庭芳】 怎不教张郎爱尔？堪与针工出色，女教为师。几千般用意，般般是可索寻思。长共短又无个样子，窄和宽想象着腰肢。无人试；想当初做时，用煞小心儿。

　　小姐寄来几件东西，都有缘故，一件件我都猜着。

【白鹤子】 这琴，教我闭门学禁指[5]，留意谱声诗，调养圣贤心，洗荡巢由耳。

【二煞】 这玉簪，纤长如竹笋，细白似葱枝，温润有清香，莹洁无瑕疵。

【三煞】 这斑管，霜枝栖凤凰，泪点渍胭脂，当时舜帝恸娥皇，今日淑女思君子。

【四煞】 这裹肚，手中一叶绵[6]，灯下几回丝，表出腹中愁，果称心间事。

【五煞】 这袜儿，针脚如虮子，绢片似鹅脂，既知礼不胡行，愿足下常如此。

　　琴童，你临行，小姐对你说什么？（童云）着官人是必

不可别继良缘。（张生云）小姐，你尚然不知我的心哩！

【快活三】冷清清客店儿，风淅淅雨丝丝，雨零风细梦回时，多少伤心事。

【朝天子】四肢不能动止，急切盼不到蒲东寺[7]。小夫人须是你见时，别有甚闲传示？我是个浪子宫人，风流学士，怎肯带残花折旧枝？自从到此，甚的是闲街市。

【贺圣朝】少甚宰相人家招婿娇姿，其间或有个人儿似尔，那里取那样温柔，这般才思？想莺莺意儿，怎不教人梦想眠思。

【耍孩儿】只在书房中颠倒个藤箱子，向里面铺几张儿纸。放时须索用心思，休教藤刺儿抓住绵丝。高摊在衣架上[8]，怕风吹了颜色，乱裹在包袱中，怕挫了褶儿。当如是，切须爱护，勿得因而。

【二煞】恰新婚才燕尔，为功名来到此。长安忆念蒲东寺。昨宵个春风桃李花开夜，今日个秋雨梧桐叶落时。愁如是，身遥心迩，坐想行思。

【三煞】这天高地厚情，到海枯石烂时，此时作念何时止？直到烛灰眼下才无泪，蚕老心中罢却思。不比轻薄子，抛夫妻琴瑟，拆鸾凤雄雌。

【四煞】不闻黄犬音，难传红叶诗[9]，路长不遇梅花使[10]。孤身作客三千里，一日思归十二时。凭阑视，听江声浩荡，看山色参差。

【煞尾】忧则忧我病中，喜则喜你来到此。投至得引人魂卓氏音书至，险将这害鬼病的相如盼望死！

西厢记

注 释

[1] 一星星说是:每一件都说得对头。

[2] 怠:懈怠。

[3] 款识(zhì):本指古代钟鼎器上铭刻的文字,此处形容莺莺的字写得好。

[4] 符箓(lù):符。

[5] 闭门学禁指:闭门弹琴。

[6] 一叶绵:谐音"一夜眠"。

[7] 蒲东寺:即普救寺。

[8] 高摊:高挂。

[9] 难传红叶诗:难通音讯。

[10] 路长不遇梅花使:此句也是说没有人捎信。

第五本

第三折 争艳

（郑恒上云）自家姓郑，名恒，字伯常。先人拜礼部尚书，在时曾定下俺姑娘的女儿莺莺为妻。不想姑夫去世，莺莺孝服未满，不曾成亲。俺姑娘引着莺莺扶灵柩回博陵安葬，为因路阻，寄居河中府。数月前，写书来唤俺，因家中无人，来迟了一步。不想到这里，听说孙飞虎要掳莺莺，得一秀才张君瑞，退了贼兵，俺姑娘把莺莺又许了他。俺如今便撞将去呵，恐没意思。这一件事都在红娘身上。俺且着人去唤他，只说哥哥从京师来，不敢造次来见姑娘，着红娘到下处来[1]，有话对姑娘行说。人去好一回了，怎么还不见来？（红娘上，云）郑恒哥哥在下处，不来见夫人，却唤俺说话。夫人着俺来，看他说什么。（红见郑科，红云）哥哥万福！夫人道，哥哥来到呵，怎不到家里来？（郑云）我怎么好就见姑娘？我唤你来说：当日姑夫在时，曾许下亲事，我今到这里，姑夫孝已满了，特地央你去夫人行说知，拣一个吉日，成合了这件事，好和一搭里[2]，下葬去。不争不成合，一路上难厮见。若说得肯呵，我重重谢你。（红云）这一节话，再也休题！莺莺已与了张生也。（郑云）道不得个一马不鞴双鞍，可怎生父在时，曾许下我，父丧之后，母却悔亲，这个道理那里有？（红云）却非如此说，当日孙飞虎将半万贼兵来时，哥哥你在那里？若不是张生呵，那里得俺一家儿性命来？

今日太平无事，却来争亲，倘被贼人掳去呵，哥哥你和谁说？（郑云）与了一个富家，也还不枉，与这个穷酸饿醋，偏我不如他？我仁者能仁、身里出身的根脚[3]，他比我甚的？（红云）他倒不如你？禁声！

【越调·斗鹌鹑】（红娘唱）卖弄你仁者能仁，倚仗你身里出身，纵教你官上加官，谁许你亲上做亲？又不曾羔雁邀媒，币帛问肯[4]，恰洗了尘，便待要过门。枉淹了他金屋银屏，枉污了他锦衾绣褥。

【紫花儿序】枉蠢了他梳云掠月，枉羞了他惜玉怜香，枉村了他滞雨尤云。当日才始判[5]，两仪初分；乾坤：清者为乾，浊者为坤，人在其中相混。君瑞是君子清贤，郑恒是小人浊民。

（郑云）贼来，他怎生退得？都是胡说！（红云）我说与你听：

【天净沙】把河桥飞虎将军，叛蒲东掳掠人民，半万贼屯合[6]寺门，手横着霜刃，高叫道，要莺莺做压寨夫人。

（郑云）半万贼，他一个人济甚事？（红云）贼围甚迫，夫人慌了，和长老商议，高叫："两廊，不论僧俗，如退得贼兵者，便将莺莺小姐与之为妻。"那时张生应声而言："我有退兵之计，何不问我？"夫人大喜，就问其计安在。张生道："我有故人白马将军，见统十万大兵，镇守蒲关。我修书一封，着人传去，必来救我。"不想书到兵来，其困即解。

【小桃红】洛阳才子善属文，火急修书信。白马将军到时分，灭了烟尘[7]。夫人小姐都心顺，则为他威而不猛，言而有信，因此上不敢慢于人。

（郑云）我自来未闻其名，知他会也不会？你这个小妮子，卖弄他偌多。

【金蕉叶】凭着他讲性理《齐论》《鲁论》，作词赋韩文柳文，识道理为人做人，俺家里有信行，知恩报恩。

（郑云）我便怎么不如他？

【调笑令】你值一分，他值百十分，萤火焉能比月轮？高低远近都休论，我拆白道字辨个清浑[8]。君瑞是肖字这壁着个立人，你是寸木马户尸巾。

（郑云）寸木马户尸巾，你道我是个村驴㞘。我祖代官宦，我倒不如那白衣穷士？

【秃厮儿】他学师友君子务本，你倚父兄仗势欺人。他齑盐日月不嫌贫[9]，治百姓新民，传闻。

【圣药王】这厮乔议论[10]，有向顺，你道是官人只合做官人。信口喷，不本分，你道是穷民到老是穷民。却不道将相出寒门。

（郑云）这节事，都是那法本秃驴弟子孩儿，我明日慢慢和他说话。

【麻郎儿】他出家人，慈悲为本，方便为门。你横死眼不识好人，招祸口不知分寸。

（郑云）这是姑夫的遗留，我拣日牵羊担酒上门去，看姑娘怎生发落我。

【后】你看讪筋[11]，发村，使狠，甚的是软疑温存？硬打夺求为眷姻，不睹事强谐秦晋。

（郑云）姑娘若不肯，着二三十个伴当[12]，抬上轿子，到下处脱了衣裳，急赶将来，还你个婆娘。

【络丝娘】你须是郑相国嫡亲的舍人[13]，倒像个孙飞虎家生的莽军。乔嘴脸，腌躯老死身分[14]，少不得有家难奔。

（郑云）兀的那小妮子，眼见得受了招安了也。我也不对你说，明日我要娶，我要娶！（红云）不嫁你，不嫁你。

【收尾】佳人有意郎君俊，教我不喝彩其实怎忍？你只好偷韩寿下风头香，傅何郎左壁厢粉！

（红娘下）（郑云）这妮子一定都和酸丁演撒。俺明日自上门去，见俺姑娘，佯做不知。只道张生在卫尚书家，做了女婿。俺姑娘最听是非，他必有话说。休说别的，只这一套衣服，也冲动他。自小京师同住，惯会寻章摘句[15]。姑夫已许成亲，谁敢将言相拒？俺若放起刁来，且看莺莺那去。且看压善欺良意，权作尤云殢雨心。（郑恒下）（夫人上云）夜来郑恒至，不来见俺，唤红娘去问亲事。据俺的心，只是与侄儿的是。况兼相公在时，已许下了。俺便是违了先夫的言语，做一个主家不正。办下酒者，今日他敢来见俺也。（郑恒上去）来到也，不索报覆，我自入去。（哭拜夫人科）（夫人云）孩儿，既到这里，怎么不来见我？（郑云）孩儿有甚面颜来见姑娘？（夫人云）莺莺为孙飞虎一节，无可解危，许了张生也。（郑云）那个张生，敢便是今科探花郎？我在京师看榜来，年纪有二十三四岁，洛阳张珙。夸官游街三日，第二日头踏正来到卫尚书家门首，尚书的小姐，结着彩楼，在那御街上，只一球正打着他。我也骑着马看，险些打着我。怕你不休了莺莺？他家粗使梅香十来个，把张生横拖倒拽入去。他口里叫道，我自有妻，我是崔相国家女婿。那尚书那里肯听，说道：我女奉圣旨结彩楼招你，莺莺是先奸后娶的，只好做个次妻罢[16]。因此闹动京师,侄儿认得他。(夫人怒云)我说这秀才不中抬举,今日果然负了俺家。俺相国之女,岂有做次妻的理。既然张生娶了妻,不要了孩儿,你择个吉日良辰,依旧入来做女婿者。(夫人下)(郑喜云)中了俺的计了。准备茶礼花红过门者。(郑恒下)

注释

[1] 下处:下榻处,住处。

[2] 一搭里:一起,一块儿。

[3] 身里出身:指能够继承父业。

[4] 币帛问肯:以财礼向女家提亲,遣媒人询问女方家许否。

[5] 始判:才分。

[6] 屯合:聚合、包围。

[7] 灭了烟尘:平定了叛乱。

[8] 清浑:清浊,此处有贤愚的意思。

[9] 齑盐日月:指清贫的苦读生活。

[10] 乔议论:胡说八道。

[11] 虬筋:因气愤激动而面红耳赤,青筋偾张。

[12] 伴当:随从的仆人。

[13] 舍人:原为官称,宋元以来通称官宦人家子弟为舍人,即公子。

[14] 腌躯老:丑陋的身躯。

[15] 寻章摘句:抓住只言片语做文章。

[16] 次妻:即妾。

第四折 团　圆

（法本上云）老僧昨日买《登科录》，看张先生果然及第，除授河中府尹。谁想夫人没主张，又许了郑恒亲事，不肯去接。老僧将着肴馔，直至十里长亭，接官走一遭。（法本下）（杜将军上云）奉圣旨，着小官主兵蒲关，提调河中府事。谁想君瑞兄弟，一举及第，正授河中府尹，一定乘此机会成亲。小官牵羊担酒，直至老夫人宅上，一来贺喜，二来主亲。左右那里？将马来，到河中府走一遭。（杜将军下）（夫人上云）谁想张生负了俺家，去卫尚书家做女婿去了。只索不负老相公遗言，还招郑恒为婿。今日是个好日子过门，准备下筵席，郑恒敢待来也。（夫人下）（张生上云）小官奉圣旨，正授河中府尹。今日衣锦还乡，小姐凤冠霞帔都将着，见呵，双手索送过去。谁想有今日也呵，文章旧冠乾坤内，姓字新闻日月边[1]。

【双调·新水令】（张生唱）一鞭骄马出皇都，畅风流玉堂人物。今朝三品职，昨日一寒儒。御笔新除，将姓名翰林注。

【驻马听】张珙如愚，酬志了三尺龙泉万卷书[2]。莺莺有福，稳受了五花官诰七香车。身荣难忘借僧居，愁来犹记题诗处。从应举，梦魂不离蒲东路。

（到寺科云）接了马者。（见夫人拜云）新探花河中府尹张珙参见。（夫人云）休拜，休拜，你是奉圣旨的女婿，我怎消受得你拜？

【乔牌儿】我躬身问起居，夫人你慈色为谁怒[3]？我只见丫鬟使数都厮觑，莫不是我身边有甚事故？

（张生云）小生去时，承夫人亲自饯行，喜不自胜。今朝得官回来，夫人反行不悦，何也？（夫人云）你如今那里想俺家，道不得个"靡不有初，鲜克有终"！我一个女孩儿，虽然妆残貌陋，他父为前朝相国。若非贼来，足下甚气力到得俺家？今日一旦置之度外，却与卫尚书家作赘，是何道理？（张生云）夫人，你听谁说来？若有此事，天不盖，地不载，害老大疔疮！

【雁儿落】若说丝鞭仕女图[4]，端的是塞满章台路[5]。小生向此间怀旧恩，怎肯别处寻亲去？

【得胜令】岂不闻君子断其初，我怎肯忘了有恩处？那一个贼畜生行嫉妒，走将来厮间阻？不能彀娇姝[6]，早晚施心数。说来的无徒[7]，迟和疾上木驴[8]！

（夫人云）是郑恒说来，绣球儿打着马，做了女婿也。你不信，唤红娘来问。（红娘上云）我巴不得见他，元来得官回来，惭愧！这是非对着也。（张生问云）红娘，小姐好么？（红云）为你做了卫尚书女婿，俺小姐依旧嫁郑恒去了也。（张生云）有这跷蹊事？

【庆东原】那里有粪堆上长出连枝树，淤泥中双游比目鱼。不明白展污了姻缘簿。莺莺呵，你嫁得个油炸猢狲的丈夫[9]。红娘呵你伏侍个烟薰猫儿的姐夫！张生呵，你撞着个水浸老鼠的姨夫！坏了风俗，伤了时务。

【乔木查】（红娘唱）妾前来拜覆，省可心头怒。自别来安乐否？你那新夫人何处居？比小姐定何如？

（张生云）和你也葫芦提了：小生为小姐受过的苦，别人不知，瞒不得你，甫能够今日，焉有是理？

【搅筝琶】小生若别有媳妇，只目下便身殂！我怎忘了待月回廊，撇了吹箫伴侣？我是受了活地狱，下了死工夫，甫能够为夫妇。我现将着夫人诰敕[10]，县君名称，怎生待欢天喜地，两只手儿亲付与。他划地把我葬诬[11]！

（红对夫人云）我道张生不是这般人，只请小姐出来自问他。（请云）小姐，张生来了，你出来，正好问他！

（莺莺上云）我来了。（相见科）（张生云）小姐，间别无恙？（莺莺云）先生万福！（红云）小姐，有的言语，和他说么？（莺莺吁云）待说甚的是？

【沉醉东风】（莺莺唱）不见时准备着千言万语，到相逢都变做短叹长吁。他急穰穰却才来，我羞答答怎生觑。腹中愁却待伸诉，及至相逢一句也无。刚道个先生万福。

（莺莺云）张生，俺家有甚负你，你见弃妾身，去卫尚书家为婿，此理安在？（张生云）谁说来？（莺莺云）郑恒在夫人行说来。（张生云）小姐，如何听这厮？小生之心，惟天可表。

【落梅风】从离了蒲东郡，来到京兆府，见佳人世不曾回顾。硬揣个卫尚书女儿为眷属[12]，曾见他影儿的也教灭门绝户。

此一桩事，都在红娘身上，我只将言语激着他，看他说什么？红娘！我问人来，说道你与小姐将简帖儿唤郑恒来。

（红云）痴人，我不合与你作成，你便看得一般了。

【甜水令】（红娘唱）君瑞先生，不索踌躇，何须忧虑？那厮本意糊涂，俺家世清白，祖宗贤良，相国名誉，我怎肯去他跟前，寄简传书？

第五本

【折桂令】（红娘唱）那吃敲才[13]，口里嚼蛆，数黑论黄[14]，恶紫夺朱。俺小姐便做道软弱囊揣，怎嫁那不值钱人样豝豿[15]。爱你个俏东君与莺花做主，怎肯将嫩枝柯折与樵夫？那厮本意嚣虚，将足下亏图，我有口难言。气夯破胸脯。

（红云）张生，你若端的不曾做女婿呵，我去夫人跟前，一力保你。等那厮来，你和他两个对证。（崔夫人云）张生并不曾人家做女婿，都是郑恒谎说，等他两个对证。（夫人云）既然他不曾呵，等郑恒来，对证了再做说话。（法本上云）谁想张生一举成名，正授河中府尹。老僧接官到了，再去夫人那里庆贺。这门亲事，当初也有老僧来。如何夫人没主张，便待要与郑恒。若与了他，府尹今日来，却怎生了也！（相见毕）（禀夫人云）夫人，今日始知老僧说得是，张先生决不是这等没行止的秀才，他如何敢忘了夫人？况兼杜将军是证见，如何悔得他这亲事？

【雁儿落】（法本唱）杜将军笑孙庞真下愚，论贾马非英物。正授着征西元帅府，兼领得陕右河中路。

【得胜令】是君前者护身符，今日有权术，来时节定把先生助，决将贼子诛。他不识亲疏，掇赚良人妇，君若不辨贤愚，便是无毒不丈夫！

（夫人云）着小姐卧房里去者。（莺莺、红娘下）（杜将军上云）小官离了蒲关，早到普救寺也。（张生见杜，拜毕）（张生云）小弟托兄长虎威，得中一举。今日回来本待做亲，有夫人侄儿郑恒，来夫人行说小弟在卫尚书家入赘。夫人怒欲悔亲，依旧要将小姐与郑恒，道不得个烈女不更二夫[16]。（杜云）夫人差矣！俺君瑞也是礼部尚书之子，况兼又得一举。夫人誓不招白衣秀士，今日反欲罢亲，莫于理上不顺！（夫人云）当初夫主在时，曾许下那厮。不想遇难，多亏张生请将军杀退贼众，老身不负前言，招他为婿。叵耐那厮说他在卫尚书家招赘，因此上我怒他，依旧要与郑恒。（杜云）他是贼心，可知妄生诽谤，老夫人如何便轻信他。（郑恒上云）打扮得齐齐整整的，只等做女婿。今日好日头，牵羊担酒，过门走一遭去。（相见科）（张生云）郑恒，你来怎么？（郑云）苦也！闻知状元回，特来贺喜！（杜云）你这厮怎么要诓骗良人的妻子，行不仁之事？我奏闻朝廷，诛此贼子。

【落梅风】（杜将军唱）你硬撞入桃源路，不言个谁是主，被东风把你个蜜蜂儿拦住。不信呵，你去绿杨荫里听杜宇[17]，一声声道不如归去。

（杜云）那厮若不去呵，只候人拿下者。（郑云）不必拿，小人自退亲事与张生罢！（夫人云）将军息怒，赶出去便罢！（郑云）今日莺莺与君瑞为夫妇，有何面目见江东父老？我要这性命何用，不如触树身死。妻子空争不到手，风流自古恋风流。何须苦用千般计，一旦无常万事休。

（倒科）（夫人云）俺虽不曾逼死他，可怜他无父母，我做主葬了者。（杜云）请小姐出来，今日做个庆贺的筵席，看他两口儿成合者。（张生、莺莺拜夫人科，又交拜科，又拜杜将军科）（红娘拜张生、莺莺科）

【沽美酒】门迎驷马车，户列八椒图[18]。娶了个四德三从宰相女,平生愿足,托赖着众亲故。

【太平令】若不是大恩人拔刀相助,怎能个好夫妻似水如鱼?好意也当时题目,正酬了今生夫妇。自古相女配夫,新探花新探花路!

（使臣上,众拜科）

【清江引】谢当今垂帘双圣主,敕赐为夫妇。永老无别离,万古常圆聚。愿天下有情的都成了眷属。

  题目 小琴童传捷报 崔莺莺寄汗衫
  正名 郑伯常干舍命 张君瑞庆团圆

  总目 张君瑞巧做东床婿
     法本师住持南禅地
     老夫人开宴北堂春
     崔莺莺待月西厢记

西厢记

注 释

[1]日月:喻帝、后。
[2]酬志:实现了博取功名的大志向。
[3]慈色:对尊长的敬称,多用于母亲。
[4]丝鞭:递接丝结的鞭子,是彩楼招亲仪式中的一个程式。
[5]章台路:本是汉代长安城繁华街道名,后代指繁华游乐之地。
[6]娇姝:美女。
[7]说来的无徒:意思是"说起这个无赖"。
[8]迟和疾上木驴:犹言早晚遭千刀万剐。
[9]油炸猢狲:轻狂。
[10]诰敕:官诰。
[11]划地:平白地。
[12]揣:强加。
[13]吃敲才:犹言"该死的东西"。
[14]数黑论黄:说三道四,搬弄是非。
[15]豭(jiā)驹:豭,猪;"人样豭驹",即有如畜牲之人。
[16]烈女不更二夫:封建社会宣扬从一而终,一女不可嫁二夫。
[17]杜宇:杜鹃鸟。
[18]户列八椒图:门上描刻着各式纹样。

Theory on Literary Translation of the Chinese School

The theory on literary translation of the Chinese school owes its origin to traditional Chinese culture, including the Confucian and the Taoist school of thought respectively represented by *Thus Spoke the Master* and *Laws Divine and Human*.

It is said in the first chapter of *Laws Divine and Human* that truth can be known, but it may not be the truth you know, and that things may be named, but names are not the things. When applied to literary translation, this may mean that the theory on literary translation can be known, but it may not the unproven theory on the one hand, nor the scientific theory on the other, for neither literary translation nor its theory is science. As the names are not equal to the things, the translation cannot be equal to the original. As there is more difference than equivalence between the Chinese and the English language, the principle of equivalence can not be applied to the translation between them as between two occidental languages.

It is said in the last chapter of *Laws Divine and Human* that truthful words may not be beautiful and beautiful words may not be truthful. That is to say, there is contradiction between truth and beauty or between equivalence and excellence. A translation where equivalents are used may be called a faithful or truthful translation. When no equivalent can be found between two languages, the translator should make use of the best expressions or excellent expressions of the target language. That may be called theory of excellence.

In *Thus Spoke the Master*, Confucius said, "At seventy, I can do what I will without going beyond what is right." Professor Zhu Guangqian said that this has shown the mature state of an artist. I think it may also show the mature state of a literary translator. The literal translator has used the equivalents without going beyond the original in sound; the liberal translator has described the image without going beyond the original in sense; the literary translator has described the scene without going beyond reality. Not to go beyond the original is to be truthful or faithful, and the translator has reached the ordinary level of translation. To do what one will without going beyond the original is not only to be faithful but also to make his translation beautiful, in that case the translator has attained a higher level. To excel the original without going beyond the reality it describes is to attain the highest level.

What is literary translation? It is an art of solving the contradiction between faithfulness (or truth) and beauty. How to solve it? There are three methods, namely, equalization, generalization and particularization. When there is little or no contradition between truth and beauty, equalization or equivalents may be used. When there is contradction between them, generalization may be used to make the meaning clear, and particularization to make a deeper impression.

Confucius said in *Thus Spoke the Master* that it would be good to be understandable, better to be enjoyable and best to be delectable or delightful. When applied to literary translation, this principle means that an understandable translation is good, an enjoyable one is better and a delightful one is best. The ontology or theory of contradition between truth and beauty, the methodology or theory of equalization, generalization and particularization, and the teleology or theory of the understandable, the enjoyable and the delectable, all owe their origin to the Confucian and Taoist schools of thoughts.

But Confucius said less about what delight is and more about how to be delightful. In the beginning of *Thus Spoke the Master* he said it is delightful to acquire knowledge and put it into practice; In Chapter Six he told us how Yan Hui could find delight in reading though living in a humble lane with only a handful of rice to eat and a gourdful of water to drink; In Chapter Eleven, Zeng Xi told us his delight in an spring excursion. From these examples we can see Confucius' theory on delight or teleology, and his theory on practice or methodology. His theory is not scientific but artistic. Since literary translation is an art but not a branch of science, his theory can not only be applied to the practice but also to the theory of literary translation. As his theory has stood the test of time, it is as durable as scientific theories. A theorist on science who studies truth and the truthful should not go beyond what is truthful. A theorist on art or an artist who studies beauty and the beautiful may go beyond what is truthful and faithful.

The contradiction between truth and beauty in Chinese theory on literary translation has developed into a contradiction between equivalence and excellence. As Keats said, "Beauty is truth, truth beauty," we may even say beauty is a virtue, a kind of excellence. When we cannot find the equivalent, we may resort to generalization or particularization.

In short, literary translation is an art to create the beautiful.

西厢记

This is the epistemology of the Chinese school. The contradition between truth and beauty or between equivalence and excellence is its ontology; the theory on equalization, generalization and particularization is its triple methodology; and the theory of the understandable, the enjoyable and the delectable or delightful is its triple teleology.

Xu Yuanchong
Oct. 2011

代后记：中国学派的文学翻译理论

中国学派的文学翻译理论源自中国的传统文化，主要包括儒家思想和道家思想，儒家思想的代表著作是《论语》，道家思想的代表著作是《老子道德经》。

《老子道德经》第一章开始就说："道可道，非常道；名可名，非常名。"联系到翻译理论上来，就是说：翻译理论是可以知道的，是可以说得出来的，但不是只说得出来而经不起实践检验的空头理论，这就是中国学派翻译理论中的实践论。其次，文学翻译理论不能算科学理论（自然科学），与其说是社会科学理论，不如说是人文学科或艺术理论，这就是文学翻译的艺术论，也可以说是相对论。后六个字"名可名，非常名"应用到文学翻译理论上来，可以有两层意思：第一层是原文的文字是描写现实的，但并不等于现实，文字和现实之间还有距离，还有矛盾；第二层意思是译文和原文之间也有距离，也有矛盾，译文和原文所描写的现实之间，自然还有距离，还有矛盾。译文应该发挥译语优势，运用最好的译语表达方式，来和原文展开竞赛，使译文和现实的距离或矛盾小于原文和现实之间的矛盾，那就是超越原文了。这就是文学翻译理论中的优势论或优化论，超越论或竞赛论。文学翻译理论应该解决的不只是译文和原文在文字方面的矛盾，还要解决译文和原文所反映的现实之间的矛盾，这是文学翻译的本体论。

一般翻译只要解决"真"或"信"或"似"的问题，文学翻译却要解决"真"或"信"和"美"之间的矛盾。原文反映的现实不只是言内之意，还有言外之意。中国的文学语言往往有言外之意，甚至还有言外之情。文学翻译理论也要解决译文和原文的言外之意、言外之情的矛盾。

《论语》说："知之者不如好之者，好之者不如乐之者。"知之，好之，乐之，这"三之论"是对艺术论的进一步说明。艺术论第一条原则要求译文忠实于原文所反映的现实，求的是真，可以使人知之；第二条原则要求用"三化"法来优化译文，求的是美，可以使人好之；第三条原则要求用"三美"来优化译文，尤其是译诗词，求的是意美、音美和形美，可以使人乐之。如果"不逾矩"的等化译文能使人知之（理解），那就达到了文学翻译的低标准，如从心所欲而不逾矩的浅化或深化的译文既能使人知之，又能使人好之（喜欢），那就达到了中标准；如果从心所欲的译文不但能使人知之，好之，还能使人乐之（愉快），那才达到了文学翻译的高标准。这也是中国译者对世界译论作出的贡献。

翻译艺术的规律是从心所欲而不逾矩。"矩"就是规矩，规律。但艺术规律却可以依人的主观意志而转移，是因为得到承认才算正确的。所以贝多芬说：为了更美，没有什么清规戒律不可打破。他所说的戒律不是科学规律，而是艺术规律。不能用科学规律来评论文学翻译。

孔子不大谈"什么是"（What?）而多谈"怎么做"（How?）。这是中国传统的方法论，比西方流传更久，影响更广，作用更大，并且经过了两三千年实践的考验。《论语》第一章中说："学而时习之，不亦说（悦，乐）乎！""学"是取得知识，"习"是实践。孔子只说学习实践可以得到乐趣，却不说什么是"乐"。这就是孔子的方法论，是中国文学翻译理论的依据。

总而言之，中国学派的文学翻译理论是研究老子提出的

"信"（似）"美"（优）矛盾的艺术（本体论），但"信"不限原文，还指原文所反映的现实，这是认识论，"信"由严复提出的"信达雅"发展到鲁迅提出"信顺"的直译，再发展到陈源的"三似"（形似，意似，神似），直到傅雷的"重神似不重形似"，这已经接近"美"了。"美"发展到鲁迅的"三美"（意美，音美，形美），再发展到林语堂提出的"忠实，通顺，美"，转化为朱生豪"传达原作意趣"的意译，直到茅盾提出的"美的享受"。孔子提出的"从心所欲"发展到郭沫若提出的创译论（好的翻译等于创作），以及钱钟书说的译文可以胜过原作的"化境"说，再发展到优化论，超越论，"三化"（等化，浅化，深化）方法论。孔子提出的"不逾矩"和老子说的"信言不美，美言不信"有同有异。老子"信美"并重，孔子"从心所欲"重于"不逾矩"，发展为朱光潜的"艺术论"，包括郭沫若说的"在信达之外，愈雅愈好。所谓'雅'不是高深或讲修饰，而是文学价值或艺术价值比较高。"直到茅盾说的："必须把文学翻译工作提高到艺术创造的水平。"孔子的"乐之"发展为胡适之的"愉快"说（翻译要使读者读得愉快），再发展到"三之"（知之，好之，乐之）目的论。这就是中国学派的文学翻译理论发展为"美化之艺术"（"三美"，"三化"，"三之"的艺术）的概况。

许渊冲
2011年10月

图书在版编目（CIP）数据

西厢记: 汉英对照 / 许渊冲译. —北京: 五洲传播出版社, 2018.1（2021.8重印）
（许译中国经典诗文集）
ISBN 978-7-5085-3899-0

Ⅰ.①西… Ⅱ.①许… Ⅲ.①杂剧—剧本—中国—元代—汉、英 Ⅳ.①H319.4：Ⅰ

中国版本图书馆CIP数据核字(2017)第323692号

西厢记

译　　者：	许渊冲　许　明
策划编辑：	荆孝敏　郑　磊
责任编辑：	王　峰
中文编辑：	张　梅　代　莉
英文编辑：	闫宇涵　张祯隆
装帧设计：	北京正视文化艺术有限责任公司
出版发行：	五洲传播出版社
地　　址：	北京市海淀区北三环中路31号生产力大楼B座6层
邮　　编：	100088
电　　话：	010—82005927，010—82007837
网　　址：	http://www.cicc.org.cn　http://www.thatsbooks.com
印　　刷：	北京市房山腾龙印刷厂
版　　次：	2012年1月第1版　2021年8月第2版第3次印刷
开　　本：	140mm×210mm　1/32
印　　张：	11.25
字　　数：	300千字
书　　号：	ISBN 978-7-5085-3899-0
定　　价：	89.00元